That Obscure Subject of Desire

Freud's Female Homosexual Revisited

~

Edited by

Ronnie C. Lesser and Erica Schoenberg

Routledge
New York and London

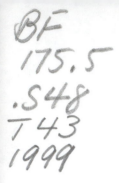

Published in 1999 by
Routledge
29 West 35th Street
New York, NY 10001

Published in Great Britain by
Routledge
11 New Fetter Lane
London EC4P 4EE

10 9 8 7 6 5 4 3 2 1

Library of Congress Cataloging-in-Publication Data

That obscure subject of desire: Freud's female homosexual revisited /
Ronnie C. Lesser & Erica Schoenberg, eds.
    p. cm.
  Includes bibliographical references and index.
    ISBN 0-415-91670-4 (hardcover : alk. paper).—ISBN 0-415-91671-2
(pbk. : alk. paper)
    1. Sex (Psychology) 2. Lesbians. 3. Homosexuality. 4. Psychoanalysis.
5. Freud, Sigmund, 1856–1939. I. Lesser, Ronnie C. II. Schoenberg, Erica.
BF175.5.S48T43 1999
155.3--dc21   98-41836
                                                                          CIP

This book is dedicated to
Ben, Gabe, Reese, and Sophie;
Marcia and Ed; Muriel and Felix;
Doug, Lea, and Mel;
and in memory of Morton and Sonia

CONTENTS

~

v

Part III. Contributions from Psychoanalysts

Part IV. Discussion

INTRODUCTION
In the Shadow of Freud

~

Ronnie C. Lesser

The essays in this collection focus on Freud's "The Psychogenesis of a Case of Homosexuality in a Woman" (1920), a paper that has been neglected by students of psychoanalysis. By presenting perspectives on this case from both psychoanalysts and academic scholars, we hope to foster a dialogue between these two groups. This is a much-needed conversation; psychoanalysts have long been isolated from scholars in other fields, and academicians are often not acquainted with the work of contemporary psychoanalysts.

Along with the isolation of psychoanalysis from scholarship in other fields comes the widespread tendency in analytic institutes to teach Freudian theory as if it emerged in a social vacuum. One of the major contributions of contemporary approaches to theory is to resist this tendency by viewing knowledge as a sociopolitical product. The essayists in this collection utilize this method in discussing Freud's case. I will further this project by discussing the ways in which the interlocking discourses of anti-Semitism and misogyny influenced Freud's treatment and conceptualization of the patient in "Psychogenesis." Rather than consider Freud's appalling behavior as simply that of a typical, patriarchal male, I will suggest that Freud was a patriarch quite without the benefits of patriarchy (to transpose a phrase of Harris, this volume). While such a view does not excuse Freud's disparagement of the patient, it does helps us understand it in a different light. Using the scholarship of Gilman (1991, 1993a, b) and Decker (1991), I will bring to the surface Freud's own status as "Other" (i.e., Jewish) in Viennese science and culture, discuss the racial trauma he experienced, and speculate about the ways Freud used his theory to both deny this trauma and work it through (Gilman, 1993).

The racism directed at Freud and other Jews is startling (see Schoenberg, this volume). Let me begin with a dramatic illustration: According to Gilman (1993), during Freud's time the clitoris was called "the Jew" in Viennese slang, and female masturbation was referred to as "playing with the Jew." This language reflected two views prevalent both inside and outside of medicine at the turn of the century: the first was of sexual homology, the belief that male and female genitalia are parallel and that the clitoris is a "truncated penis," analogous to the circumcised ("truncated") penis of the Jewish male; the second, related view was that Jewish males are feminized and, thus, homosexual. The "real" male was the opposite of both the female and the Jewish male. According to Gilman, Freud repressed this disparaging stereotype of Jewish men and projected it into the category of woman (i.e., women are castrated).

With this example, and with others I will discuss in later sections, I hope to show the indissociability of the discourses of anti-Semitism and misogyny in Freud's world and his attempts to deal with these hateful stereotypes in his theory. I will relate these themes to Freud's well-documented ambivalence about homosexuality (de Lauretis, 1994; Harris, this volume).

Freud as a Victim of Racial Trauma

Racialized hatred of Jews cast its shadow on Freud's life and work. It was because of anti-Semitism that Freud's parents migrated in 1859 from the Czech province of Moravia. The history of the Jews in this area is one not only of continuous injustice that led to massacre, but also of continuous uncertainty (Decker, 1991). What was constant was a long period of "state-decreed inferiority, familial upheaval, and spasms of dubious quiet and the trauma of hopes raised only to be brutally dashed" (Decker, 1991 p. 15).

Consider the traumatic history of Eastern European Jews from the eighteenth through the nineteenth centuries. In the early part of the eighteenth century, an edict to curtail the Jewish population was put into effect. The Familiants Laws of 1726 severely limited the number of Jews who could marry and have a family. Among those Jews who were legally recognized, only the eldest son was allowed to marry—and only after the age of twenty-four *and* after the death of his father. If children other than the eldest son wanted to marry legally, they were forced to leave the country, as many did. For those who stayed, the Familiants Law created a group of Jews who were illegal; the children of these marriages were illegitmate, were not allowed to settle anywhere permanently, and could not pursue a livelihood. They survived by begging (Decker, 1991).

With the accession of a new emperor (Joseph II) who wanted to make Jews more useful to the state, these policies changed. With the Edict of Tolerance of 1782, Jews were able to enter the wider world, but only if they gave up their Jewish heritage. Jewish children had to have a German secular education, and business, legal, and communal records could no longer be kept in Yiddish or Hebrew. High schools and universities opened their doors to Jewish boys who could enter certain professions when they graduated. Until this point existing laws had decreed dress codes for Jews, banned them from going outside during Christian festivals and requiring that both Jews and livestock pay a body tax when entering a city. With the nullification of these laws came an increasingly assimilated nineteenth-century Jewry, proud to be progressive and to abandon their Jewish heritage (Decker, 1991).

At the same time that these positive changes occurred in the 1880s and 1890s, a new kind of anti-Jewish feeling arose, now called anti-Semitism. It was fueled by fears and anger toward Jews about economic competition, as the ills of urban, technological life came to be symbolized by the activities of recently emancipated Jews (Decker, 1991).

Freud was not only exposed to hatred of Jews in popular culture; racialized hatred of Jews also pervaded science. In his extensive studies of the central role of racism in nineteenth-century biological and medical paradigms and its influence on Freud, Gilman (1993) stresses the contrast of human types: Aryan Christians, who represented "the perfected prototype," and Jews, who represented degeneration and disease. Within this nosology, Jews were believed to constitute a different race, measurably inferior to Aryan Christians.

Any Jew who became a physician (a profession that Jews were allowed to pursue for the first time in the nineteenth century) had to deal with racism in science. Gilman (1993) sees an answer to the Jew's stigmatization being worked out in the rhetoric of psychoanalysis. Consider that Freud moved away from the prevailing view of degeneracy as a pathology unique to the Jews. In Freud's *Three Essays* (1905) degeneracy is an illness of all people. By bringing the sexual activities of the "pervert" into the realm of the "normal" adult, Freud folded the marginal into the universal.

While Freud dealt with racism by universalizing negative stereotypes of Jews in his theory, at other times he projected racist views into the category of woman. Consider this description of women in *Three Essays*: (1905).

> [T]he significance of the factor of sexual overvaluation can best be studied in men, for their erotic life alone has become accessible to research. That of women—partly owing to the stunting effect of civilized conditions and partly owing to their convention of secretiveness and insincerity—is still veiled in an impenetrable obscurity. (p. 17)

Gilman (1993) holds that this pejorative tone mirrors anti–Semitic rhetoric, which described Jews not only as genetically tainted, but also as carriers of the ills of modern, industrialized conditions. Jews were said to hide their practices and conspiracies and to lie as part of their character.

Branding women insincere is repeated in "Psychogenesis," where Freud described his patient as disdaining "no means of deception" when she appeared in public with her "irreputable" friend against her parents' wishes. Unable to identify with the patient, Freud apparently never thought that she might be struggling to have freedom of movement and not be crushed by cultural expectations of women. Later in "Psychogenesis," he repeated the same charge: The "deceitful" patient was now lying not only to her parents but also to him. Freud interpreted his patient's dreams about being with a man and having children as deceptions meant to make him hopeful, only to disappoint him later on. Apparently, Freud was so blindsided by his need to see the patient as insincere and untrustworthy that he forgot his own theory of bisexuality.

By the end of the century, anti-Semitism and hatred of women had become indissociable in the popular mind. Seventeen years before Freud wrote his case study, Otto Weininger's *Sex and Character* was published in Austria. As astonishing as it seems to us today, the book was the talk of Vienna. Widely reviewed, believed by some to be a masterpiece, and admired by contemporaries such as Kafka, *Sex and Character* is important for the links it made between misogyny and Judaism. Weininger argued that women's pure sexuality contaminated men. Even the most superior woman ranked below the lowest man, as the highest Jew ranked below the lowest Christian. Judaism was contemptible because it was so feminine. Just as women lacked souls, so did Jews. Weininger, himself a Jew who had converted to Protestantism, killed himself because he thought he could never overcome the woman and the Jew in him. As Decker (1991) remarks,

> [I]t would, therefore, be simple to dismiss Weininger as an extremist and his book as the outcome of a psychotic depression. . . . The truth is that Weininger had only expressed flamboyantly what many believed: that women were an inferior order of being and that all other inferior groups could be compared with women when one was trying to explain the essence of their deficiencies. (p. 39)

Misogyny and the Budding Feminist Movement

Misogyny, like anti–Semitism, was also pervasive in Viennese society. It was not merely a prejudice but also a codified system of subjugation, set down in the Austrian Legal Code of 1811. According to its dictates, the husband was the legal "head of the family" and "director of the household," whose orders had to be obeyed by his wife. Without a husband's consent, women were not entitled to educate their children, run their households, go to court, or engage in commercial activities (Gay, 1988). Women were commonly depicted in middle-class newspaper articles as irrational, illogical, and dishonest. Since this was an attitude accepted by society at large, it is not surprising that it was shared by most early members of the Vienna Psychoanalytic Society (Decker, 1991).

Some of the attitudes expressed in "Psychogenesis" by both Freud and the patient's father, while as troubling and distasteful as ever, are in light of my argument herein, more comprehensible. Both tended to regard her strong-mindedness as "unnatural" as well as embarrassing and ill-advised. Not only did the patient insist on a female lover and the right to be seen with her in public, but she also insisted on her right to choose. The social reality was this: Women did not act. They waited, hoped, and tried in small ways to influence their fate, but did not create their futures. According to Gay (1988), Viennese women were brought up to be

> foolish and untaught, well-bred and unsuspecting, inquisitive and shy, uncertain and impractical, and predetermined by this unwordly education to be shaped and led in marriage by their husbands without a will of their own. (p. 511).

Freud's patient wildly violated these expectations. Her willfullness needed to be tamed; it was not only inconvenient, but was also not feminine. Freud required but a small step and an obvious one to disparage the patient's feminism by linking it with a "masculinity complex": "She was in fact a feminist; she felt it to be unjust that girls should not enjoy the same freedom as boys, and rebelled against the lot of woman in general"(p. 29, in this volume).

Freud's disparagement of the patient's feminism was not unique to him. Throughout the Western world by the mid-nineteenth century, feminists had started organizing to fight legal, social, and economic disadvantages. They faced an intense backlash (Gay, 1988). The first declaration of women's rights was voted on in 1848 in Seneca Falls, New York. According to Gay, it was almost timid in its tone. Despite its conciliatory attitude, it met with widespread anger. The authors were labelled "perverts" who were out to destroy the family and the natural relations between the sexes. Feminists were forced to confront an opposition that was securely rooted in church, state, and society (Gay, 1988).

In Austria, progress made by feminists was even slower than in other countries. An 1867 law prohibited women from participating in political actions; organizing to secure the vote was out of the question. When Austrian women organized at all, they chose safer causes that were traditionally associated with women: education and charity. Austrian women who wanted an education or an independent life were subject to severe ridicule. Middle-class women were unprepared to fight for their rights since Viennese "polite society" monitored both what they read and where they could go (Gay, 1988).

Toward an Understanding of Freud's Ambivalence toward Homosexuality

Thus far I have talked about the virulent anti-Semitism and misogyny that were prevalent in Freud's time. I have discussed how Freud projected hateful stereotypes about Jews into the category of women. With this information we are in a position to examine Freud's well-documented ambivalence toward homosexuality. Several authors (Harris, this volume; de Lauretis, 1994; Young-Bruehl, personal communication to de Lauretis, 1994) have pointed out the schism between the radical and the conventional Freud. The former is represented in *Three Essays* (1905), in which Freud wrote about both heterosexuality and homosexuality as constructions and stated, "We must loosen the bond between instinct and object that exists in our thoughts as it's probable that the sexual instinct to begin with is independent of its objects" (p. 11).

The conventional Freud, who dominates "Psychogenesis" with his heavy-handed, disparaging treatment of the patient and his advancement of a pathology model to explain her lesbianism, was already waiting in the wings in *Three Essays*. There Freud used a developmental model to describe heterosexuality as an ideal norm, a seed that will mature into normal sexuality (de Lauretis, 1994). As Young-Bruehl put it (personal communication to de Lauretis, 1994):

> Freud was forever fighting with himself, trying not [to] be a simple (or even an unsimple, Darwinian) teleologist, but being one all the same. His radicality . . . is his anti-teleology side; his conventionality rises when teleology wins back territory in him.

Could a Jewish man ever be in a position to depathologize homosexuality without risking that he himself would be seen as fitting the stereotype of a feminine, homosexual Jew? In many ways Freud was in a situation similar to the one in which we lesbian and gay psychoanalysts find ourselves today; our views about the anti-homosexual tenor of psychoanalytic theory are often marked "political" and dismissed, while the views of heterosexual homophobes are seen as unmarked and objective. Freud had good reason to be afraid (Lesser, 1997).

Freud's ambivalence about the relationship between gender and sexual object choice may also be seen in this context. While the radical Freud of the *Three Essays* broke with the sexologists of the day—who saw gender and sexual object choice as indissociable—by stating that there is no necessary connection between the two, the conservative Freud of "Psychogenesis" backed down from this position. In the latter he stated that the independence of gender and sexual object choice does not hold as completely for women as for men, for in women, "bodily and mental traits belonging to the opposite sex are apt to coincide" (p. 19, in this volume). By taking the masculine position in her style of loving another woman, the patient, according to Freud, "changed into a man and took her mother in place of her father as the object of her love" (p. 22, in this volume). Freud seemed so determined that men should be men and women women that he succumbed to social convention by equating activity in women with masculinity and pathology. It is a small stretch to understand why a representative of a group (i.e., Jewish males) slandered as feminine and homosexual would be at pains to keep the sexes separate and make activity the province of men.

How difficult it must have been for Freud to deal with his own homosexual feelings and his identification with women, much less go public with them, given the prevailing racist climate that slandered Jewish men for just these characteristics. Freud's homosexual feelings toward Fliess have been well-documented (Bernheimer, 1985; Boyarin, 1995). Bernheimer cites a letter Freud wrote to Fliess a few months before their final meeting, in which he stated, "[T]here can be no substitute for the close contact with a friend which a particular—almost a feminine—side of me calls for" (p. 16).

Bernheimer (1985) describes Freud as being aware of the erotic aspect of his relationship with Fliess from the outset, as in another letter Freud writes, "I am looking foward to our congress as to the slaking of hunger and thirst. I bring two open ears and one temporal lobe lubricated for reception" (p. 318). These letters suggest that Freud had overcome what he later called "the rebellious over-compensation of the male, [that] produces one of the strongest transference-resistances" (as quoted in Bernheimer, 1985): assuming a passive role toward another male. Yet in the Dora case it is apparent that Freud was unable to identify with Dora, repudiating as Other the feminine aspects of himself that he had been able to see in his relationship with Fliess. We find a similar inability on Freud's part to identify with the patient in "Psychogenesis."

Boyarin (1995) reflects that Freud's ability to consider his own "femininity" and homosexual feelings toward Fliess was undone by his turn to the positive Oedipus complex with its view of masculinity as active, phallic, and heterosexual. This model saved him from the anxiety created by his own ideas about the indeterminacy of the sexes, as well as from the charges that Jewish men are feminine and homosexual. Boyarin views the positive Oedipal complex as itself a repression of homosexual desire—a response to cultural representations of Jewish men as passive, feminine, and homosexual. While for

Freud's father, passivity connoted dignity and spiritual superiority, for the emancipated, secular Jewish male of Sigmund Freud's generation, passivity received its meaning within the context of the intensification of misogyny and antihomosexuality at the end of the century. Jewish male passivity, connected to homosexuality, was dangerously charged in the climate of Weininger, the Wilde scandal of 1895, and two homosexual scandals in Germany in 1902 and 1906 (Boyarin, 1995).

Reading "Psychogenesis"

"Psychogenesis" is a key text for understanding the development of psychoanalytic theory about lesbians. Yet, as Fuss notes, it "may well be Freud's most overlooked case study: certainly compared to the volume of criticism generated by the Dora case, the 'Psychogenesis' paper has received surprisingly little attention" (in this volume). The lack of critical consideration mirrors the marginalization of lesbians within both psychoanalytic theory and popular culture.

As O'Connor and Ryan (1993) note, the themes Freud presented in "Psychogenesis" came to dominate subsequent analytic debate about female homosexuality: whether its origination is acquired or congenital; the question of pathology vs. normalcy; its putative link to masculinity; its hypothesized causation in disappointment with and rejection by men and/or early fixation on the mother; the difficulties the analyst has with the patient's transference as well as his own countertransference; and the issue of whether "cure" is possible.

One of the reasons the coeditors wanted to assemble a collection of essays on "Psychogenesis" is that we wished to remove the patient from Freud's shadow and give her a voice. Consider how she was denied subjecthood by Freud's refusal to grant her a pseudonym, and never got to speak in her own voice within Freud's narrative. Perhaps, as Dimen suggests (in this volume), this was not entirely Freud's doing: It is possible that the patient's resistance to Freud took the form of her not making herself known (which, in my opinion, was good thinking on the patient's part). All of the essayists struggle with the difficulty, if not the impossibility, of giving a voice to a woman we never come to know by reading Freud's case study.

The coeditors had hoped to publish the interview that Kurt Eissler, M.D., is reported to have conducted with her. Unfortunately, the interview is locked within the Freud Archives, and Dr. Eissler has refused to discuss it with us for this book.

We hope that this volume will contribute to a reconsideration of "Psychogenesis" in terms of the pivotal role it played in the development of psychoanalytic theory of female homosexuality, the purposes that its biased views toward lesbians served, and the way that these biases became codified into the psychoanalytic canon.

References

Bernheimer, C. (1985). Introduction: Part I. In C. Bernheimer & C. Kahane (Eds.), *In Dora's case: Freud-hysteria-feminism*. New York: Columbia University Press.

Boyarin, D. (1995). Freud's baby, Fliess' maybe: Homophobia, anti-Semitism, and the invention of Oedipus. *GLQ: A Journal of Lesbian and Gay Studies, 2*, 1–12.

Decker, H. (1991). *Freud, Dora, and Vienna 1900*. New York: Free Press.

de Lauretis, T. (1994). *The practice of love: Lesbian sexuality and perverse desire*. Bloomington IN: Indiana University Press.

Freud, S. (1953–1974). Three essays on the theory of sexuality. In J. Strachey (Ed. and Trans.), The *Standard edition of the complete psychological works of Sigmund Freud*. (Vol. 7, pp. 123–245). London: Hogarth. (Original work published 1905)

Gay, P. (1988). *Freud: a life for our times*. New York: W.W. Norton & Co.

Gilman, S. (1991). *The Jew's body*. New York: Routledge.

Gilman, S. (1993a). *The case of Sigmund Freud: Medicine and identity at the fin de siècle*. Baltimore: The Johns Hopkins University Press.

Gilman, S. (1993b). *Freud, race, and gender*. Princeton, NJ: Princeton University Press.

Lesser, R. (1997). On the politics of writing sex: Response to commentaries on *Disorienting sexuality*. *Gender and Psychoanalysis, 2*.

O'Connor, N. & Ryan, J. (1993). *Wild desires & mistaken identities: Lesbianism & Psychoanalysis*. New York: Columbia University Press.

Young-Bruehl, E. Personal communication to de Lauretis as cited in de Lauretis (1994), *The practice of love: Lesbian sexiality and perverse desire*. Bloomington, IN: Indiana University Press.

Part I

~

THE PSYCHOGENESIS OF A CASE OF HOMOSEXUALITY IN A WOMAN

1

THE PSYCHOGENESIS OF A CASE OF HOMOSEXUALITY IN A WOMAN (1920)*

Sigmund Freud

I

Homosexuality in women, which is certainly not less common than in men, although much less glaring, has not only been ignored by the law, but has also been neglected by psychoanalytic research. The narration of a single case, not too pronounced in type, in which it was possible to trace its origin and development in the mind with complete certainty and almost without a gap may, therefore, have a certain claim to attention. If this presentation of it furnishes only the most general outlines of the various events concerned and of the conclusions reached from a study of the case, while suppressing all the characteristic details on which the interpretation is founded, this limitation is easily to be explained by the medical discretion necessary in discussing a recent case.

A beautiful and clever girl of 18, belonging to a family of good standing, had aroused displeasure and concern in her parents by the devoted adoration with which she pursued a certain lady "in society" who was about 10 years older than herself. The parents asserted that, in spite of her distinguished name, this lady was nothing but a *cocotte*. It was said to be well known that she lived with a married woman as her friend, having intimate relations with her, while at the same

---

* First published in *Zeitschrift*, Bd. VI., 1920; reprinted in *Sammlung,* Fünfte Folge. [Translated by Barbara Low and R. Gabler.]

time she carried on promiscuous affairs with a number of men. The girl did not contradict these evil reports, but neither did she allow them to interfere with her worship of the lady, although she herself was by no means lacking in a sense of decency and propriety. No prohibitions and no supervision hindered the girl from seizing every one of her rare opportunities of being together with her beloved, of ascertaining all her habits, of waiting for her for hours outside her door or at a tram-halt, of sending her gifts of flowers, and so on. It was evident that this one interest had swallowed up all others in the girl's mind. She did not trouble herself any further with educational studies, thought nothing of social functions or girlish pleasures, and kept up relations only with a few girl friends who could help her in the matter or serve as confidantes. The parents could not say to what lengths their daughter had gone in her relations with the questionable lady, whether the limits of devoted admiration had already been exceeded or not. They had never remarked in their daughter any interest in young men, nor pleasure in their attentions, while, on the other hand, they were sure that her present attachment to a woman was only a continuation, in a more marked degree, of a feeling she had displayed of recent years for other members of her own sex which had already aroused her father's suspicion and anger.

There were two details of her behavior, in apparent contrast with each other, that most especially vexed her parents. On the one hand, she did not scruple to appear in the most frequented streets in the company of her questionable friend, being thus quite neglectful of her own reputation; while, on the other hand, she disdained no means of deception, no excuses and no lies that would make meetings with her possible and cover them. She thus showed herself too brazen in one respect, and full of deceitfulness in the other. One day it happened, indeed, as was sooner or later inevitable in the circumstances that the father met his daughter in the company of the lady. He passed them by with an angry glance which boded no good. Immediately after, the girl rushed off and flung herself over a wall down the side of a cutting on to a railway line. She paid for this undoubtedly serious attempt at suicide with a considerable time on her back in bed, though fortunately little permanent damage was done. After her recovery she found it easier to get her own way than before. The parents did not dare to oppose her with so much determination, and the lady, who up till then had received her advances coldly, was moved by such an unmistakable proof of serious passion and began to treat her in a more friendly manner.

About 6 months after this episode the parents sought medical advice and entrusted the physician with the task of bringing their daughter back to a normal state of mind. The girl's attempted suicide had evidently shown them that the instruments of domestic discipline were powerless to overcome the existing disorder. Before going further it will be desirable, however, to deal separately with the attitude of her father and of her mother to the matter. The father was an earnest, worthy man, at bottom very tender-hearted, but he had to some extent estranged his children by the sternness he had adopted toward them. His treatment of his only daughter was too much influenced by consideration for his wife. When he first came to know of his daughter's homosexual tendencies he flared up in rage and tried to suppress them by threatening her; at that time perhaps he hesitated between different, though equally painful, views—regarding her either as vicious, as degenerate, or as mentally afflicted. Even after the attempted suicide he did not achieve the lofty resignation shown by one of our medical colleagues who remarked of a similar irregularity in his own family, "It is just a misfortune like any other." There was something about his daughter's homosexuality that aroused the deepest bitterness in him, and he was determined to combat it with all the means in his power; the low estimation in which psychoanalysis is so generally held in Vienna did not prevent him from turning to it for help. If this way failed he still had in reserve his strongest countermeasure; a speedy marriage was to awaken the natural instincts of the girl and stifle her unnatural tendencies.

The mother's attitude toward the girl was not so easy to grasp. She was still a youngish woman, who was evidently unwilling to relinquish her own claim to find favor by means of her beauty. All that was clear was that she did not take her daughter's passion so tragically as did the father, nor was she so incensed at it. She had even for a long time enjoyed her daughter's confidence concerning the love affair, and her opposition to it seemed to have been aroused mainly by the harmful publicity with which the girl displayed her feelings. She had herself suffered for some years from neurotic troubles and enjoyed a great deal of consideration from her husband; she was quite unfair in her treatment of her children, decidedly harsh toward her daughter and overindulgent to her three sons, the youngest of whom had been born after a long interval and was then not yet 3 years old. It was not easy to ascertain anything more definite about her character, for, owing to motives that will only later become intelligible, the patient was always reserved in what she said about her mother, whereas in regard to her father she showed no feeling of the kind.

To a physician who was to undertake psychoanalytic treatment of the girl, there were many grounds for a feeling of discomfort. The situation he had to deal with was not the one that analysis demands, in which alone it can demonstrate its effectiveness. As is well known, the ideal situation for analysis is when someone who is otherwise master of himself is suffering from an inner conflict, which he is unable to resolve alone, so that he brings his trouble to the analyst and begs for his help. The physician then works hand in hand with one part of the personality which is divided against itself, against the other partner in the conflict. Any situation but this is more or less unfavorable for psychoanalysis and

adds fresh difficulties to those already present. Situations like that of a proprietor who orders an architect to build him a villa according to his own tastes and
desires, or of a pious donor, who commissions an artist to paint a picture of
saints, in the corner of which is to be a portrait of himself worshipping, are
fundamentally incompatible with the conditions of psychoanalysis. It constantly
happens, to be sure, that a husband informs the physician as follows, "My wife
suffers from nerves, so that she gets on badly with me; please cure her, so that
we may lead a happy married life again." But often enough it turns out that such
a request is impossible to fulfill, i.e., that the physician cannot bring about the
result for which the husband sought the treatment. As soon as the wife is freed
from her neurotic inhibitions, she sets about dissolving the marriage, for her
neurosis was the sole condition under which maintenance of the marriage was
possible. Or else parents expect one to cure their nervous and unruly child. By
a healthy child they mean one who never places his parents in difficulties, but
only gives them pleasure. The physician may succeed in curing the child, but
after that it goes its own way all the more decidedly, and the parents are now
far more dissatisfied than before. In short, it is not a matter of indifference
whether someone comes to analysis of his own accord or because he is brought
to it, whether he himself desires to be changed, or only his relatives, who love
him (or who might be expected to love him), desire this for him.

Further unfavorable features in the present case were the facts that the girl
was not in any way ill—she did not suffer from anything in herself, nor did she
complain of her condition—and that the task to be carried out did not consist
in resolving a neurotic conflict but in converting one variety of the genital organization of sexuality into the other. The removal of genital inversion or homosexuality is in my experience never an easy matter. On the contrary, I have
found success possible only under specially favorable circumstances, and even
then the success essentially consisted in being able to open to those who are
restricted homosexually the way to the opposite sex, which had been till then
barred, thus restoring to them full bisexual functions. After that it lay with themselves to choose whether they wished to abandon the other way that is banned
by society, and in individual cases they have done so. One must remember that
normal sexuality also depends upon a restriction in the choice of object; in general, to undertake to convert a fully developed homosexual into a heterosexual
is not much more promising than to do the reverse, only that for good practical reasons the latter is never attempted.

In actual numbers the successes achieved by psychoanalytic treatment of the
various forms of homosexuality, which, to be sure, are manifold, are not very
striking. As a rule the homosexual is not able to give up the object of his pleasure,
and one cannot convince him that if he changed to the other object he would

find again the pleasure that he has renounced. If he comes to be treated at all, it is mostly through the pressure of external motives, such as the social disadvantages and dangers attaching to his choice of object, and such components of the instinct of self-preservation prove themselves too weak in the struggle against the sexual impulses. One then soon discovers his secret plan, namely, to obtain from the striking failure of his attempt the feeling of satisfaction that he has done everything possible against his abnormality, to which he can now resign himself with an easy conscience. The case is somewhat different when consideration for beloved parents and relatives has been the motive for his attempt to be cured. Then there really are libidinal tendencies present which may put forth energies opposed to the homosexual choice of object, though their strength is rarely sufficient. It is only where the homosexual fixation has not yet become strong enough, or where there are considerable rudiments and vestiges of a heterosexual choice of object, i.e., in a still oscillating or in a definitely bisexual organization that one may make a more favorable prognosis for psychoanalytic therapy.

For these reasons I declined altogether holding out to the parents any prospect of their wish being fulfilled. I merely said I was prepared to study the girl carefully for a few weeks or months, so as then to be able to pronounce how far a continuation of the analysis might influence her. In quite a number of cases, indeed, the analysis divides itself into two clearly distinguishable stages: In the first, the physician procures from the patient the necessary information, makes him familiar with the premises and postulates of psychoanalysis, and unfolds to him the reconstruction of the genesis of his disorder as deduced from the material brought up in the analysis. In the second stage the patient himself lays hold of the material put before him, works on it, recollects what he can of the apparently repressed memories, and behaves as if he were living the rest over again. In this way he can confirm, supplement, and correct the inferences made by the physician. It is only during this work that he experiences, through overcoming resistances, the inner change aimed at, and acquires for himself the convictions that make him independent of the physician's authority. These two stages in the course of the analytic treatment are not always sharply divided from each other; this can only happen when the resistance maintains certain conditions. But when this is so, one may institute a comparison with two stages of a journey. The first comprises all the necessary preparations, today so complicated and hard to effect, before, ticket in hand, one can at last go on to the platform and secure a seat in the train. One then has the right, and the possibility, of travelling into a distant country, but after all these preliminary exertions one is not yet there—indeed, one is not a single mile nearer to one's goal. For this to happen one has to make the journey itself from one station to the other, and this part of the performance may well be compared with the second stage in the analysis.

The analysis of the patient I am discussing took this course of two stages, but it was not continued beyond the beginning of the second stage. A special constellation of the resistance made it possible, nevertheless, to gain full confirmation of my inferences and to obtain an adequate insight on broad lines into the way in which her inversion had developed. But before relating the findings of the analysis I must deal with a few points which have either been touched upon already by myself or which will have roused special interest in the reader.

I had made the prognosis partly dependent on how far the girl had succeeded in satisfying her passion. The information I gleaned during the analysis seemed favorable in this respect. With none of the objects of her adoration had the patient enjoyed anything beyond a few kisses and embraces; her genital chastity, if one may use such a phrase, had remained intact. As for the lady who led a double life and who had roused the girl's most recent and by far her strongest emotions, she had always treated her coldly and had never allowed any greater favor than kissing her hand. Probably the girl was making a virtue of necessity when she kept insisting on the purity of her love and her physical repulsion against the idea of any sexual intercourse. But perhaps she was not altogether wrong when she vaunted of her wonderful beloved that, aristocrat as she was, forced into her present position only by adverse family circumstances, she had preserved, in spite of her situation, a great deal of nobility. For the lady used to recommend the girl every time they met to withdraw her affection from herself and from women in general, and she had persistently rejected the girl's advances up to the time of the attempted suicide.

A second point, which I at once tried to investigate, concerned any possible motives in the girl herself which might serve to support a psychoanalytic treatment. She did not try to deceive me by saying that she felt any urgent need to be freed from her homosexuality. On the contrary, she said she could not conceive of any other way of being in love, but she added that for her parents's sake she would honestly help in the therapeutic endeavor, for it pained her very much to be the cause of so much grief to them. I had to take this as a propitious sign to begin with; I could not divine the unconscious affective attitude that lay behind it. What came to light later in this connection decisively influenced the course taken by the analysis and determined its premature conclusion.

Readers unversed in psychoanalysis will long have been awaiting an answer to two other questions. Did this homosexual girl show physical characteristics plainly belonging to the opposite sex, and did the case prove to be one of congenital or acquired (later developed) homosexuality?

I am aware of the importance attaching to the first of these questions. Only one should not exaggerate it and obscure in its favor the fact that sporadic secondary characteristics of the opposite sex are very often present in normal individuals and that well-marked physical characteristics of the opposite sex may be found in persons whose choice of object has undergone no change in the direction of inversion; in other words, that in both sexes *the degree of physical hermaphroditism is to a great extent independent of the psychical hermaphroditism.* In modification of this statement it must be added that this independence is more evident in men than women, where bodily and mental traits belonging to the opposite sex are apt to coincide in their incidence. Still I am not in a position to give a satisfactory answer to the first of our questions about my patient: the psychoanalyst customarily forgoes thorough bodily examination of his patients in certain cases. Certainly there was no obvious deviation from the feminine physical type, nor any menstrual disturbance. The beautiful and well-developed girl had, it is true, her father's tall figure, and her facial features were sharp rather than soft and girlish, traits which might be regarded as indicating a physical masculinity. Some of her intellectual attributes also could be connected with masculinity: for instance, her acuteness of comprehension and her lucid objectivity, in so far as she was not dominated by her passion, though these distinctions are conventional rather than scientific. What is certainly of greater importance is that in her behavior toward her love-object she had throughout assumed the masculine part: that is to say, she displayed the humility and the sublime overestimation of the sexual object so characteristic of the male lover, the renunciation of all narcissistic satisfaction, and the preference for being lover rather than beloved. She had thus not only chosen a feminine love-object, but had also developed a masculine attitude toward this object.

The second question, whether this was a case of inherited or acquired homosexuality, will be answered by the whole history of the patient's abnormality and its development. The study of this will show how fruitless and inappropriate this question is.

II

After an introduction which digresses in so many directions, the sexual history of the case under consideration can be presented quite concisely. In childhood the girl had passed through the normal attitude characteristic of the feminine Oedipus complex[1] in a way that was not at all remarkable, and had later also begun to substitute for her father a brother slightly older than herself. She did not remember any sexual traumata in early life, nor were any discovered by the analysis. Comparison of her brother's genital organs and her own, which took place about the beginning of the latency period (at 5 years old or perhaps a little earlier), left a strong impression on her and had far-reaching after effects. There were only slight hints pointing to infantile onanism, or else the analysis did not go deep enough to throw light on this point. The birth of a second brother when she was between 5 and 6 years old left no special influence upon her development. During the prepubertal years at school she gradually became acquainted with the facts of sex, and she received this knowledge with mixed feelings of fascination and frightened aversion, in a way which may be called normal and was not exaggerated in degree. This amount of information about her seems meager enough, nor can I guarantee that it is complete. It may be that the history of her youth was much richer in experiences; I do not know. As I have already said, the analysis was broken off after a short time, and therefore yielded an anamnesis not much more reliable than the other anamneses of homosexuals, which there is good cause to question. Further, the girl had never been neurotic and came to the analysis without even one hysterical symptom, so that opportunities for investigating the history of her childhood did not present themselves so readily as usual.

At the age of 13 to 14 she displayed a tender and, according to general opinion, exaggeratedly strong affection for a small boy, not quite 3 years old, whom she used to see regularly in a playground in one of the parks. She took to the child so warmly that in consequence a permanent friendship grew up between herself and his parents. One may infer from this episode that at that time she was possessed of a strong desire to be a mother herself and to have a child. However, after a short time she grew indifferent to the boy and began to take an interest in mature, but still youthful, women; the manifestations of this in her soon led her father to administer a mortifying chastisement to her.

It was established beyond all doubt that this change occurred simultaneously with a certain event in the family, and one may therefore look to this for some explanation of the change. Before it happened, her libido was focused on motherhood, while afterward she became a homosexual attracted to mature women, and has remained so ever since. The event which is so significant for our understanding of the case was a new pregnancy of her mother's and the birth of a third brother when she was about 16.

The network of causes and effects that I shall now proceed to lay bare is not a product of my gift for combination; it is based on such trustworthy analytic evidence that I can claim objective validity for it; it was in particular a series of interrelated dreams, easy of interpretation, that proved decisive in this respect.

The analysis revealed beyond all shadow of doubt that the beloved lady was a substitute for—the mother. It is true that she herself was not a mother, but then she was not the girl's first love. The first objects of her affection after the birth of her youngest brother were really mothers, women between 30 and 35 whom she had met with their children during summer holidays or in the family circle of acquaintances in town. Motherhood as a "condition of love" was later on given up, because it was difficult to combine in real life with another one, which grew more and more important. The specially intensive bond with her latest love, the "Lady," had still another basis which the girl discovered quite easily one day. On account of her slender figure, regular beauty, and offhand manner, the lady reminded her of her own brother, a little older than herself. Her latest choice corresponded, therefore, not only with her feminine but also with her masculine ideal; it combined gratification of the homosexual tendency with that of the heterosexual one. It is well known that analysis of male homosexuals has in numerous cases revealed the same combination, which should warn us not to form too simple a conception of the nature and genesis of inversion and to keep in mind the extensive influence of the bisexuality of mankind.[2]

But how are we to understand the fact that it was just the birth of a child who came late in the family, at a time when the girl herself was already mature and had strong wishes of her own, that moved her to bestow her passionate tenderness upon her who gave birth to this child, i.e., own mother, and to express that feeling toward a substitute for her mother? From all that we know we should have expected just the opposite. In such circumstances mothers with daughters of about a marriageable age usually feel embarrassed in regard to them, while the daughters are apt to feel for their mothers a mixture of compassion, contempt, and envy, which does nothing to increase their tenderness for them. The girl we are considering, however, had altogether little cause to feel affection for her mother. The latter, still youthful herself, saw in her rapidly developing daughter an inconvenient competitor; she favored the sons at her expense, limited her independence as much as possible, and kept an especially strict watch against any close relation between the girl and her father. A yearning from the beginning for a kinder mother would, therefore, have been quite intelligible, but why it should have flamed up just then, and in the form of a consuming passion, is not comprehensible.

The explanation is as follows: The girl was just experiencing the revival of the infantile Oedipus complex at puberty when she suffered a great disappointment. She became keenly conscious of the wish to have a child, and a male one; that it was her father's child and his image that she desired, her consciousness was not allowed to know. And then—it was not she who bore the child, but the unconsciously hated rival, her mother. Furiously resentful and embittered, she turned away from her father and from men altogether. After this first great reverse she forswore her womanhood and sought another goal for her libido.

In doing so she behaved just as many men do who after a first painful experience turn their backs forever upon the faithless female sex and become woman-haters. It is related of one of the most attractive and unfortunate princes of our time that he became a homosexual because the lady he was engaged to marry betrayed him with a stranger. I do not know whether this is true histor-

ically, but much psychological truth lies behind the rumor. In all of us, throughout life, the libido normally oscillates between male and female objects; the
bachelor gives up his men friends when he marries, and returns to club life when
married life has lost its savor. Naturally, when the swingover is fundamental and
final, we suspect some special factor which has definitely favored one side or the
other and which perhaps only waited for the appropriate moment in order to
turn the choice of object finally in its direction.

After her disappointment, therefore, this girl had entirely repudiated her wish
for a child, the love of a man, and womanhood altogether. Now it is evident that
at this point the developments open to her were very manifold; what actually
happened was the most extreme one possible. She changed into a man and took
her mother in place of her father as her love object.[3] Her relation to her mother
had certainly been ambivalent from the beginning, and it proved easy to revive
her earlier love for her mother and with its help to bring about an overcompensation for her current hostility toward her. Since there was little to be done
with the real mother, there arose from the conversion of feeling described the
search for a mother-substitute to whom she could become passionately attached.[4]

In her actual relations with her mother there was a practical motive further-
ing the change of feeling which might be called an "advantage through illness."
The mother herself still attached great value to the attentions and the admiration of men. If, then, the girl became homosexual and left men to her mother
(in other words, "retired in favor of" the mother), she removed something
which had hitherto been partly responsible for her mother's disfavor.[5]

The attitude of the libido thus adopted was greatly reinforced as soon as the girl
perceived how much it displeased her father. Once she had been punished for an
over-affectionate overture made to a woman she realized how she could wound
her father and take revenge on him. Henceforth she remained homosexual out of
defiance against her father. Nor did she scruple to lie to him and to deceive him
in every way. Toward her mother, indeed, she was only so far deceitful as was
necessary to prevent her father from knowing things. I had the impression that
her behavior followed the principle of the talion: "Since you have betrayed me,
you must put up with my betraying you." Nor can I come to any other conclusion about the striking lack of caution displayed by this otherwise ingenious and
clever girl. She *wanted* her father to know occasionally of her intercourse with the
lady, otherwise she would be deprived of satisfaction of her keenest desire—
namely revenge. So she saw to this by showing herself openly in the company of
her adored one, by walking with her in the streets near her father's place of business, and the like. This maladroitness was by no means unintentional. It was
remarkable by the way, that both parents behaved as though they understood the
secret psychology of their daughter. The mother was tolerant, as though she

appreciated the favor of her daughter's "retirement" from the arena; the father was furious, as though he realized the deliberate revenge directed against himself.

The girl's inversion, however, received its final reinforcement when she found in her "Lady" an object which promised to satisfy not only her homosexual tendency, but also that part of her heterosexual libido still attached to her brother.

III

Consecutive presentation is not a very adequate means of describing complicated mental processes going on in different layers of the mind. I am therefore obliged to pause in the discussion of the case and treat more fully and deeply some of the points brought forward earlier.

I mentioned the fact that in her behavior to her adored lady the girl had adopted the characteristic masculine type of love. Her humility and her tender lack of pretensions, "*che poco spera e nulla chiede,*" her bliss when she was allowed to accompany the lady a little way and to kiss her hand on parting, her joy when she heard her praised as beautiful—while any recognition of her own beauty by another person meant nothing at all to her—her pilgrimages to places once visited by the loved one, the oblivion of all more sensual wishes: All these little traits in her resembled the first passionate adoration of a youth for a celebrated actress whom he regards as far above him, to whom he scarcely dares lift his bashful eyes. The correspondence with the "type of object choice in men" that I have described elsewhere, whose special features I traced to the attachment to the mother[6] held good even to the smallest details. It may seem remarkable that she was not in the least repelled by the evil reputation of her beloved, although her own observations sufficiently confirmed the truth of such rumors. She was after all a well-brought-up and modest girl who had avoided sexual adventures for herself and who regarded coarsely sensual gratification as unaesthetic. But already her first passions had been for women who were not celebrated for specially strict propriety. The first protest her father made against her love-choice had been evoked by the pertinacity with which she sought the company of a cinematograph actress at a summer resort. Moreover, in all these affairs it had never been a question of women who had any reputation for homosexuality and who might, therefore, have offered her some prospect of homosexual gratification; on the contrary, she illogically courted women who were coquettes in the ordinary sense of the word, and she rejected without hesitation the willing advances made by a homosexual friend of her own age. The bad reputation of her "Lady," however, was positively a "condition of love" for her, and all that is enigmatical in this attitude vanishes when we remember that in the case of the masculine type of object-choice derived from the mother it is also an essential condition that the loved object should be in some way or other "of bad repute" sexually, one who really may be called a "light woman." When the girl learned later on how far her adored lady deserved to be called by this title and that she lived simply by giving her bodily favors, her reaction took the form of great compassion and of fantasies and plans for "rescuing" her beloved from these ignoble circumstances. We have been struck by the same endeavors to "rescue" in the men of the type referred to earlier, and in my description of it I have tried to give the analytical derivation of this tendency.

We are led into quite another realm of explanation by the analysis of the attempt at suicide, which I must regard as seriously intended, and which, by the way, considerably improved her position both with her parents and with the lady she loved. She went for a walk with her one day in a part of the town and at an hour at which she was not unlikely to meet her father on his way from his office. So it turned out. Her father passed them in the street and cast a furious look at her and her companion, whom he had by that time come to know. A few moments later, she flung herself on to the railway cutting. Now the explanation she gave of the immediate reasons determining her resolution sounded quite plausible. She had confessed to the lady that the man who had given them such an irate glance was her father and that he had absolutely forbidden their friendship. The lady became incensed at this and ordered the girl to leave her then and there and never again to wait for her or to address her—the affair must now come to an end. In her despair at having thus lost her loved one forever, she wanted to put an end to herself. The analysis, however, was able to disclose another and deeper interpretation behind the one she gave, which was confirmed by the evidence of her own dreams. The attempted suicide was, as might have been expected, determined by two other motives besides the one she gave: it was a "punishment-fulfilment" (self-punishment), and a wish-fulfilment. As a wish-fulfilment it signified the attainment of the very wish which, when frustrated, had driven her into homosexuality—namely, the wish to have a child by her father, for now she "fell"[7] through her father's fault.[8] The fact that at this moment the lady had spoken to the same effect as the father and had uttered the same prohibition, forms the connecting link between this deeper interpretation and the superficial one of which the girl herself was conscious. From the point of view of self-punishment, the girl's action shows us that she had developed in her unconscious strong death wishes against one or other of her parents: perhaps against her father, out of revenge for impeding her love, but, more likely, also against her mother when she was pregnant with the little brother. For analysis has explained the enigma of suicide in the following way: Probably no one finds the mental energy required to kill himself unless, in the first place, he is in doing this at the same time killing an object with whom he has identified himself and, in the second place, is turning against himself a death wish which had been directed against someone else. Nor need the regular discovery of these unconscious death wishes in those who have attempted suicide surprise us as strange (any more than it need make an impression as confirming our deductions), since the unconscious of all human beings is full enough of such death wishes, even against those we love.[9] The girl's identification of herself with her mother, who ought to have died at the birth of the child denied to herself, makes this "punishment-fulfilment" itself again into a "wish-fulfilment." Lastly, a discovery that several quite different motives, all of great strength, must have cooperated to make such a deed possible is only in accord with what we should expect.

In the girl's account of her conscious motives the father did not figure at all, there was not even any mention of fear of his anger. In the motivation laid bare by the analysis he played the principal part. Her relation to her father had this same decisive importance for the course and outcome of the analytic treatment, or rather, analytic exploration. Behind her pretended consideration for her parents, for whose sake she had been willing to make the attempt to be transformed, lay concealed her attitude of defiance and revenge against her father which held her fast to her homosexuality. Secure under this cover, the resistance allowed a considerable degree of freedom to the analytic investigation. The analysis went forward almost without any signs of resistance, the patient participating actively with her intellect, though absolutely tranquil emotionally. [Once when I expounded to her a specially important part of the theory, one touching her nearly, she replied in an inimitable tone, "How very interesting," as though she were a *grande dame* being taken over a museum and glancing through her lorgnon at objects to which she was completely indifferent.] The impression one had of her analysis was not unlike that of an hypnotic treatment, where the resistance has in the same way withdrawn to a certain limit, beyond which it then proves to be unconquerable. The resistance very often pursues similar tactics—Russian tactics, as they might be called[10]—in cases of the obsessional neurosis, which for this reason yield the clearest results for a time and permit of a penetrating inspection of the causation of the symptoms. One begins to wonder how it is that such marked progress in analytic understanding can be unaccompanied by even the slightest change in the patient's compulsions and inhibitions, until at last one perceives that everything accomplished had been admitted only under the mental reservation of doubt,[11] and behind this protective barrier the neurosis may feel secure. "It would be all very fine," thinks the patient, often quite consciously, "if I were obliged to believe what the man says, but there is no question of that, and so long as that is not so I need change nothing." Then, when one comes to close quarters with the motivation of this doubt, the fight with the resistances breaks forth in earnest.

In the case of our patient, it was not doubt, but the affective factor of revenge against her father that made her cool reserve possible, that divided the analysis into two distinct stages and rendered the results of the first stage so complete and perspicuous. It seemed, further, as though nothing resembling a transference to the physician had been effected. That, however, is of course absurd, or, at least, is a loose way of expressing it; for some kind of relation to the analyst must come about, and this is usually transferred from an infantile one. In reality she transferred to me the deep antipathy to men which had dominated her ever since the disappointment she had suffered from her father. Bitterness against men is as a rule easy to gratify upon the analyst; it need not evoke any violent emotional manifestations; it simply expresses itself in rendering futile all his endeavors and in clinging to the neurosis. I know from experience how difficult it is to make the patient understand just this mute kind of symptomatic behavior and to make him aware of this latent, and often exceedingly strong, hostility without endangering the treatment. So as soon as I recognized the girl's attitude to her father, I broke off the treatment and gave the advice that, if it was thought worth while to continue the therapeutic efforts, it should be done by a woman. The girl had in the meanwhile promised her father that at any rate she would not communicate with the "Lady," and I do not know whether my advice, the motive for which is evident, will be followed.

Only once in the course of this analysis did anything appear which I could regard as a positive transference, a greatly weakened revival of the original passionate love for the father. Even this manifestation was not quite free from other motives but I mention it because it brings up, in another direction, an interesting problem of analytic technique. At a certain period, not long after the treatment had begun, the girl brought a series of dreams which, distorted as is customary and couched in the usual dream-language, could nevertheless be easily translated with certainty. Their content, when interpreted, was, however, remarkable. They anticipated the cure of the inversion through the treatment, expressed her joy over the prospects in life then opened before her, confessed her longing for a man's love and for children, and so might have been welcomed as a gratifying preparation for the desired change. The contradiction between them and the girl's utterances in waking life at the time was very great. She did not conceal from me that she meant to marry, but only in order to escape from her father's tyranny and to follow her true inclinations undisturbed. As for the husband, she remarked rather contemptuously, she would easily deal with him and besides, one could have sexual relations with a man and a woman at one and the same time, as the example of the adored lady showed. Warned through some slight impression or other, I told her one day that I did not believe these dreams, that I regarded them as false or hypocritical, and that she intended to deceive me just as she habitually deceived her father. I was right; after this exposition this kind of dream ceased. But I still believe that, beside the intention to mislead me, the dreams partly expressed the wish to win my favor; they were also an attempt to gain my interest and my good opinion—perhaps in order to disappoint me all the more thoroughly later on.

I can imagine that to point out the existence of lying dreams of this kind, destined to please the analyst, will arouse in some readers who call themselves analysts a real storm of helpless indignation. "What!" they will exclaim, "so the unconscious, the real center of our mental life, the part of us that is so much nearer the divine than our poor consciousness, so that too can lie! Then how can we still build on the interpretations of analysis and the accuracy of our findings?" To which one must reply that the recognition of these lying dreams does not constitute an astounding novelty. I know, indeed, that the craving of mankind for mysticism is ineradicable and that it makes ceaseless efforts to win back for mysticism the playground it has been deprived of by the *Traumdeutung,* but in the case under consideration surely everything is simple enough. A dream is not the "unconscious" itself; it is the form into which a thought from the preconscious, or even from waking conscious life, can, thanks to the favoring conditions of sleep, be recast. During sleep this thought has been reinforced by unconscious wish-excitations and thus has experienced distortion through the "dream-work," which is determined by the mechanisms valid for the unconscious. With our dreamer, the intention to mislead me, just as she did her father, certainly emanated from the preconscious, or perhaps even from consciousness; it could come to expression by entering into connection with the unconscious wish-impulse to please the father (or father-substitute), and in this way it created a lying dream. The two intentions, to betray and to please the father, originate in the same complex; the former resulted from the repression of the latter, and the later one was reduced by the dream-work to the earlier one. There can therefore be no question of any devaluation of the unconscious, nor of a shaking of our confidence in the results of our analysis.

I will not miss this opportunity of expressing for once my astonishment that human beings can go through such great and momentous phases of their love life without heeding them much, sometimes even, indeed, without having the faintest suspicion of them: or else that, when they do become aware of these phases, they deceive themselves so thoroughly in their judgment of them. This happens not only with neurotics, where we are familiar with the phenomenon, but seems also to be common enough in ordinary life. In the present case, for example, a girl develops a devotion for women, which her parents at first find merely vexatious and hardly take seriously; she herself knows quite well that her feelings are greatly engaged, but still she is only slightly aware of the sensations of intense love until a certain disappointment is followed by an absolutely excessive reaction, which shows everyone concerned that they have to do with a consuming passion of elemental strength. Even the girl herself had never perceived anything of the conditions necessary for the outbreak of such a mental upheaval. In other cases we come across girls or women in a state of severe depression, who on being asked for a possible cause of their condition tell us that they have, it is true, had a little feeling for a certain person, but that it was nothing deep and that they soon got over it when they had to give up hope. And yet it was this renunciation, apparently so easily borne, that became the cause of serious mental disturbance. Again, we have to do with men who have passed through casual love affairs and then realize only from the subsequent effects that they had been passionately in love with someone whom they had apparently regarded lightly. One is also amazed at the unexpected results that may follow an artificial abortion which had been decided upon without remorse and without hesitation. One must agree that the poets are right who are so fond of portraying people in love without knowing it, or uncertain whether they do love, or who think that they hate when in reality they love. It would seem that the knowledge received by our consciousness of what is happening to our love-instincts is especially liable to be incomplete, full of gaps, or falsified. Needless to say, in this discussion I have not omitted to allow for the part played by subsequent failures of memory.

IV

I now come back, after this disgression, to the consideration of my patient's case. We have made a survey of the forces which led the girl's libido from the normal Oedipus attitude into that of homosexuality, and of the paths thus traversed by it in the mind. Most important in this respect was the impression made by the birth of her little brother, and we might from this be inclined to classify the case as one of late acquired inversion.

But at this point we become aware of a state of things which also confronts us in many other instances in which light has been thrown by psychoanalysis on a mental process. So long as we trace the development from its final stage backward, the connection appears continuous, and we feel we have gained an insight which is completely satisfactory or even exhaustive. But if we proceed the reverse way, if we start from the premises inferred from the analysis and try to follow these up to the final result, then we no longer get the impression of an inevitable sequence of events which could not be otherwise determined. We notice at once that there might have been another result and that we might have been just as well able to understand and explain the latter. The synthesis is thus not so satisfactory as the analysis; in other words, from a knowledge of the premises we could not have foretold the nature of the result.

It is very easy to account for this disturbing state of affairs. Even supposing that we thoroughly know the etiological factors that decide a given result, still we know them only qualitatively and not in their relative strength. Some of them are so weak as to become suppressed by others and therefore do not affect the final result. But we never know beforehand which of the determining factors will prove the weaker or the stronger. We only say at the end that those which succeeded must have been the stronger. Hence it is always possible by analysis to recognize the causation with certainty, whereas a prediction of it by synthesis is impossible.

We do not, therefore, mean to maintain that every girl who experiences a disappointment of this kind, of the longing for love that springs from the Oedipus attitude during puberty, will necessarily on that account fall a victim to homosexuality. On the contrary, other kinds of reaction to this trauma are probably commoner. Then, however, there must have been present in this girl special factors that turned the scale, factors outside the trauma, probably of an internal nature. Nor is there any difficulty in pointing them out.

It is well known that even in the normal person it takes a certain time before a decision in regard to the sex of the love-object is finally achieved. Homosexual enthusiasms, unduly strong friendships tinged with sensuality, are common enough in both sexes during the first years after puberty. This was also so with our patient, but in her these tendencies undoubtedly showed themselves to be stronger, and lasted longer, than with others. In addition, these presages of later homosexuality had always occupied her conscious life, while the attitude arising from the Oedipus complex had remained unconscious and had appeared only in such signs as her tender fondling of the little boy. As a schoolgirl she was for a long time in love with a strict and unapproachable mistress, obviously a mother-substitute. A long time before the birth of her brother and still longer before the first reprimand at the hands of her father, she had taken a specially keen interest in various young mothers. From very early years, therefore, her libido had flowed in two streams, the one on the surface being one that we may unhesitatingly designate homosexual. This latter was probably a direct and unchanged continuation of an infantile mother-fixation. Possibly the analysis described here actually revealed nothing more than the process by which, on an appropriate occasion, the deeper heterosexual libido stream was also deflected into the manifest homosexual one.

The analysis showed, further, that the girl had suffered from childhood from a strongly marked "masculinity complex." A spirited girl, always ready to fight, she was not at all prepared to be second to her slightly older brother; after inspecting his genital organs she had developed a pronounced envy of the penis, and the thoughts derived from this envy still continued to fill her mind. She was in fact a feminist; she felt it to be unjust that girls should not enjoy the same freedom as boys and rebelled against the lot of woman in general. At the time of the analysis the idea of pregnancy and childbirth was disagreeable to her, partly, I surmise, on account of the bodily disfigurement connected with them. Her girlish narcissism had betaken itself to this refuge[12] and ceased to express itself as pride in her good looks. Various clues indicated that she must formerly have taken great pleasure in exhibitionism and scoptophilia. Anyone who is anxious that the claims of environment in etiology should not come short, as opposed to those of heredity, will call attention to the fact that the girl's behavior, as described herein, was exactly what would follow from the combined effect in a person with a strong mother-fixation of the two influences of her mother's indifference and of her comparison of her genital organs with her brother's. It is possible here to trace back to the impression of an effective external influence in early life something which one would have been ready to regard as a constitutional peculiarity. But a part even of this acquired disposition, if it has really been acquired, has to be ascribed to the inborn constitution. So we see in practice a continual mingling and blending of what in theory we should try to separate into a pair of opposites—namely, inherited and acquired factors.

An earlier, more tentative, conclusion of the analysis might have led to the view that this was a case of late-acquired homosexuality, but deeper consideration of the material undertaken later impels us to conclude that it is rather a case of inborn homosexuality which, as usual, became fixed and unmistakably manifest only in the period following puberty. Each of these classifications does justice only to one part of the state of affairs ascertainable by observation, but neglects the other. It would be best not to attach too much value to this way of stating the problem.

Publications on homosexuality usually do not distinguish clearly enough between the questions of the choice of object, on the one hand, and of the sexual characteristics and sexual attitude of the subject, on the other, as though the answer to the former necessarily involved the answers to the latter. Experience, however, proves the contrary: A man with predominantly male characteristics and also masculine in his love life may still be inverted in respect to his object, loving only men instead of women. A man in whose character feminine attributes evidently predominate, who may, indeed, behave in love like a woman, might be expected, from this feminine attitude, to choose a man for his love-object, but he may nevertheless be heterosexual and show no more inversion in respect of his object than an average normal man. The same is true of women; here also mental sexual character and object-choice do not necessarily coincide. The mystery of homosexuality is therefore by no means so simple as it is commonly depicted in popular expositions, e.g., a feminine personality, which therefore has to love a man, is unhappily attached to a male body; or a masculine personality, irresistibly attracted by women, is unfortunately cemented to a female body. It is instead a question of three series of characteristics, namely—

Physical sexual characteristics—Mental sexual characteristics
(physical hermaphroditism) (masculine, or feminine, attitude)
Kind of object-choice

which up to a certain point, vary independently of one another and are met with in different individuals in manifold permutations. Tendencious publications have obscured our view of this interrelationship by putting into the foreground, for practical reasons, the third feature (the kind of object-choice), which is the only one that strikes the layman, and in addition by exaggerating the closeness of the association between this and the first feature. Moreover, they block the way leading to a deeper insight into all that is uniformly designated homosexuality by rejecting two fundamental facts which have been revealed by psychoanalytic investigation. The first of these is that homosexual men have experienced a specially strong fixation in regard to the mother; the second, that in addition to their manifest heterosexuality, a very considerable measure of latent or unconscious homosexuality can be detected in all normal people. If these findings are taken into account, then, to be sure, the supposition that nature in a freakish mood created a "third sex" falls to the ground.

It is not for psychoanalysis to solve the problem of homosexuality. It must rest content with disclosing the psychical mechanisms that resulted in determination of the object-choice and with tracing the paths leading from them to the instinctual basis of the disposition. There its work ends, and it leaves the rest to biological research, which has recently brought to light, through Steinach's[13] experiments, such very important results concerning the influence exerted by the first factor mentioned above on the second and third. Psychoanalysis has a common basis with biology, in that it presupposes an original bisexuality in human beings (as in animals). But psychoanalysis cannot elucidate the intrinsic nature of what in conventional or in biological phraseology is termed "masculine" and "feminine"; it simply takes over the two concepts and makes them the foundation of its work. When we attempt to reduce them further, we find masculinity vanishing into activity and femininity into passivity, and that does not tell us enough. In what has gone before I have tried to explain how far we may reasonably expect, or how far experience has already proved, that the elucidations yielded by analysis furnish us with the means for altering inversion. When one compares the extent to which we can influence it with the remarkable transformations that Steinach has effected in some cases by his operations, it does not make a very imposing impression. Thus it would be premature, or a harmful exaggeration, if at this stage we were to indulge in hopes of a "therapy" of inversion that could be generally used. The cases of male homosexual-

ity in which Steinach has been successful fulfilled the condition, which is not
always present, of a very patent physical "hermaphroditism." Any analogous
treatment of female homosexuality is at present quite obscure. If it were to consist in removing the probably hermaphroditic ovaries and in implanting others,
which would, it is hoped, be of a single sex, there would be little prospect of its
being applied in practice. A woman who has felt herself to be a man and has
loved in masculine fashion will hardly let herself be forced into playing the part
of a woman when she must pay for this transformation, which is not in every
way advantageous, by renouncing all hope of motherhood.

Notes

1. I do not see any progress or advantage in the introduction of the term "Electra
complex," and do not advocate its use.

2. Cf. J. Sadger, *Jahresbericht über sexuelle Perversionen*.

3. It is by no means rare for a love relation to be broken off by means of a process
of identification on the part of the lover with the loved object, a process equivalent to
a kind of regression to narcissism. After this has been accomplished, it is easy in making
a fresh choice of object to direct the libido to a member of the sex opposite to that of
the earlier choice.

4. The displacements of the libido here described are doubtless familiar to every
analyst from investigation of the anamneses of neurotics. With the latter, however, they
occur in early childhood, at the beginning of the love life; with our patient, who was in
no way neurotic, they took place in the first years following puberty, though, by the
way, they were just as completely unconscious. Perhaps one day this temporal factor
may turn out to be of great importance.

5. As "retiring in favor of someone else" has not previously been mentioned among
the causes of homosexuality, or in the mechanism of libido-fixation in general, I will
adduce here another analytical observation of the same kind which has a special feature
of interest. I once knew two twin brothers, both of whom were endowed with strong
libidinal impulses. One of them was very successful with women and had innumerable
affairs with women and girls. The other went the same way at first, but it became
unpleasant for him to be trespassing on his brother's beat, and, owing to the likeness
between them, to be mistaken for him on intimate occasions, so he got out of the difficulty by becoming homosexual. He left the women to his brother, and thus "retired"
in his favor. Another time I treated a young man, an artist, unmistakably bisexual in disposition, in whom the homosexual trend had come to the fore simultaneously with a
disturbance in his work. He fed from both women and work together. The analysis,
which was able to bring him back to both, showed that the fear of the father was the
most powerful psychic motive for both the disturbances which were really renunciations. In his imagination all women belonged to the father, and he sought refuge in men
out of submission, so as to "retire from" the conflict in favor of the father. Such a motivation of the homosexual object-choice must be by no means uncommon; in the
primeval ages of the human race all women presumably belonged to the father and head
of the primal horde.

Among brothers and sisters who are not twins this "retirement" plays a great part in other spheres as well as in that of the love choice. For example, an elder brother studies music and is admired for it; the younger, far more gifted musically, soon gives up his own musical studies, in spite of his longing, and cannot be persuaded to touch an instrument again. This is one example of a very frequent occurrence, and investigation of the motives leading to this retirement rather than to open rivalry discloses very complicated conditions in the mind.

6. See *supra,* essay IV.

7. [In the text there is a play on the word *niederkommen,* which means both "to fall" and "to be delivered of a child." There is also in English a colloquial use of the verb "to fall," meaning pregnancy or childbirth.—Trans.]

8. That the various means of suicide can represent sexual wish-fulfilments has long been known to all analysts. (To poison oneself = to become pregnant; to drown = to bear a child; to throw oneself from a height = to be delivered of a child.)

9. Cf. "Reflections upon War and Death," *Character and Culture,* Collier Books, edition BS 193 V.

10. [A reference to the European War, 1914–18.—Trans.]

11. [i.e., believed on condition that it is regarded as not certain—Trans.]

12. Cf. Kriemhilde's confession in the *Nibelungenlied.*

13. Cf. A. Lipschütz, *Die Pubertätsdrüse und ihre Wirkungen.*

Part II

~

CONTRIBUTIONS FROM ACADEMIC SCHOLARS

2

LETTER TO AN UNKNOWN WOMAN

∽

Teresa de Lauretis

Prologue

When I was invited to contribute to this volume, I saw an opportunity for reconsidering what I had written on this singular case history a few years ago in *The Practice of Love* (1994). In that book I revisited the classic texts of Freudian psychoanalysis on female homosexuality (Freud, Jones, Lampl-de Groot, Deutsch, and Lacan) as part of a larger project concerned with theorizing lesbian sexuality and desire. To that end, I reexamined Freud's theory of sexuality and what little he and others had said specifically on the topic of female homosexuality, in conjunction, in contrast, and in counterpoint with texts of lesbian self-representation—literary, filmic, and critical texts. My project was not clinically based but was conceptually framed in psychoanalytic terms and elaborated a model of desire that, while not disregarding the psychic structure of the Oedipus complex, did nevertheless exceed its terms. I called it *perverse desire*.

Shortly before and since my book was published, several essays devoted to Freud's "Psychogenesis" [1920] have appeared.[1] All of them contribute to the ongoing critical discourse on female (homo)sexuality, many referring to the Dora case history as well. They are insightful critiques of Freud's text, demonstrating the inadequacy of his conceptual framework and the blind spots of his analytical method, and raising issues of countertransference and personal or ideological bias. But, even as their authors prove as capable of astute textual analyses as Freud himself and often, as it were, beat him at his own game, they remain

within the confines of a textual reading or an exegesis of the case history itself.
None of them ventures beyond the master's narrative or seeks to theorize
beyond the limitations they describe in it. My own reading of "Psychogenesis,"
coming as it did early on in the writing of the book, was also cast as a critique
of Freud's text: It remarked its incoherence and distress in the face of a question,
What does the homosexual woman want?, and in the face of a girl who did not
respond to treatment, to his theory of the Oedipus, or to him personally.

And yet the larger project of my book did intend to go beyond Freud, to
elaborate a model of desire beyond the Oedipus, to understand lesbian sexuality beyond the commonplace of the masculinity complex and the pre-Oedipal
fixation on the mother. Such a theory, I argued in *The Practice of Love,* Freud
could not envision but in some way suggested in the *Three Essays on the Theory
of Sexuality.* In the first essay, if only dimly, by negation, and clothed in ambiguity, he adumbrated a theory of sexuality as perversion, on which then, in the
last two essays, he imposed the structuring narrative of the Oedipus complex.
And it was finally Freud's later conception of disavowal [*Verleugnung*] and the
psychic mechanism he named "splitting of the ego" [*Ichspaltung*] that allowed
me to work out progressively, through several chapters of the book, a model of
perverse or fetishistic desire that I saw reflected in the lesbian texts. But I never
went back to reconsider Freud's singular "case of homosexuality in a woman"
in light of that model.

My first thought, when I agreed to contribute to this volume, was to do just
that, to reread the story of Freud's "girl" against my model of perverse desire.
Soon, however, I realized that that could not be done because a case history
belongs to its writer, not to its case: It is the history of a case, the reconstruction
of a psychic trajectory, an interpretation, a representation, a text of fiction, and
not a "true story." It is a text that bears the inscription of a subjectivity, a desire,
that are much more its writer's, Freud's, than those of its central character,
whether named or unnamed. As Madame Bovary "is" Flaubert, as Heathcliff
"is" Emily Brontë, so is the girl a mirror reflecting Freud in his efforts to work
out his theory of psychoanalysis, to refine his clinical technique, to further his
understanding of homosexuality and/or bisexuality, and above all to confirm his
belief in the Oedipus complex. What we know about the girl is what he tells us,
what she says is in answer to his questions; even her indifference is a sign of *his*
feeling rejected, unrecognized, irrelevant.

Thus, at the same time, I also realized why all the other commentators on this
case history remained caught in the textual web of ambiguities, inconsistencies,
contradictions, or evasions spun by Freud: If only exegetic one-upmanship or
rhetorical escalation could provide an adequate reading, it was because Freud's
text was the only game in town. Conversely, if I had been able to understand

lesbian desire as structured by fetishism and disavowal rather than, as Freud does, by the (inverted) Oedipus complex, it was because the texts I was reading, unlike Freud's, inscribed a lesbian subjectivity and authorial desire. Were I now to undertake a second reading of "Psychogenesis," I could do no more than produce yet another exegesis of the case, perhaps another critique of Freud, but no advance would be made in illuminating "the mystery of [the girl's] homosexuality" (Freud [1920], p. 170).

For my contribution to this volume, then, I will extend my earlier reading of "Psychogenesis" (which will appear here in the section entitled "The Master's Narrative") to emphasize how Freud's understanding of the case was overdetermined by his own project—on the one hand, by his preoccupation with homosexuality and, on the other, by a passionate fiction, the Oedipus complex, which, after all, was the enabling fiction of his invention of psychoanalyis. For it is this Oedipal fantasy that structures the narrative of "Psychogenesis," although, as we shall see, Freud himself was dissatisfied with it. In the second part of this chapter, I will suggest that something else besides the Oedipus is going on in homosexual desire, and I will propose another, non-Oedipal model of sexual structuring that may account for the "psychogenesis" of lesbianism in some women.

I call this chapter "Letter to an Unknown Woman" in reference to a film by Max Ophuls [Oppenheimer], *Letter From an Unknown Woman* (United States, 1948), adapted from a 1924 novella by Stefan Zweig, a Viennese writer and friend of Freud's. The letter is written by Lisa (played by Joan Fontaine) just before dying to the man she has loved in silence all her life and by whom she conceived a child in the one night they spent together. The film is a single, uninterrupted flashback of scenes spread over a lifetime and joined together by Lisa's voiceover narration. Not unlike a psychoanalysis, the film represents a subject, Lisa, existing only through memory and desire; it reconstructs her from disconnected images and words by selecting events or scenes and giving them narrative continuity, as secondary elaboration does with the fragments of a dream.

"By the time you read this I'll be dead," Lisa's letter begins. Through the fiction of the letter addressed to Stefan (played by Louis Jourdan), the film recreates her now-ended existence and unending love for him, thus making Lisa and her desire known to the spectator as well. As my title suggests, I will be speaking of a woman who remains unknown, although Freud tells her story in "Psychogenesis." This is the only major case history of Freud's in which the patient is not given a (fictitious) name, and thus not given the status of fictional character; he simply calls her the girl, "*das Mädchen.*" But it is not only the girl's name that remains unknown to the reader; it is also the nature of her desire, which Freud attempts to analyze but is finally unable to explain to his satisfaction—or to mine. What I want to address here is the problem of representing (naming) the desire of a woman such as the girl in Freud's story and the conditions of its representability. My "letter," therefore, is addressed to whom it may concern.

The Master's Narrative

"A beautiful and clever girl of 18, belonging to a family of good standing, had aroused displeasure and concern in her parents by the devoted adoration with which she pursued a certain 'society lady' who was about ten years older than herself." Thus begins, in the best fashion of the genre, the master's narrative of "The Psychogenesis of a Case of Homosexuality in a Woman." Immediately before this sentence, in the first paragraph of the case history, Freud makes his customary invocation to the muse of method: Since female homosexuality has been heretofore neglected by psychoanalytic theory as it has been by the law, then even "the narration of a single case, not too pronounced in type, in which it was possible to trace its origin and development in the mind with complete certainty and almost without a gap may, therefore, have a certain claim to attention" (p. 147). But the presumption of "complete certainty" that opens what promises to be a full account ("almost without a gap") of the heroine's homosexual development is cast in serious doubt several pages later:

> This amount of information about her seems meagre enough, nor can I guarantee that it is complete. It may be that the history of her youth was much richer in experiences; I do not know. As I have already said, the analysis was broken off after a short time, and therefore yielded an anamnesis not much more reliable than the other anamneses of homosexuals, which there is good cause to question. Further, the girl had never been neurotic, and came to the analysis without even one hysterical symptom, so that opportunities for investigating the history of her childhood did not present themselves so readily as usual" (p. 155).

This pattern of alternating assertion and disclaimer, certainty and doubt, presumption and condescension recurs in each of the four parts that make up the story and the analysis. Each part contains elements of both: a diegetic section about the girl's history is preceded or followed by an exegetic or interpretive section, often augmented by considerations of a theoretical nature in the form of digressions on analytic technique and dream interpretation, as well as digressions on bisexuality and homosexuality itself. For example, part II opens with these words: "After this highly discursive introduction I am only able to present a very concise summary of the sexual history of the case under consideration. In childhood the girl had passed through the normal attitude characteristic of the feminine Oedipus complex" (p. 155); and the paragraph ends with the disclaimer about the unreliable anamnesis I cited earlier. Part IV also begins with the words, "I now come back, after this digression, to the consideration of my patient's case" (p. 167).

While the pattern may recall the actual movement of the analysis, with its slow progress, setbacks, and occasional breakthroughs, it also underscores the contrast between Freud's confidence in his doctrinal premises and the need to have recourse to them in moments of uncertainty, as if to find reassurance and interpretive strength against the difficulties caused by the patient's unreliability, her unforthcoming or negative transference, and his own problematic (unavowed) countertransference.

The latter difficulties are not new to Freud, since he encountered them in the analysis of "Dora" and recorded them in "Fragment of an Analysis of a Case of Hysteria," (*SE,* Vol. 7, pp. 1–122), originally published in 1905. There, too, the stumbling block was the patient's resistance to an interpretation in which the father "played the principal part" both in the diegesis (the girl's father or his substitutes) and in the exegesis (Freud, the analyst, with his undisguised wish to be loved): "In reality she transferred to me the sweeping repudiation of men which had dominated her ever since the disappointment she had suffered from her father. . . . But I still believe that, beside the intention to mislead me, the dreams partly expressed the wish to win my favour" ([1920] pp. 164–165). Like Dora, this patient resists Freud's attribution of her problems to her resistance against the Oedipal imperative and will not gratify him by assenting to what he can only see as "her keenest desire—namely, revenge" (p. 160) against her father(s). Dora's "revenge" had been to break off the analysis, to give him a 2-week notice as one would a paid employee, one socially inferior; and so does this girl, in effect, "by rendering futile all his endeavours and by clinging to the illness" (p. 164); so much so that he is forced to break off treatment himself and recommend *a woman doctor* as someone better equipped to continue the treatment.

However, whereas Dora apparently had problems, manifested by her various hysterical symptoms, this girl clearly does not.[2] So Freud now must explain why her homosexuality is a problem. It would be simple enough to repeat that it is a problem only for her parents, who sought his advice because they were preoccupied with social conventions (although the father is more than just angry with her, as Freud perceptively notes: "There was something about his daughter's homosexuality that aroused the deepest bitterness in him" [p. 149]). But Freud does not leave it at that. He has some stake in proving that it is a problem for the girl as well. For one might ask: So what, if "she changed into a man and took her mother [substitute] in place of her father as the object of her love" (p. 158)—what's wrong with that? What's wrong with a woman's masculinity complex provided she is not in the least neurotic and has no symptoms? Why is this not simply one outcome of that "universal bisexuality of human beings" (p. 157), which Freud has just defined, a moment ago, with olympian serenity: "In all of us, throughout life, the libido *normally* oscillates between male and female objects" (p. 158, emphasis added). Pressed closely by such feminist arguments, however, his answer is adamant: No, the problem is that in her the libido did not oscillate, and "[h]enceforth she *remained* homosexual out of defiance against her father" (p. 159, emphasis added). Defiance and resistance, in other words, are the specific symptoms of female homosexuality; they are what makes it perverse and such that, unlike neurosis and hysteria, psychoanalysis is impotent to alter it.

From the start, it must be added in all fairness, Freud did caution us that this was not "the ideal situation for analysis." The girl was not ill, had no symptoms, no complaint of her condition, and no will to change: "She did not try to deceive me by saying that she felt any urgent need to be freed from her homosexuality. On the contrary, she said she could not conceive of any other way of being in love" (p. 153). Thus his analytic task was most difficult, for it consisted not in resolving a neurotic conflict but in converting one variety of genital organization into the other. And "such an achievement," Freud pleads, if possible at all, is

> never an easy matter. On the contrary I have found success possible only in specially favourable circumstances, and even then the success essentially consisted in making access to the opposite sex (which had hitherto been barred) possible to a person restricted to homosexuality, thus restoring his full bisexual functions. (p. 151)

At this point in the text, the narrative has given way to a theoretical digression on the topic of homosexuality, where Freud discusses various cases in his experience, their causal factors, their prognoses, and their resolutions. If one has the definite impression that he is speaking of male patients here, it is less by dint of the masculine pronoun, or the familiarity one may have with his only other written case of (presumed) female homosexuality, "A Case of Paranoia" [1915], than because of Freud's dispassionate and almost benevolent tone, which is set early on by his equanimous admission of having a rather poor track record in successful treatments.[3] It is as if these failures, these patients' "abnormalities" and their bisexual or homosexual genital organizations, did not affect his professional self-esteem or make his analytic task particularly difficult, as does the case of the girl.

On the positive side, however, at least as far as the reader is concerned, the difficulties brought about by this case make Freud work harder, both as analyst and as theorist. Somehow he is impelled by this girl to come to terms with homosexuality in its female form, to try to figure out how it fits into his overall theory, to explain why "full bisexuality" is not really an option, or a cure, for this patient, and just what kind of perversion it is. For all his troubles, he scores one victory and one defeat. The victory is diegetic and analytic: The enigma of the story is solved by the birth of a brother, when the girl was 16, and the dénouement provides the explanation for her homosexuality as a rejection of the Oedipal imperative compounded by revenge against the father. The enigma, as the narrative presents it, is: Why did the girl become "a homosexual attracted to mature women, and remained so ever since" (p. 156) when, in fact, her mother favored the girl's brothers, generally acted unkindly toward her, and vied with her for the father's love? Freud answers:

> The explanation is as follows. It was just when the girl was experiencing the revival of her infantile Oedipus complex at puberty that she suffered her great disappointment. She became keenly conscious of the wish to have a child, and a male one; that what she desired was her *father's* child and an image of *him,* her consciousness was not allowed to know. And what happened next? It was not *she* who bore the child, but her unconsciously hated rival, her mother. Furiously resentful and embittered, she turned away from her father and from men altogether. After this first great reverse she forswore her womanhood and sought another goal for her libido. In doing so she behaved just as many men do who after a first distressing experience turn their backs for ever upon the faithless female sex and become woman-haters. (p. 157)

There are as many holes in this explanation as there are turns in the narrative: The girl is conscious of wanting a child but unconscious of wanting the father's child (his image); she is unconscious of hating the mother/rival yet consciously rejects her and, with her, both femininity and motherhood; she consciously hates and defies the father but unconsciously (still loves and) identifies with him; she consciously falls in love with a woman and becomes a woman-hater. Because the toggle-switch term *conscious/unconscious*—which Freud here uses in the common, rather than technical or systemic sense—acts as a sort of joker in the exegetic game, the holes turn out to be, rather, loopholes, and make it as difficult to disprove or argue against each of these propositions as it would be to prove them. However, it is clear that the whole house of cards rests on the founding stone of the positive Oedipus complex (the wish for a child by the father). This is the first move of Freud's interpretive "journey" here as elsewhere with regard to female sexuality. He imagines it as the (asymmetrical) counterpart of the male's positive Oedipus complex, which leads him to the conclusive parallel with men and the last, paradoxical proposition: Women who love women hate women. (Freud's notorious disregard for a girl's erotic attachment to the mother—what he would later call the negative Oedipus complex—was subsequently redressed and amended by women analysts such as Lampl-de Groot and Deutsch but with no significant gain as regards changing the Oedipal paradigm.)

On the strength of this interpretation, finally, it would seem that the girl's masculinity complex, already "strongly marked" since childhood, was reinforced and perverted by the "occasion" of the mother's late pregnancy, which pushed it over the brink and made the girl "fall a victim to homosexuality" (p. 168). Freud's hard-won interpretive victory, however, is a Pyrrhic victory in that it is accompanied by a defeat in the theoretical project of explaining homosexuality. For in part IV of the text, as he retraces forward the steps that the analysis had followed backward, he must admit that "we no longer get the impression of an inevitable sequence of events which could not have been otherwise determined. We notice at once that there might have been another result" (p. 167). This statement all but unravels the complicated exegetic skein: The causes of the girl's homosexuality, which the analytic narration reconstructed "with complete certainty and almost without a gap" into a seamless narrative, where every "external factor" could be accounted for, are now said to be by no means a necessary or sufficient condition of her homosexual disposition, a disposition that may or may not have been acquired but, at any rate, at least in part, "has to be ascribed to inborn constitution" (p. 169). And if we search the text for signs of what that inborn constitution might be, we can only find that "strongly marked 'masculinity complex'," which the girl "had brought along with her from her childhood":

> A spirited girl, always ready for romping and fighting, she was not at all prepared to be second to her slightly older brother; after inspecting his genital organs [. . .] she had developed a pronounced envy for the penis, and the thoughts derived from this envy still continued to fill her mind. She was in fact a feminist; she felt it to be unjust that girls should not enjoy the same freedom as boys, and rebelled against the lot of woman in general. (pp. 155, 169)

Freud's concern with theorizing homosexuality beyond the context of this particular case—and hence what I have called his theoretical defeat—is evident in the digressions on the topic that appear in parts I and IV, where he makes reference to the sexological arguments he had addressed in the *Three Essays* [1905] 15 years earlier, and which, by 1920, had already become known or popularized outside the domain of medical knowledge. Thus, in part I, Freud entertains the queries he expects from the lay reader: "Readers unversed in psycho-analysis will long have been awaiting an answer to two other questions. Did this homosexual girl show physical characteristics plainly belonging to the opposite sex, and did the case prove to be one of congenital or acquired (later-developed) homosexuality?" (p. 153). He answers no to the first question and offers the case history itself as his answer to the second: "[W]hether this was a case of congenital or acquired homosexuality, will be answered by the whole history of the patient's abnormality and its development. The study of this will show how far this question is a fruitless and inapposite one" (p. 154).

But lo and behold, the fruitless question reappears in part IV, where Freud unabashedly contradicts himself by reproposing its terms as still viable instead of displacing or replacing them with something more apposite. He states that, if at first the analysis indicated that this might be "a case of late-acquired homosexuality," a fuller "consideration of the material impels us to conclude that it is rather a case of congenital homosexuality" (p. 169). The subsequent cautionary remark, that "it would be best not to attach too much value to this way of stating the problem" (p. 170), does not sufficiently undercut the previous statement to dispel the reader's sense of having just read a diagnosis of congenital homosexuality. In a similar way, in the third of the *Three Essays,* he had reintroduced and continued to use as valid the notions of perversion and genital primacy that, in the first essay, he had criticized and effectively shown to be theoretically untenable.[4]

In "Psychogenesis," the final appeal to an inborn constitution that might have affected what appeared to be an "acquired disposition (if it *was* really acquired)," as Freud perversely insinuates (p. 169), leaves the reader with no clearer view of homosexuality—or, for that matter, bisexuality—than could be gleaned from the *Three Essays* and, if anything, with greater uncertainty. It leaves Freud's position on homosexuality enmeshed in that same structural ambiguity or inconsistency that is so conspicuous in the *Three Essays.* Once again, the pivot on which the inconsistency turns is the imposition of a structuring narrative, or a structuring fantasy, onto the "material" of the case history. In other words, again the theory strains against the structure but is finally contained, as perhaps all theories must be, by a passionate fiction. In this case, the fiction is the fantasy of the "positive" Oedipus complex—the fantasy that a girl must desire the father and wish to bear a child in his image.

The Mystery of Homosexuality

Other critics have noted the inconsistencies, reversals, or exegetic somersaults in Freud's account of female homosexuality in this case history, which in some respects resembles that of Dora written 20 years earlier, although here homosexuality, and not hysteria, is the explicit problem to be addressed.[5] But if both times Freud failed to cure or resolve the patients' problems, here he takes on directly the issue of female homosexuality, which he had relegated to the footnotes, almost an afterthought, in Dora's case ([1905], pp. 105, 120); and if the unconscious "homosexual current of feeling" he surmised in Dora could be ignored in the analysis of hysteria, even as he remarked on the evidence of a "fairly strong homosexual predisposition" in neurotics ([1905], p. 60), here he can no longer evade the issue because "the mystery of homosexuality" ([1920], p. 170) stares him in the face.

Although Freud was to articulate the complete Oedipus complex, in its positive and negative form—positive, when the object of the erotic cathexis is the parent of the other sex, negative when it is the parent of the same sex—only a few years later in "The Ego and the Id" ([1923], pp. 31–34) the conception of a fourfold structure is already present in the interpretation of "Psychogenesis":

> From very early years [the girl's] libido had flowed in two currents, the one on the surface being one that we may unhesitatingly designate as homosexual. This latter was probably *a direct and unchanged continuation of an infantile fixation on her mother.* Probably the analysis described here actually revealed nothing more than the process by which, on an appropriate occasion, the deeper heterosexual current of libido, too, was deflected into the manifest homosexual one. ([1920] pp. 168–169, emphasis added)

Here the Oedipus complex is mentioned explicitly only in relation to the girl's father that is, as positive; however, the "fixation" on the mother is precisely what Freud will later imagine as the girl's negative Oedipus complex. In short, he argues that the two currents of the libido are present in the girl: The homosexual is manifest and conscious (perversion), while the heterosexual, arising from the positive Oedipus complex, is deeper and unconscious.[6] And in light of the observation that "homosexual men have [also] experienced a specially strong fixation on their mother," Freud then concludes that "a very considerable measure of latent or unconscious homosexuality can be detected in all normal people" ([1920], p. 171).

Given these "fundamental facts" devolving from the Oedipus complex, however, it would seem that homosexuality should hardly be a "mystery," for it is fundamentally a manifestation of what Freud calls the "universal bisexuality of human beings." The libido or instinctual disposition is bisexual, he asserts, and can flow both ways; which direction will prevail is a matter of the contingencies and vagaries of individual life. And yet Freud continues to perceive it as a problem. Why? Through the years he will reiterate that homosexuality is not a psychic illness, and such that psychoanalysis cannot cure it.[7] And yet he ends "Psychogenesis" with an admission of defeat, analogous to the sense of failure that haunts his papers on female sexuality in the 1930s; just as, there, in the matter of the riddle of femininity, psychoanalysis must turn to the poets, so here, in the matter of homosexuality, it must yield to biological science.

I think Freud is aware that something else is going on in homosexuality, although he cannot quite grasp it. I propose that the reason why he cannot grasp it lies at the very foundation of his theory, in the founding fiction of the Oedipus complex. However, the unresolved contradictions in his thinking about "the mystery" of homosexuality are, to my mind, related to a contradiction in his thinking about sexuality which is equally founding, in the sense that it dates back to the *Three Essays* [1905]—a contradiction I discussed at length in chapter 1 of *Practice of Love*. To summarize it briefly, in the first essay Freud argued that the sexual drive does not have a preassigned or natural object and that its aim is solely pleasure. But he also held another, contradictory belief, which is apparent in the second and third essays: the belief that something in human sexuality obeys the biological command to reproduce the species, as manifested in the sexual drive and in those psychic structures he calls phylogenetic, such as the primal scene and the Oedipus complex. I am not interested in discussing this point now, but I say this because it was that inconsistency in Freud that prompted my project.

Perverse Desire

In *Practice of Love* I wanted to understand conceptually a form of desire that I saw represented in many texts written by lesbians and that I have experienced in my own life: the sexual desire for another woman. I wanted to understand how it could occur or come about. The contradiction in Freud prompted me to leave aside the normative Oedipal narrative to follow instead the path traced by the perversions (in particular, fetishism). That enabled me to articulate a model of perverse desire, that is to say, to imagine how a desire that is non-Oedipal and nonreproductive may be constituted and structured. I call such a desire *perverse* in the etymological sense of perversion as deviation from a given path.

The "normal" path of sexual desire is the reproductive one, Freud wrote in the *Three Essays* [1905]:

> The normal sexual aim is regarded as being the union of the genitals in the act known as copulation. (p. 149)
>
> Perversions are sexual activities which either (a) extend, in an anatomical sense, beyond the regions of the body that are designed for sexual union, or (b) linger over the intermediate relations to the sexual object which should normally be traversed rapidly on the path toward the final sexual aim. (p. 150)

In this view, *perversion* means deviation from the path leading to the "final" or "normal" sexual aim of copulation, a deviation from the path linking the drive to the reproductive object (i.e., a person of the other sex). But if we follow up Freud's other argument, that the sexual drive does not have a natural or pre-assigned object and that its aim is not reproduction but pleasure, then *perversion* describes the very nature of the sexual drive, its mobility with regard to objects and its not being determined by a reproductive aim.

Let me say it another way: If the sexual drive is independent of its object, and the object is variable and chosen for its ability to satisfy, as Freud maintains, then the concept of perversion loses its meaning of deviation from nature (and hence loses the common connotation of pathology) and takes on the meaning of deviation from a socially constituted norm. This norm is precisely "normal" sexuality, which psychoanalysis itself, ironically, proves to be nothing more than a projection, a presumed default, an imaginary mode of being of sexuality that is in fact contradicted by psychoanalysis' own clinical evidence.

Perversion, on the other hand, is the very mode of being of *sexuality* as such, while the projected norm, in so-called normal sexuality, is a requirement of social *reproduction,* both reproduction of the species and reproduction of the social system. Now, the conflation, the imbrication, of sexuality with repro-duction in Western history has been shown by Foucault to come about through what he called "the technology of sex" and has been analyzed by feminist the-ory in the concept of compulsory heterosexuality.[8] And it is, obviously, still a widely held or hegemonic notion. But my point is that the specific character of *sexuality* (as distinct from *reproduction*) and the empirically manifested form of sexuality, *as far as psychoanalysis knows it,* is indeed perversion, with its negative or repressed form, neurosis.

This second view of perversion suggests to me another model of sexual struc-turing, one based on perverse desire, that stands in contrast to the model of sex-ual structuring implied by the first definition of perversion, namely, the model based on Oedipal desire.[9] Freud himself contributed further to the articulation of what I call perverse desire with his analysis of the psychic mechanism of dis-avowal (*Verleugnung*) in "Fetishism" (1927) and "Splitting of the Ego in the Process of Defence" (1940), although he restricted fetishistic desire to men. Disavowal is a psychic process that, at the same time, recognizes *and* refuses to recognize a traumatic perception. What the male fetishist disavows is the per-ception of a body without penis (the mother's body), for such perception threat-ens the body-ego, or the subject's bodily integrity and pleasure.

The body is the starting point of Freud's reflection, and this is indeed one of the main attractions that his psychoanalysis has for me and may have had for many other women since the time of Freud. But precisely because the body was so central to his theory, the theory had to be constructed from his own experi-ence of the body; that is, the body as experienced and understood by a man of his culture and of his sociohistorical and personal situation. In such a body, he tells us (and I can do nothing else but take him at his word), the penis is the foremost organ of pleasure. Therefore, the threat of castration for a male child is as strong as the threat of loss of life; it is a threat to his body-image and body-ego, a threat of nonbeing (Lacan's *manque à être*).

A female body, however, usually has no such organ, and since the penis is not part of her body-ego, a female child has no perceptions or pleasure from it or fear of losing it (here I can do nothing else but take me at my word). To the boy, a body without penis may appear damaged, wounded, imperfect, inadequate to give pleasure or to be loved, inferior; the absence of the penis is like a wound to the integrity of his body-ego, and thus a narcissistic wound. What can cause a narcissistic wound and the threat of nonbeing to a girl? They cannot depend on losing or not having a body part of which she has no perception; for this reason, the often literal understanding of the castration complex in women has been justly contested. I think, however, that the narcissistic wound and the threat of castration also depend, as they do for the boy, on a damaged body-image, the fantasy of having a body that is imperfect, faulty, or inadequate to give pleasure and to be loved. And since the body-image constitutes the first matrix of the ego, an inadequate or unlovable body is a threat to the body-ego, a threat of nonbeing. This narcissistic wound, for the girl, is equivalent to the boy's fear of castration, but it is not due to the loss or lack of a penis, and it is not perceived as such, at least initially.

Here, then, is how I would revise Freud's story of femininity. As the girl child grows up, her sense of having a body that is inadequate, imperfect, or inferior finds confirmation and an explanation in the family practices, the social arrangements, and the cultural forms that privilege men both socially and sexually—in short, the whole choreography of gender. Since the penis is a relatively small bodily difference, but one that is taken as the symbol of male privilege, she herself may (or may not) come to accept the explanation and attribute her sense of being imperfect to the fact that she does not have a penis (whence Freud's impression of women's penis envy). Indeed, as she grows older, all those around her direct her to expect pleasure from the penis in a man's body and to look forward to the attainment of a perfect female body through motherhood; everything in her culture tells her that she can regain her narcissistic pride in becoming a mother. (In this sense Freud says that the baby she can have is the compensation and the equivalent of the penis she does not have. For this reason maternity is an extremely important fantasy for all women, as evidenced by the many lesbians who seek artificial insemination, a technology that has been developed to favor the reproduction of "normal" middle-class and upper-class white families.)

In Freud's theory of the Oedipus complex, the boy can heal his narcissistic wound and restore the narcissistic ego-instincts [*Ichtriebe*] or self-love that are necessary for psychic survival by identifying with his father or a father-figure who represents the phallus he can aspire to have when he grows up (the phallus is the penis endowed with *social and sexual* power). The girl's wound can be healed or repaired, and her narcissistic ego-instincts restored, by identifying with her mother or a mother-figure and wanting to be loved as a mother. In a way, this is to say that the threat of castration, the narcissistic wound, in both the boy and the girl, is healed or repaired by identification with a figure of power; the phallus and the mother are both figures of power, more or less power depending on the particular culture.[10]

The male fetishist described by Freud sees that a female body (the mother's) has no penis but refuses to believe in that perception, which threatens him with his own possible castration. His erotic investment in the mother's body and his own body is then displaced onto something else, a fetish, which temporarily repairs the narcissistic wound and suspends the threat to his body-ego and his pleasure. As is well known, Freud says that women cannot be fetishists because they are already castrated; that is, they have no penis to lose. But if the female equivalent of castration, her narcissistic wound, is understood as the perception of an inadequate or unlovable body-image, then she, too, can disavow that perception (i.e., recognize it *and* not recognize it) and thus displace her erotic investment from the mother's and her own body onto something else. For the female, as for the male fetishist, the something else (the fetish) is an object or sign that signifies not only the lost object of desire—the beloved, lovable body—but also the subject's capacity to desire. It takes the place of the phallus as signifier of desire.

Thus the phantasmatic "lost object" of female perverse desire is neither the mother's body nor the paternal phallus; it is the subject's own lost body, which can be recovered in fantasy, in sexual practice, *in and with* another woman. This perverse desire is not based on the masculinity complex (the denial of sexual difference), nor is it based on a regressive attachment to the mother (a regression to the pre-Oedipal or the phallic phase). It is based on the post-Oedipal disavowal of that loss—the loss of one's body-ego, the loss of being. By "post-Oedipal disavowal" I mean that the desiring subject has gone through the Oedipus complex but the form of desiring is not dependent on its binary terms; as a result of disavowal, it attaches itself to other objects, fetish-objects, which sustain and represent her *being-in-desire;* in Freud's terms, these would engage at once both object-libido and ego-libido.

The model of perverse desire that I have sketched here and articulated more elaborately in *Practice of Love* is different from the Oedipal model of normal or inverted desire (positive or negative Oedipus complex). As a *conceptual* model of sexual structuring, perverse desire places sexuality beyond the terms of the family schema—mother, father, child—and its reproductive teleology. But one model does not merely replace or exclude the other. Perverse desire may co-exist with some of the effects of the Oedipus complex, and the latter indeed may play an important role in the subject's identifications, notably in gender identity and possibly in racial or ethnic identity as well.

The psyche is a complex and dynamic phenomenon, subject to historical and personal vicissitudes, shaped and reshaped by fantasies public and private. The Oedipal narrative, which framed Freud's understanding of human life and enabled his invention of psychoanalysis (and still dominates the practice and most of the theory of psychoanalysis), is a passionate fiction, a fantasmatic scenario that informs the social imaginary and incites subjective desires. Now, at a time when the institution of the family and the reproduction of the white middle class seem endangered, the Oedipal narrative is being emphatically reproposed in Hollywood movies and the popular media in the most benign and sentimental forms. But at the same time, concurrently with the Oedipal fantasy, it is quite possible to imagine other scenarios of desire.

I have no doubt that other cultural narratives can produce other fantasies and other desires. In non-Western cultures there may be no Oedipal narrative, or it may have no effect in structuring sexuality, as Franz Fanon (1967) asserts in *Black Skin, White Masks*. In Western cultures, too, the Oedipus fantasy may be eventually superseded in the wake of technological and social change. My own attempt to theorize, to articulate conceptually, the ways and "psychogenesis" of a desire that exceeds and eludes the confines of the Oedipal script is the construction of another passionate fiction, one that now represents my life and my desire much better than the Oedipal fantasy does. But I would not say that Freud was "wrong," since I myself experienced the positive Oedipus complex through adolescence, and I completely identified with Oedipus when I first read Freud at age 30. In some perverse way, I still do.

Notes

1. See Merck (1993), Roof (1991), Fuss (1993), O'Connor and Ryan, (1993), and Jacobus (1995).

2. Or rather, did not upon entering treatment, for in the course of the analysis she produces "a lying dream": "The intention to mislead me, just as she did her father, certainly emanated from the preconscious, and may indeed have been conscious; it could come to expression by entering into connection with the unconscious wishful impulse to please her father (or father-substitute), and in this way it created a lying dream. The two intentions, to betray and to please her father, originated in the same complex" (p. 166). I suggest that the attempted suicide may be seen precisely in this light. Like the

occasional "lying dreams," the attempted suicide lacked the repetitive and uncontrollable character of actual neurotic symptoms. The presence of neurotic behavior due to (the resistance to) the Oedipal imperative does not contradict the girl's homosexuality (perversion or inversion, in Freud's terms). On the coexistence of neurosis and perversion, see Sachs (1991).

3. In "A Case of Paranoia Running Counter to the Psycho-Analytic Theory of the Disease" [1915], the woman's homosexuality is merely presumed by Freud and nowhere admitted or suggested by the subject in question, and the case for homosexuality is even less convincingly argued than in the feminist readings of Dora. As even the customarily sober, scholarly, and factual editors of the *Standard Edition* are impelled to introduce it, this case history is "an object-lesson to practitioners on the danger of basing a hasty opinion of a case on a superficial knowledge of the facts" (Vol. 14, p. 262). It is less an analysis than a peroration *pro domo sua* on the part of Freud, who is seeking confirmation of his freshly formulated theory of paranoia in the case of President Schreber—the "theory that the delusion of persecution invariably depends on homosexuality" (p. 266).

4. I discuss this at length in chapter 1 of *The Practice of Love* (1994).

5. The similarities, also noted by Merck (1993) and Roof (1991) include the length of the analysis and its early termination, the patient's attempted suicide, her choice of an older female object, her resistance or failed transference, and Freud's unavowed countertransference. Unlike the girl of "Psychogenesis," Dora has become a feminist heroine. The symbol of feminine resistance to patriarchy, she has inspired a play, two films, a biographical memoir, and a mass of critical essays, some of them collected in Bernheimer and Kahane (1985). What is especially intriguing is that a major theme in many of these works is Dora's alleged homosexuality, whereas Freud's only case history of a female homosexual has received much less feminist attention and almost exclusively by lesbian critics. Why have feminists equated Dora's hysteria with homosexuality? Is it only because Lacan treated the two cases as virtually interchangeable, or are there other possible explanations? I discuss these questions in chapter 2 of *The Practice of Love* and offer an interpretation in chapter 4 under the heading of "The Seductions of Lesbianism."

6. This, we note, is the exact reversal of the situation Freud had described in Dora's case, where the homosexual current was the unconscious one. But, *mutatis mutandis,* the Oedipal structure remain in place.

7. Cf. the letter Freud wrote to an American mother in 1935, cited in Abelove (1993).

8. The concept was first articulated in Adrienne Rich (1986). I discuss it and amplify it in my "Eccentric Subjects" (1990).

9. I use this somewhat awkward phrase, *sexual structuring,* to emphasize the permanently under-construction character of sexuality in the sociosexual subject, its being a process and not a stable structure that is set in place once and for all in childhood or adolescence. I would not, however, use terms such as *sexual orientation* or *sexual identity* because these do not sufficiently convey the overdetermination of sexuality by psychic and fantasmatic structures.

10. It should perhaps be added that, contrary to current views, femininity can also be a figure of power, when it is socially and culturally valorized; there are women in whose personal experience and family or social situation femininity is something of value. In heterosexual relations femininity confers power, specifically the power of seduction, and in some lesbian subcultures the femme is a figure of empowered femininity, as is the drag queen in contemporary U.S. gay subcultures.

References

Abelove, H. (1993). Freud, male homosexuality, and the Americans. In H. Abelove, M. Barale, & D. Halperin (Eds.). *Lesbian and gay studies reader* (pp. 381–393). New York: Routledge.

Bernheimer, C. & Kahane C. (Eds). (1985). *Dora's case: Freud—hysteria—feminism*. New York: Columbia University Press.

de Lauretis, T. (1994). *The practice of love: Lesbian sexuality and perverse desire*. Bloomington: Indiana University Press.

de Lauretis, T. (1990). Eccentric subjects: Feminist theory and historical consciousness. *Feminist Studies, 16* (1), 115–150.

Fanon, F. (1967). *Black skin, white masks*. (C.L. Markmann, Trans.). New York: Grove Weidenfeld.

Freud, S. (1953–1974). A case of paranoia running counter to the psycho-analytic theory of the disease. In J. Strachey (Ed. and Trans.), *The standard edition of the complete psychological works of Sigmund Freud*. (Vol. 14, pp. 261–272). London: Hogarth. (Original work published 1915)

Freud, S. (1953–1974). The psychogenesis of a case of homosexuality in a woman. In J. Strachey (Ed. and Trans.), *The standard edition of the complete psychological works of Sigmund Freud*. (Vol. 18, pp. 145–172). London: Hogarth. (Original work published 1920)

Freud, S. (1953–1974). Three essays on the theory of sexuality. In J. Strachey (Ed. and Trans.), *The standard edition of the complete psychological works of Sigmund Freud*. (Vol. 7, pp. 123–245). London: Hogarth. (Original work published 1905)

Freud, S. (1953–1974). Fetishism. In J. Strachey (Ed. and Trans.), *The standard edition of the complete psychological works of Sigmund Freud*. (Vol. 21, pp. 152–157). London: Hogarth. (Original work published in 1927)

Freud, S. (1953–1974). The ego and the id. In J. Strachey (Ed. and Trans.), *The standard edition of the complete psychological works of Sigmund Freud*. (Vol. 19, pp. 12–66). London: Hogarth. (Original work published in 1923)

Freud, S. (1953–1974). Splitting of the ego in the process of defense. In J. Strachey (Ed. and Trans.) *The standard edition of the complete psychological works of Sigmund Freud*. (Vol. 23, pp. 275–278). London: Hogarth. (Original work published in 1940 [posthumously], written 1938)

Fuss, D. (1993). Freud's fallen women: Identification, desire, and "*A case of homosexuality in a woman.*" *Yale Journal of Criticism, 6*(1), 1–23.

Jacobus, M. (1995). Russian tactics: Freud's "Case of homosexuality in a woman." *GLQ. A Journal of Lesbian and Gay Studies, 2*(1–2), 65–79.

Merck, M. (1993). The train of thought in Freud's "Case of homosexuality in a woman." In *Perversions: Deviant readings*. (pp. 13–32). New York: Routledge.

O'Connor, N. & Ryan, J. (1993). *Wild desires and mistaken identities: Lesbianism and psychoanalysis*. London: Virago.

Rich, A. (1986). Compulsory heterosexuality and lesbian existence. In *Blood, bread, and poetry: Selected prose 1979–1985*. (pp. 23–75). New York: Norton. (Original work published 1980)

Roof, J. (1991). *A lure of knowledge: Lesbian sexuality and theory*. New York: Columbia University Press.

Sachs, H. (1991). On the genesis of perversion. *American Imago, 48,* 283–293. (Original work published 1923)

3

FALLEN WOMEN
"The Psychogenesis of a Case of Homosexuality in a Woman"

～

Diana Fuss

This chapter selects for discussion one of the most underdiscussed texts in the psychoanalytic library, Sigmund Freud's case history of 1920, "The Psychogenesis of a Case of Homosexuality in a Woman."[1] Working from my initial premise that no scientific language can escape the pull of metaphor, I would like to suggest in the following reading that the cognitive paradigm of "falling," which Freud provides in this case study to "explain" female homosexuality, is already a rhetorical figure. The allegory of the fall—upon which Freud's entire theory of female inversion hinges—activates in psychoanalysis a certain Newtonian metalogics of force, counterforce, attraction, repulsion, and reversal. These figurative traces of psychodynamics in psychoanalytic theory name more than the subject's fall into (or out of) sexuality; they critically define and delimit the operations of the two psychical mechanisms Freud locates as central to the formation of any sexual identity identification and desire. Specifically for Freud, a gravitational fall back into preoedipality, secured through an identification with the father and a concomitant desire for the mother, accounts for the "psychogenesis of a case of homosexuality in a woman." The case history Freud published under this name represents his most sustained attempt to engage with the subject of female homosexuality. Freud's efforts to trace and to codify the "preoedipalization" of the homosexual subject is largely responsible for establishing the perimeters of a sexology, which is founded upon questions of space, time, duration, gravity, and motion, and which continues to set the terms of the psychoanalytic debates on sexuality today.

In the history of psychoanalysis, female homosexuality is theorized almost exclusively in terms of the "pre": the preoedipal, the presymbolic, the prelaw, the premature, even the presexual. The critical presupposition that female homosexuality occupies the space and time of an origin—that it is widely assumed to be, in a word, pretheoretical—could account for its long-term neglect in revisionist theoretical work ordinarily devoted to challenging normative definitions of sexual desire. Part of the general critical disregard for homosexuality in contemporary theories of sexual difference may well be occasioned by a judicious devaluation of false foundationalisms and a healthy suspicion of theories of primacy—those very theories of primacy within which homosexuality has historically been understood. However, such antifoundationalisms, while crucially challenging the dangerous ideology of natural origins, need also to investigate how a concept like "preoedipality" is itself constituted as an effect of a cultural symbolics and, more particularly, to ask how homosexuality comes to be so routinely assigned to the regressive, conservative space of this fictive origin. How and why do psychoanalytic theories of female homosexuality position their subjects *as* foundational, as primeval, as primitive, and indeed as presubjects, presubjects before the normative, heterosexualizing operations of the Oedipus complex, that "legal, legalising coordinate."[2] This chapter will attempt to confront the limits and the dangers of preoedipality as an explanatory model for female homosexuality, focusing specifically upon the instrumental role identification and desire play in Freud's theorization of sexual identity formation.

Liminal Foundations

Let me begin by posing the following historical and institutional question: Where is female homosexuality to be found in psychoanalysis? The answer is in psychoanalysis' very foundations. Of the six case studies Freud completed, both the first case study, *Fragment of an Analysis of a Case of Hysteria* (1905), and the last, "The Psychogenesis of a Case of Homosexuality in a Woman" (1920), are studies of inversion in women, studies of deviations with respect to a woman's object choice. Jacques Lacan's dissertation on paranoid psychosis, his 1932 thesis in medicine, betrays a similar fascination with female paranoiacs whose lack of distance from other women and from themselves (attributed by Lacan to their presymbolic, prelinguistic, preseparation relation to the mother) constitutes the very source of their paranoia. So deep is Lacan's early preoccupation with the question of homosexuality in women that one would have to amend Catherine Clément's general observation, "In the beginning Lacan was interested only in women,"[3] to the more precise formulation, "In the beginning

Lacan was interested only in *homosexual* women." More recently, Julia Kristeva's work on sexual difference is noteworthy for its relative disinterest, not to say dismissal, of female homosexuality, work that addresses the question of homosexuality in women only in occasional postscriptural asides. But it is in her earliest books where female homosexuality emerges as "foundational" and as preparatory to her later depreciation of it—especially in *About Chinese Women* (1974), where the first third of the book defers the question of the Orient to elaborate instead a theory of orientation.[4]

From Sigmund Freud to Julia Kristeva, preoedipality defines the fundamental psychical organization of the homosexual subject who never, it seems, fully accedes to the position of subject but who remains in the ambiguous space of the precultural. Beginning with Freud's study of the "sexual aberrations," upon which he bases his entire theory of sexuality, moving through Lacan's thorough subsumption of female homosexuality into a preoedipalized paranoid psychosis, and reaching toward Kristeva's theory of female homosexuality as a refusal, rather than a fulfillment, of the revolutionary potential of the semiotic, we see in psychoanalysis' positioning and repositioning of homosexuality a critical fall back to the earliest stages of the subject's formation. The progressive movement in psychoanalysis is backward, deep into the subject's prehistory. The most recent work on the question of subjectivity has pushed back the point of sexual identity formation to a time before the preoedipal; the trajectory from Freud to Lacan to Kristeva advances a fast fall from oedipal to preoedipal to semiotic (or what one might call the prepreoedipal). The very history of the institution of psychoanalysis enacts a critical temporal inversion: The preoedipal is theorized after the oedipal, suggesting that any "pre" is a construct of the "post."[5] Ironically, psychoanalysis itself performs the very regressive movement that Freud, and Lacan in his famous "return to Freud," describe as constitutive of what might be called homosexuality's "devolutionary" process—that is, a temporal fall back, a return to a time before the beginning of time, before culture, before oedipality, and before history. Inverted in its progression, psychoanalysis uncannily follows a developmental path strikingly similar to the etiology of homosexuality first set out by Freud.

What this essay does not address is the question of female homosexuality's "etiology" (the "cause" or "origin" of inversion)—a question that can only assume in advance what it purports to demonstrate. Rather, it seeks to understand how female homosexuality is not only structurally situated in the inaugural moments of psychoanalysis but is also theoretically located at the site of an origin, the origin of *any* female sexual identity. These latter questions will tell us far more about what Patricia Williams has recently termed "inessentially speaking"[6] than what even Freud recognizes as the pointless resuscitation of debates over etiology (i.e., is homosexuality innate or acquired?).[7] Inessentiality is a particularly useful figure for describing homosexuality's foundational yet liminal position in psychoanalytic accounts of identity formation. The preposition "in" in "inessential," which here doubles as a prefix, connotes at once a relation of exteriority or nonessentiality (in the sense of incidental, superfluous, peripheral, unimportant, immaterial, lesser, minor, secondary . . .) and a relation of interiority, of being inside essentiality (in the sense of indispensable, central, important, fundamental, necessary, inherent, vital, primary . . .). Homosexuality is "inessential" in this double sense, positioned within psychoanalysis as an essential waste ingredient: The child's homosexual desire for the parent of the same sex, essential to the subject's formation as sexed, is nonetheless simultaneously figured as nonessential, a dispensable component of desire that ultimately must be repudiated and repressed. Could repeated emphasis on the essential inessentiality of homosexuality, its status as repressed excess, reflect a secondary reaction-formation against psychoanalysis' own attraction to an economy of the same, its desire for the homo, and indeed its narcissistic fascination with its own origins?

Homosexuality, Law, Excess

I want to turn now to Freud's "The Psychogenesis of a Case of Homosexuality in a Woman"[8] to begin to work through this question of the essential inessentiality of homosexuality in women. We are faced immediately with a certain ambiguity in the title, where "The Psychogenesis of a Case of Homosexuality in a Woman" can be glossed as either the psychogenesis of an *instance* of homosexuality in a woman or the psychogenesis of Freud's own *study* of homosexuality in a woman. In the first case, Freud characteristically bases an entire theory of female sexual inversion on a single case history: that of an 18–year-old girl, "beautiful and clever," from a family of "good standing," who has become infatuated with a woman 10 years her senior, a "lady" of "fallen" circumstances known for her "promiscuous" behavior. In the second case, Freud traces, also in characteristic fashion, the genesis of his own work, reminding us that psychoanalysis has always been fascinated with beginnings, especially its own, and preoccupied with its relation to the law, indeed its status *as* law. The case begins: "Homosexuality in women, which is certainly not less common than in men, although much less glaring, has not only been ignored by the law, but has also been neglected by psychoanalytic research" (p. 147). In their specific relation to the question of homosexuality in women, psychoanalysis and the law are analogously related: Neither is able to see what is immediately before it. Homosexuality constitutes not an absence, strictly speaking, but an overpresence, an excess, a surplus, or an overabundance; homosexuality may be "less glaring" in women than in men, but it is still "glaring" (*lärmend*). Freud's choice of the word *lärmend* (riotous, noisy, unruly) to describe homosexuality insinuates that the blindness issues from homosexuality itself, its very excess an assault upon the senses, a blinding and deafening spectacle. The law has "ignored" homosexuality in women and psychoanalysis has "neglected" it not because homosexuality is invisible but because, apparently, it is too visible, too audible, too present. The precise characterization of homosexuality as "glaring" permits Freud to deflect psychoanalysis' concentrated "work of elucidation" (p. 171) away from its own powers of definition and concealment, for it is the law of psychoanalysis to establish the frame of reference, the conditions of visibility and audibility, by which sexual identities can be seen and heard in the first place and, in the case of homosexuality, *as* first places, as sites of origin.

Freud continues: "The narration of a single case, not too pronounced in type, in which it was possible to trace its origin and development in the mind with complete certainty and almost without a gap may, therefore, have a certain claim to attention" (p. 147). Although elsewhere, in *Three Essays on the Theory of Sexuality,* Freud theorizes three different kinds of inverts—absolute (inverts whose "sexual objects are exclusively of their own sex"), amphigenic ("psychosexual hermaphrodites" whose "sexual objects may equally well be of their own or of the opposite sex"), and contingent (inverts who "under certain external conditions . . . are capable of taking as their object someone of their own sex"),[9] he prefers to psychoanalyze in his practice only the latter kind, contingent inverts, cases "not too pronounced in type," where libidinal change is possible and a turn away from the same-sex love object can be effected by the analysis. It is crucial to point out here that there is at least an implied distinction in Freud's work between "homosexual women" and "homosexuality in women." At the end of this particular case study, Freud concludes that "a very considerable measure of latent or unconscious homosexuality can be detected in all normal people" (p. 171), that "latent" homosexuality is, in fact, a central precondition of all "manifest" heterosexuality. But whereas homosexuality can be found in all women, not all women are homosexual. For Freud there must be some "special factor" (p. 168), some libidinal remainder or surplus, which converts the contingent homosexuality in women into homosexual women.

Here we need to turn to the case history itself to understand the dynamics of this object conversion. Freud's patient is an adolescent girl, the only daughter in a family with three sons, brought to Freud by a strict and puritanical father in the hopes that analysis might "cure" his daughter of an infatuation with a lady of questionable social standing and loose sexual mores. In the course of the analysis Freud uncovers the girl's "exaggeratedly strong affection" in early puberty for a small boy, not quite 3 years old, an affection which gradually evolved into an interest in "mature, but still youthful women" (p. 156) who are themselves mothers. The motivation for this curious shift in the girl from a "maternal attitude" (p. 156) (wanting to *be* a mother) to a homosexual one (wanting to *have* a mother) Freud attributes to the unexpected pregnancy of the girl's own mother and the birth of her third brother. The girl is, in short, in love with her own mother and redirects this tabooed desire toward a series of mother-substitutes. Freud immediately disavows, however, this homosexual daughter–mother incest by reading it as a displacement of a preceding hetero-sexual daughter–father incest. The "origin" of the girl's (preoedipal) mother-love is a prior (oedipal) father-love; she turns away from her father and toward her mother out of disappointment and resentment that it is her "hated rival," her mother, and not herself who can give the father what it is assumed he most desires, a son. The daughter, in Freud's account, to diffuse the identificatory rivalry with her mother, falls back, "retires in favor of" her mother and her mother's hatred by taking her mother instead of her father as love-object (p. 159). The daughter's desire for the mother is read by Freud as a ruse or a screen to protect the girl against her frustrated oedipal desire for the father. But why is it presumed from the outset that desire for the mother is a displaced artic-ulation of unfulfilled desire for the father, and not the other way around? Why is the daughter's "disappointment" imagined to be provoked by her inability to have the father's baby and not her failure to give her mother one (a possibility Freud later allows for in "Femininity" [1933]) Why is the daughter's resentment and bitterness surmised to be directed toward the mother as competitor for the father's affections and not toward the father as interloper into the mother–daughter relation? Why, in short, is the daughter's "rivalry" assumed to be with the mother and not with the father?

Falling

Freud deploys a complicated rhetoric of "turns" in his work to explain these ambiguous shifts in sexual object choice, theorizing sexual identities and the sexual identifications that produce them in terms of returns, revivals, regressions, retirements, renunciations, and restorations. In the present case history, the analysand's turn toward a same-sex love object is triggered in adolescence by a change in the family configuration (the mother's pregnancy and the birth of a new brother) and a coinciding "revival" of the girl's infantile Oedipus complex. For Freud a revival is a peculiar kind of return: Every revival of the girl's un-resolved Oedipus complex is a regression—a fall back into a preoedipal identi-fication with the father and desire for the mother. In "Femininity," Freud explains the turn back toward the mother as a response to an "inevitable dis-appointment" from the father:

> Female homosexuality is seldom or never a direct continuation of
> infantile masculinity. Even for a girl of this kind it seems necessary
> that she should take her father as an object for some time and enter
> the Oedipus situation. But afterwards, as a result of her inevitable dis-
> appointments from her father, she is driven to regress into her early
> masculinity complex.[10]

Freud was not, of course, the only psychoanalyst to understand female homosexuality as a backward motion, although his theory of regression remains one
of the most elaborately developed. Helene Deutsch, for example, also reads the
female homosexual's apparent preoedipal attachment to the mother as a post-
oedipal regression—"not a question of a simple fixation on the mother as the
first love object but rather a complicated process of returning." And Otto
Fenichel puts the case even more bluntly:

> In women, the turning away from heterosexuality is a regression that
> revives memory traces of the early relations to the mother. Female
> homosexuality therefore has a more archaic imprint than male homo-
> sexuality. It brings back the behavior patterns, aims, pleasures, but also
> the fears and conflicts of the earliest years of life.[11]

For the homosexual presubject, every "pre" contains the spectre of a "re":
Female homosexuality is posited as regressive and reactive, primitive and primal, undeveloped and archaic. Moreover, any gesture of "retirement" signals a
form of renunciation, a refusal to compete and a retreat from conflict; inability
to sustain psychical conflict and desire to ward off "open rivalry" (p. 195) actu-
ate the girl's return to the preoedipal. Turning back in this reading is always read
as a turning away, a retrenchment rather than an advance, a retreat *from* the
father rather than a move *toward* the mother.

But there is a second and equally important sense of "turning" in Freud's
work on homosexuality, namely psychoanalysis's own attempts to effect a conversion in the homosexual patient, a turning of one genital organization into
another through the actual work of analysis. In his discussion of the proper conditions for a successful analysis, Freud admits that such conversions of sexual
identifications in the subject are futile; the most psychoanalysis can do, he
writes, is to "restore" the invert to his or her "full bisexual functions" (p. 151).
The earlier the inversion takes hold, the less likely a conversion can be effected:

> It is only where the homosexual fixation has not yet become strong
> enough, or where there are considerable rudiments and vestiges of a
> heterosexual choice of object, i.e., in a still oscillating or in a defi-
> nitely bisexual organization, that one may make a more favorable
> prognosis for psychoanalytic therapy. (p. 151)

Just as homosexuality is figured as a return, a fall back, so is its apparent psychoanalytic resolution, but whereas the one is posited as a regression, a retiring in favor of a rival, the other is presented as a restoration, a process of recuperation and reconsolidation. One can legitimately ask here why the return to a homosexual object-choice is seen as "regressive" when the return proferred as the means to "cure" homosexuality is seen as "restorative."[12] What marks the difference between these two types of returns? And how, exactly, is a turn from one sexual object to another produced in the subject?

A third sense of "turning" in psychoanalysis speaks to these questions: the turn as fall. For Freud, a woman's return to desire for the mother enacts a fall—not a prelapsarian fall which was, after all, a fall into heterosexuality, but a postlapsarian fall into homosexuality. The female subject passes through the Symbolic, through the process of oedipalization, but because of a series of "inevitable disappointments from her father" lapses back into the preoedipal. It is hardly insignificant to Freud that the event that immediately precedes the beginning of the analysis, and indeed the crisis that occasions it, is the girl's attempted suicide. Strolling on the street one day in the company of the lady, the girl encounters her father who passes the couple by with "an angry glance" (p. 148) [*zornigen Blick*]; incurring the sudden wrath of both father and beloved, the infatuated girl throws herself over a wall and falls onto a suburban railway track. Freud reads the suicide attempt as the fulfillment of the girl's unconscious wish—"the attainment of the very wish which, when frustrated, had driven her into homosexuality—namely, the wish to have a child by her father, for now she 'fell' through her father's fault" (p. 162). Freud here plays on the double signification of the German word for "fall," *niederkommen*, which means both "to fall" and "to be delivered of a child" (p. 162). The girl's fall back into a homosexual desire for the mother actually constitutes a particular kind of maternity in Freud's reading—a fall equivalent to a deliverance.

Cathy Caruth has suggested that "the history of philosophy after Newton could be thought of as a series of confrontations with the question of how to talk about falling,"[13] a proposition that takes on considerable force in light of Freud's own compulsive returns to the problem of the subject's "fall" into sexual difference. Scenes of falling in Freud's work frame sexuality as an injurious event. While working on "A Case of Homosexuality in a Woman," Freud added a passage to *The Interpretation of Dreams* that recounts one of his earliest childhood memories of an accident that befell him between the ages of 2 and 3 years old:

> I had climbed up on to a stool in the store-closet to get something nice that was lying on a cupboard or table. The stool had tipped over and its corner had struck me behind my lower jaw; I might easily, I reflected, have knocked out all my teeth.[14]

A lesson of the retribution inflicted upon young boys attempting to reach covertly into their mothers' cupboards, this remembrance of an early fall functions as a parable for the symbolic threat of permanent injury that precipitates Freud's own painful and sudden entry into oedipality. For the already castrated woman, however, *falling* symbolically registers another kind of injury. In "Dreams and Telepathy" (1922), published shortly after "A Case of Homosexuality in a Woman," Freud recounts a woman patient's recurrent nightmare of falling out of bed, where falling is taken to represent specifically a "fresh representation of childbirth"[15]—for Freud, the very mark of female heterosexual desire. "If a woman dreams of falling," he explains in *The Interpretation of Dreams,* "it almost invariably has a sexual sense: she is imagining herself as a '*fallen woman*'" (p. 202). Or elsewhere, unable to resist summoning an old misogynistic proverb, Freud concludes that "when a girl falls she falls on her back."[16] And in the case history presently under discussion, "A Case of Homosexuality in a Woman," Freud notes with more than a physician's anecdotal detail that his homosexual patient "paid for this undoubtedly serious attempt at suicide with a considerable time on her back in bed" (p. 148). Fear of falling for a woman apparently represents in this thinking both a fear of heterosexuality and a dread of one of its potential consequences, pregnancy, and yet it is precisely the motion of falling that Freud takes as constitutive of female homosexuality. The theoretical problem that insistently poses itself to any reader trying to make sense of Freud's often incoherent writings on female homosexuality is the question of what a woman's *homosexual* identity formation has to do with *maternity,* with "fresh representations of childbirth."

It cannot be a matter of indifference to feminist readers of Freud that "A Case of Homosexuality in a Woman" begins with the word "homosexuality" and concludes with the word "motherhood"—perhaps the most obvious staging of Freud's inability to think homosexuality outside the thematics of maternity. But how do we read the relation between these two poles of sexual identity formation: between homosexuality and motherhood, or between, in Freud's questionable theoretical alignment, same-sex desire and same-sex identification? Freud could be suggesting a symmetrical relation between the two, an irresolvable psychical tension in the young girl's life between wanting to *be* a mother and wanting to *have* her. Or he could be following a more conventional Victorian logic that posits motherhood as a possible antidote to homosexuality, the "answer" to the question that female homosexuality poses for that psychoanalysis which sees itself as a science of restoration. Still another possibility to explain the homosexuality-motherhood alliance in this particular case study could be Freud's attempt to formulate an evolutionary sexual continuum with homosexuality as the originary "before" and motherhood as the developmental "after." Then again, Freud could also be suggesting that homosexuality represents a regressive return *to* the mother—a desire to have the mother by figuratively becoming the mother—a return achieved through a literal fall enacting a symbolic delivery. Details of the case history rule out none of these possibilities; in fact, the analyst's contradictory twists and turns in logic appear to mimic the unfolding drama of the analysand's own infinitely reversible and reactive identifications. The more difficult question for interpreters of Freud is determining precisely how the agencies of identification and desire are invoked to fashion this particular structural relation of dependency between homosexuality and motherhood and why the first term (homosexuality) must always be read in relation to, and must eventually give way to, the second term (motherhood).

Identification and Desire

The return as fall, as deliverance, marks female homosexuality as not simply the subject's return *to* the mother but the subject's turn *as* mother. But this reading of the homosexual turn suggests that the daughter must *become* the mother in order to *have* her. It undermines one of the fundamental laws of psychoanalysis, preserved from Freud through Kristeva, which holds that desire and identification are structurally independent of one another, the possibility of one always presupposing the repression of the other. A subject's desire for one sex can only be secured through a corresponding identification with the other sex; a simultaneous desire for and identification with the same object would be a logical impossibility for Freud.[17] A year after publication of his "Homosexuality in a Woman" case study, Freud completed *Group Psychology and the Analysis of the Ego* (1921), where he first begins to systematize the complicated dialectical relation between identification and object-choice in the formation of the sexed subject:

> It is easy to state in a formula the distinction between an identification with the father and the choice of the father as an object. In the first case one's father is what one would like to *be,* and in the second he is what one would like to *have.* The distinction, that is, depends upon whether the tie attaches to the subject or to the object of the ego. The former kind of tie is therefore already possible before any sexual object-choice has been made.[18]

To identify with the father is to wish to be him, whereas to desire the father is to wish to have him. The very notion of identification appears to be gendered for Freud, modeled on a masculine oedipality even when Freud is most concerned with theorizing the child's preoedipal (presexual) identification with the mother. Philippe Lacoue-Labarthe's shrewd observation that Freud "cannot help 'identifying' the figure of identification with the father figure"[19] further

strengthens the suspicion that it is a postoedipal "secondary" identification that
instantiates and organizes the preoedipal "primary" identification in the first
place. A woman's desire for a woman, Freud maintains throughout his work,
can only be thought in terms of the subject's fall back into a preoedipal identification with the father. But even Freud comes eventually to recognize, in *New
Introductory Lectures on Psycho-Analysis* (1932–1933), that the structural "independence" of identification and object-choice is never so neatly symmetrical as
this "formula" would suggest, and is only ever precariously achieved. It is desire,
for Freud, that continually risks turning (back) into identification:

> Identification and object-choice are to a large extent independent of
> each other; it is however possible to identify oneself with someone
> whom, for instance, one has taken as a sexual object, and to alter one's
> ego on his model.[20]

This turn from object–choice to identification is no simple turn; it operates, in
fact, as a *return* and more properly a *regression*; "object-choice has regressed to
identification," Freud writes on thinking back to his first case study of homosexuality in a woman, the Dora case.[21]

But Freud still needs to account for what motivates these turns in sexual
object-choice, for what provokes the fall of desire into sexual identification. The
answer to the problem of the turn in the "Homosexuality in a Woman" case
study comes, as so many answers do in Freud, in a footnote:

> It is by no means rare for a love-relation to be broken off through a
> process of identification on the part of the lover with the loved object,
> a process equivalent to a kind of regression to narcissism. After this
> has been accomplished, it is easy in making a fresh choice of object
> to direct the libido to a member of the sex opposite to that of the ear-
> lier choice. (p. 158)[22]

Freud attributes the turn to an excess of desire, a surplus of love, or some other
"overcompensation" (p. 158). Why do some subjects have this "overness," this
essential inessential psychical component, and not others? Freud is unable to
answer the question he himself implicitly poses, but what is perhaps even more
significant is that in the very attempt to prove that identification and desire are
counterdirectional turns, Freud in fact demonstrates their necessary collusion
and collapsability, the ever-present potential for the one to metamorphose into,
or turn back onto, the other. The instability of sexual identity lies in the capacity of its psychical mechanisms *to desire and to identify with each other*.

Identification in Freud's work is typically figured in terms of height:
Identification works as a displacement *upward*; the ego elevates itself through

identification, imagines itself always in relation to a higher ideal.[23] Situated at the very bottom of Freud's developmental scale, homosexuals are caught in the Sisyphean labor of pulling themselves up toward the ego-ideal only to be repeatedly disappointed by the object once attained. Sexuality in this scene of falling is neither given nor achieved but *lost*. Desire continually collapses back into identification under the weight of the subject's "disappointment," a disappointment prompted by the inadequacy of the object to fill the measure of its desire. This fall appears to be no different from the deflation any subject experiences when the fantasized object of desire is finally encountered. Slavoj Žižek rightly points out that the found object never coincides with the referent of desire; when faced with the object of desire, the desiring subject inevitably experiences a feeling of "this is not it."[24] What makes this homosexual fall, this fall into homosexuality, more precipitous is the fact that the subject's aspirations are more ambitious. This particular subject has overstepped its bounds and desired too much. Those who progress farthest in oedipalization apparently tumble hardest, with enough momentum and force to reenter the preoedipal stage, leaving desire, lack, and even injury behind. But what kind of fall, in this pseudoscientific gravitational model, produces a homosexual subject? "We do not . . . mean to maintain," Freud insists, "that every girl who experiences a disappointment such as this of the longing for love that springs from the Oedipus attitude at puberty will necessarily on that account *fall a victim to homosexuality*" (p. 168, emphasis added). Do some subjects carry within them a kind of Icarus complex,[25] an inherent proclivity for falling? Or are certain unpredictable Newtonian forces at work to pull any subject at any moment back into the center of gravity Freud calls primary identification? If falling is the tropological model Freud selects to describe homosexual identity formations, then what can be said exactly to precipitate the fall?

Freud's excesses make their reentry at this point, for falling is conceptualized as a response to a heavy burden: One falls under an excessive weight, the weight of desire—a desire that can only ultimately function in such a symbolics as synonymous with heterosexuality. For Freud, homosexual desire is oxymoronic; like women, homosexuals (male and female) lack lack,[26] or lack a certain mature relation to lack. By temporally positing homosexuality as antecedent to the lack that inaugurates desire, Freud in effect drops the sexuality out of homosexuality. It is not lack that defines a homo(sexual) subject but excess, the lack of lack: the surplus that precedes and delimits need, the unintelligible remainder that circumscribes the boundaries of the rational, the overness that must always come first to mark off the deviant from the normal. The excess associated with homosexuality, in Freud's inversive logic (his logic of inversion), holds the position of a "left-over" which comes "right-before," with homosexuality assigned to the place of the firstness of any supplement.

In its popular incarnations, the surfeit that marks off homosexuality from its normative Other, heterosexuality, is "gleaned" from the surface of the body: Homosexuals are said to distinguish themselves by their extravagant dress, their exaggerated mannerisms, their hysterical intonations, their insatiable oral sex drives, and their absurd imitations of "feminine" and "masculine" behavior.[27] What we have in Freud's grammar of excess is a critical displacement of excess from the exterior to the interior; no longer a catalog of enculturating signs such as clothes, language, or style, excess shifts from surface index to subterranean force. Freud writes that his own patient betrayed none of the outward signs a Viennese medical profession expected to find in a homosexual woman, showing "no obvious deviation from the physical type, nor any menstrual disturbance" (p. 154). It is true, Freud confesses, that the "beautiful and well-made girl" had her father's tall figure and sharp facial features, as well as his intellectual acuity, but "these distinctions are conventional rather than scientific," he concludes (p. 154). Moreover, unlike her famous predecessor Dora, Freud's latest homosexual patient "had never been neurotic, and came to the analysis without even one hysterical symptom" (p. 155). In every superficial respect, his new patient strikes Freud as completely unexceptional. Yet it is the very absence of conventional hysterical symptoms (coughing, aphasia, weeping, spasms, tics . . .) or other external signs of neurosis that draw Freud ultimately to the conclusion that this woman's very normality is most irregular, her lack of "even one hysterical symptom" an indicator of the most abnormal or peculiar of states for a woman. This particular woman is excessively normal, her deviancy secured through an apparent psychological refusal of abnormality. Mimicry is transposed from the surface of the body to its psychical infrastructure as excess comes to designate something more than a style or a performance; excess for Freud marks a certain internal relation that defines the very structure of an emotional identification.

Mikkel Borch-Jacobsen, following Freud, explains the desire–identification dynamics this way: Identification always *anticipates* desire: identification, rather than an object, "governs" (p. 32), "orients" (p. 34), "induces," and "predicts" desire (p. 47). Identification, in effect, comes first, and the subject "dates" itself from this mimetic turn:

> Desire (the desiring subject) does not come first, to be *followed* by an identification that would allow the desire to be fulfilled. What comes first is a tendency toward identification, a primordial tendency which then gives rise to a desire; and this desire is, from the outset, a (mimetic, rivalrous) desire to oust the incommodius other from the place the pseudo-subject already occupies in fantasy. . . . Identification brings the desiring subject into being, and not the other way around.[28]

This approach de-essentializes sexuality in a particularly useful way, for to show that desires are never originary is also to imply that there are no "natural" or "normal" libidinal impulses that may later get rerouted or "perverted" through an identification gone astray. However, what remains completely ungrounded in this explanation of desire and identification is the problematical notion of *identification* as a "primordial tendency." Freud leans heavily on a scientific model of entropy that posits the motor force of psychological change and sexual development as a drive toward sameness, a tendency toward mimesis: homophilic identification. While crucially naming the indispensability of homophilic identification to the production of sexual identity, Freud nonetheless sees mimeticism as a continual threat to the stability and the coherency of that identity. For Freud, I would suggest, the real danger posed by the desire/identification codependency is not the potential for an excess of desire to collapse back into an identification, but the possibility for new forms of identification to generate ever proliferating and socially unmanageable forms of desire.

"A Case of Homosexuality in a Woman" attributes the girl's sexual interest in young mothers to the eventual, perhaps even inevitable, collapse of her "strong desire to be a mother herself" (p. 156), a change in object-choice brought about by the girl's oedipal disappointment at her failure to have her father's child—a failure made all the more visible by her own mother's midlife pregnancy. The first objects of the girl's sexual desire after the birth of her youngest brother, Freud tells us, are therefore "really mothers, women between 30 and 35 whom she had met with their children," and even though the girl eventually gives up actual motherhood as the "*sine qua non* in her love object," analysis proves to Freud "beyond all shadow of doubt that the lady-love was a substitute for—her mother" (p. 156). While Freud directs his theoretical remarks, and the reader's attention, to the problem of an excess of desire reverting (back) into an identification, the example proferred by the details of the case history itself demonstrates exactly the opposite phenomenon: the possibility for an overly zealous identification ("the strong desire to be a mother") to give way to an equally powerful desire ("motherhood as a *sine qua non* in her love-object"). Apparently Freud's patient assumes her role too well, her excessive desire to be a mother the very trigger for her sudden desire to sleep with one. Yet the lurking danger posed by a too successful oedipalization signals exactly the paradox Freud refuses to see in his own reading, for to recognize this possibility would involve also, at the very least, entertaining the idea of heterosexuality as an inessential supplement and originary excess, or, in an even more radical (and, for Freud, untenable) formulation, allowing for the possibility that it is "absolute" or "exclusive" *hetero*sexuality that may be intolerable to the ego.[29] Moreover, Freud's tactical misreading of the actual workings of identification and desire in this particular case history permits him to deflect attention away from the enculturating and normative work of psychoanalysis: the attempt to effect "curative restorations" by carefully monitoring and limiting the range of a subject's identifications. The job of psychoanalysis, after all, is typically to reorient a culturally tabooed desire by first redirecting the identification that produced it—a task usually accomplished through the therapeutic use of transference.

Fallen Women

Freud's insistence upon the homosexual woman's "fall" into primary identification (preoedipal absorption with the mother) works effectively to exclude the woman who desires another woman from the very category of "sexuality," and it does so by ensuring that any measure of sexual maturity will be designated as heterosexual object-choice "achieved" through the act of secondary identification (oedipal incorporation of a parental ideal). Freud sustains the notion of female homosexuality's presexual status by assuming, first, that same-sex desire is principally and finally an act of primary identification and, second, that primary identification is completely uninflected by the cultural markers associated with secondary identification. When the girl leaves the Oedipus complex, which marked her original entry into history and culture, and falls into the shadowy netherworld of primary identification, she drops out of sexual difference as well. But "primary" identification is itself a social process, already presupposing in the subject prior knowledge of the culturally weighted distinction between maternal and paternal roles, and assuming in advance at least an "intuition" of sexual difference.[30] Preoedipality is firmly entrenched in the social order and cannot be read as before, outside, or even after the Symbolic; the mother–daughter relation, no less than the father–daughter relation, is a Symbolic association completely inscribed in the field of representation, sociality, and culture.

Freud explains his patient's homoerotic attachment to older women of childbearing age as a rehearsal of the girl's early "mother-complex," a preoedipal, presexual state of nondifferentiation with the mother, while at the same time making this homosexual object-choice entirely dependent upon a (preceding) paternal identification. This contradictory insistence upon homosexuality's postoedipal return to a precultural fixation flatly contradicts the case history's repeated disclosures of the importance, in the formation of the girl's sexual identity, of specifically social ties between the girl, her family members, and the extrafamilial objects of her affections. Exactly whom the girl identifies *with* in her homosexual attachment to the lady is never entirely clear. While Freud ostensibly concludes that a masculine, paternal identification permits the girl's homosexual object-choice ("she changed into a man and took her mother in place of her father as the object of her love," [p. 158]), his patient's suicidal plunge, which temporarily replaces the father's punitive anger with parental solicitude, suggests a feminine, maternal identification in which the girl continues to compete with her mother as rival for her father's love and attention (the mother "had herself suffered for some years from neurotic troubles and enjoyed a great deal of consideration from her husband," [p. 149]). Equally indeterminate is the gendered identity of the love object, insofar as the lady corresponds as much to the girl's masculine as to her feminine ideal: "Her lady's slender figure, severe beauty, and downright manner reminded her of the brother who was a little older than herself" (p. 156).[31] With what in the other does the subject identify if not a particular familial or social ideal? Put slightly differently, what does the subject desire in the other if not a cultural reflection of what she herself aspires to be?

The scale of identification, in which the desiring subject rises and falls according to the strength of the pull and resistance of its elusive object, carries along with it a strong class connotation for Freud's patient. The girl, a member of the rising middle class, finds herself irresistably attracted to "fallen women." Her current object of desire, a "*demimondaine*" (p. 153) who has lost her reputation and fallen into "ignoble circumstances," inspires in the enamored young girl fantasies of chivalric rescue. The case history provides a strong suggestion that the "lady" is, in fact, a "lady-of-the-evening," a woman who maintains some semblance of her former class status by earning a living as a high-class prostitute: "[S]he lived simply by giving her bodily favours." But even before her devotion to the lady, the girl's "first passions had been for women who were not celebrated for specially strict propriety" (p. 161). These early infatuations include "a film actress at a summer resort" (who first incites the ire of the girl's father, [p. 161]) and "a strict and unapproachable mistress" (who, Freud adds, is "obviously a substitute mother," [p. 168]). For the girl, "bad reputation" in the love object is "positively a 'necessary condition for love'" (p. 161). All three of these mother-substitutes—the prostitute, the actress, and the teacher—occupy a class below the girl, but they also represent collectively a class of women who earn their living independently, outside of marriage and the heterosexual contract. Could it be that the force of the attraction exerted on the girl by these figures of desire is, in part, the lure of the economic independence and social mobility that they represent? The real provocation of the girl's impassioned devotion to these working ladies may issue not simply from the sex of her love objects but from their "low" social standing as well. To a class-conscious Viennese society, the greatest threat posed by the girl's "homosexual enthusiasms" (p. 168) is the ever-present possibility of what Freud diagnoses elsewhere as "the dangers of sexual relations with people of an inferior social class."[32]

This figuration of identification as a problem of height and scale, a matter of the ego's striving to reach up to an elevated object, further recalls the image of the young Freud reaching for the unattainable goods in his mother's cupboard. That one of Freud's earliest memories should summon up a fall during the pre-oedipal stage, a fall that inflicted a wound whose scar he bears with him into adulthood, may suggest Freud's unconscious fear that he has already been cas-trated and placed on a homosexual continuum along with the mother. Indeed, what Freud seems most anxious to disavow in his analysis of the young girl is his own identification with the feminine. Freud more or less admits directly to an identification with his patient's stern but loving father, "an earnest, worthy man, at bottom very tender-hearted" (p. 149), and he seems convinced that his patient, as he tellingly puts it, "intended to deceive me just as she habitu-ally deceived her father" (p. 165). But this masculine identification masks a deeper, more disturbing feminine identification with the mother who "enjoyed her daughter's confidence concerning her passion" (p. 149). The transferential role Freud frequently found himself playing in his therapeutic sessions was not exclusively nor even principally the familiar role of paternal prohibitor but more often the less comfortable role of maternal educator: sub-stitute mother figure imparting sexual knowledge to adolescent girls. In fact, as a male doctor speaking candidly on sexual subjects to girls in his professional care, regularly opening himself to charges of social impropriety and sexual prurience, Freud could not entirely escape (despite his best attempts to seek refuge behind the mantle of scientific knowledge) the "taint" of a feminine identification with the mother whose proper role is to educate her daughter on matters of sexual and social conduct. This is not the first time Freud has dis-avowed a strong feminine identification. For example, in addition to Freud's much-discussed identification with Dora's hysteria, Jim Swan has uncovered Freud's unconscious identification with a pregnant woman in the dream of Irma's injection and an equally strong identification with his childhood nurse in the dream of "a little sheep's head." Freud himself was unable to make these connections, even though, as Swan points out, the idea of the therapist as a nurse to his patients is not in the least an uncommon theme in psychoanalytic literature.[33]

Fighting continually against the "low estimation" (p. 149) in which psycho-analysis is held in Vienna, Freud perhaps more closely resembles the lady than any other stock figure in this extended family romance. Freud's own marginal social standing and his life-long economic anxieties, in addition to his frank dis-cussion of sexuality, all situate him structurally in the position of the lady, the fallen woman. But unlike the lady, Freud is unable to achieve any stature or prominence in his patient's eyes:

> Once when I expounded to her a specially important part of the the-
> ory, one touching her nearly, she replied in an inimitable tone, "How
> very interesting," as though she were a *grande dame* being taken over
> a museum and glancing through her lorgnon at objects to which she
> was completely indifferent. (p. 163)

This overly clever comparison of his patient to a *grande dame* glancing through her lorgnon betrays Freud's sensitivity to the girl's cutting pretenses to class superiority. When, in a psychodrama like this one, the look carries such potent and castrating powers, not even Freud is immune to the discomfiture provoked by his patient's class condescension—an irritation that ultimately leads Freud to terminate the girl's treatment and to counsel his patient to see a woman doctor instead (p. 164). "Retiring in favor of someone else" (p. 159),[34] Freud beats a fast retreat, acting out the very rhetorical move that he identifies in this case history as one of the "causes" of homosexuality (p. 159). Fixed by his patient's arrogant glance, much like the girl is herself arrested on the street by her father's disapproving look, Freud "falls" through his patient's fault. In a case history where reversible and elastic identifications keep the family neurosis in motion, Freud interestingly gets to play all the principal parts: father, mother, beloved, *and* girl.

Conclusion

The subject, governed by a drive to consume and to possess the object of its desire, must resist the call of primary identification (homophilia) if it is to succeed in its climb toward maturity, defined as object-relatedness (heterophilia). Primary identification—something of a redundancy in Freud—operates as the gravitational pull that perpetually threatens to capsize the subject under the excessive weight of its own regressive desires. In short, identification both precedes desire and strives to exceed it, propelled by its insatiable oral drive to swallow desire whole. In Freud's reading of identification and desire, homosexual desire is not even, properly speaking, desire. Rather, homosexuality represents an instance of identification gone awry—identification in overdrive (or, one might say, oral drive). This overdrive is also implicitly a death drive: *Cadere* (Latin for "to fall") etymologically conjures cadavers. For Freud every fall into homosexuality is *inherently suicidal* since the "retreat" from oedipality entails not only the loss of desire but also the loss of a fundamental relation to the world into which desire permits entry—the world of sociality, sexuality, and subjectivity.

While desire is the province and the privilege of heterosexuals, homosexuals are portrayed as hysterical identifiers and expert mimics.[35] By strategically aligning "homo" with identification and "hetero" with desire, Freud, in spectacularly circular fashion, resubmits homosexuality to its own alleged entropic

"tendencies," so that "homo" subsumes "sexuality" and identification incorporates desire. What Freud gives us in the end is a Newtonian explanation of sexual orientation in which falling bodies are homosexual bodies, weighted down
by the heaviness of multiple identifications, and rising bodies are heterosexual
bodies, buoyed up by the weightlessness of desires unmoored from their (lost)
objects. This chapter has attempted to demonstrate that such a mechanistic
explanatory model is itself overburdened and constrained by the heaviness of its
terms, terms that increasingly come to exceed the bounds and conditions of their
founding logic. Precisely because desire and identification cannot be securely separated or easily prevented from turning back on one another, Freud's persistent
attempt to read sexual orientation according to the laws of gravity and motion
ultimately falls apart, splintering under the pressure of its own rhetorical weight.

Notes

1. Sigmund Freud, "The Psychogenesis of a Case of Homosexuality in a Woman"
(1920), *Standard Edition,* 18:145–172. The original text, "Über die Psychogenese eines
Falles von weiblicher Homosexualität," can be found in volume 12 of *Gesammelte Werke*
(Frankfurt am Main: S. Fischer Verlag, 1968), 271–302.

2. The phrase is Jacques Lacan's, from Seminar I on *Freud's Papers on Technique,
1953–1954,* ed. Jacques-Alain Miller, trans. John Forrester (New York and London:
W. W. Norton and Company, 1988), 198. In its interest in the inverted, disorientating
logic of the "pre" and the "post," this essay addresses, albeit from a different direction,
many of the same theoretical problems discussed in Lee Edelman's analysis of the Wolf
Man. In "Seeing Things: Representation, the Scene of Surveillance, and the Spectacle
of Gay Male Sex," Edelman returns to the question of "sexual suppositions" in the
psychoanalytic constitution of male subjectivity, while my own reading of female homosexuality anticipates the problem of sexual presuppositions. A comparative reading might
also conclude that Edelman's (be)hindsight finds an epistemological counterpart in my
own focus upon a circumscribed (be)foresight. While the cultural representations of lesbian sexuality as "foreplay" and gay male sexuality as "behindplay" (see Edelman, 104)
may well overdetermine the staging of these particular theoretical "scenes," it strikes me
that such investigations of the before and the behind (my own confrontation with the
before post-dating Edelman's entry into the behind) might more profitably be read back-
to-back. See Lee Edelman's contribution to *Inside/Out: Lesbian Theories, Gay Theories,*
ed. Diana Fuss (New York: Routledge, 1991).

3. Catherine Clément, *The Lives and Legends of Jacques Lacan,* trans. Arthur Gold-
hammer (New York: Columbia University Press, 1983), 60.

4. See Sigmund Freud, *Dora: Fragment of an Analysis of a Case of Hysteria* (1905),
Standard Edition, 7:125–243; Jacques Lacan, *De la psychose paranoïaque dans ses rapports avec
la personalité suivi de Premiers écrits sur la paranoïa* (Paris: Editions du Seuil, 1975); and Julia
Kristeva, *About Chinese Women,* trans. Anita Barrows (New York: Marion Boyars, 1977).

5. Judith Butler is especially adept at relentlessly interrogating the specious logic of
a before and an after, exposing how every before (what ostensibly comes first) is really

an effect of the after (what it was thought to precede): for example, the preoedipal an effect of the oedipal, the prediscursive an effect of the discursive, the prejuridical an effect of the juridical, and so on. *Pre*formatives are read as *per*formatives in Butler's deconstruction of false foundationalisms. See *Gender Trouble: Feminism and the Subversion of Identity* (New York: Routledge, 1990).

6. I am grateful to Patricia Williams for her suggestion of this particular term and for her invitation to think more about the figure of inessentiality at the annual meeting of the American Association of Law Schools; some of the following remarks were formulated for that occasion on a panel devoted to the problem of "inessentially speaking."

7. Although unable to resist speculating on etiological foundations throughout his work on sexual inversion, Freud nonetheless seems peculiarly aware of the futility of doing so. He writes in the present case history: "So long as we trace the development from its final outcome backwards, the chain of events appears continuous, and we feel we have gained an insight which is completely satisfactory or even exhaustive. But if we proceed the reverse way, if we start from the premises inferred from the analysis and try to follow these up to the final result, then we no longer get the impression of an inevitable sequence of events which could not have been otherwise determined" (167).

8. "The Psychogenesis of a Case of Homosexuality in a Woman" may well be Freud's most overlooked case study; certainly compared to the volume of criticism generated by the Dora case history, the "Psychogenesis" paper has received surprisingly little attention. For some important exceptions to this critical silence, see Luce Irigaray, "Commodities Among Themselves" in *This Sex Which Is Not One,* trans. Catherine Porter (Ithaca, NY: Cornell University Press, 1985); Mandy Merck, "The Train of Thought in Freud's 'Case of Homosexuality in a Woman,'" *m/f* 11/12 (1986): 35–46; Judith A. Roof, "Freud Reads Lesbians: The Male Homosexual Imperative," *Arizona Quarterly* 46:1 (Spring 1990): 17–26; Diane Hamer, "Significant Others: Lesbians and Psychoanalytic Theory," *Feminist Review* 34 (Spring 1990): 134–151; and Mary Jacobus, "Russian Tactics: Freud's 'Case of Homosexuality in a Woman,'" in *First Things: Reading the Maternal Imaginary* (New York: Routledge, 1995).

9. Sigmund Freud, *Three Essays on the Theory of Sexuality (1905), Standard Edition,* 7:136–137.

10. Sigmund Freud, "Femininity," in *New Introductory Lectures on Psychoanalysis* (1933), *Standard Edition,* 22:130.

11. Helene Deutsch, "On Female Homosexuality," in *Psychoanalysis and Female Sexuality,* ed. Hendrik Ruitenbeek (New Haven, CT: College and University Press, 1966), 125. Deutsch's essay was originally published in *The International Journal of Psychoanalysis* 14 (1933), the same year Freud's *New Introductory Lectures* appeared in print. See also Deutsch's *The Psychology of Women,* vol. 1 (New York: Bantam, 1973), 332–361. The Fenichel citation is taken from his volume on *The Psychoanalytic Theory of Neurosis* (New York: W.W. Norton and Company, 1945), 340.

12. For an interesting inversion of the regression/restoration binary, see John Fletcher's "Freud and His Uses: Psychoanalysis and Gay Theory," in *Coming On Strong: Gay Politics and Culture,* eds. Simon Shepherd and Mick Wallis (London: Unwin Hyman, 1989), 90–118. Fletcher sees lesbianism, and not its proposed psychoanalytic "cure," as the true restoration. To the degree that lesbianism *contests* castration, it can be read as "a restorative strategy which seeks to repair the losses, denigrations, thwartings that a patriarchal culture inflicts on the girl in her primary relation to the mother" (105).

13. Cathy Caruth, "The Claims of Reference," *The Yale Journal of Criticism* 4:1 (Fall 1990): 194.

14. Freud, *The Interpretation of Dreams* (1900), *Standard Edition,* 5:560. See also "Dreams and Telepathy" (1922), *Standard Edition,* 18:198.

15. Freud, "Dreams and Telepathy," 213.

16. Sigmund Freud, *The Psychopathology of Everyday Life* (1901), *Standard Edition,* 6:175.

17. I have discussed the implications of Freud's persistent attempts to dichotomize desire and identification in "Fashion and the Homospectatorial Look," *Critical Inquiry* 18 (Summer 1992): 713–737. For a similar critique of Freud's insistence on the mutual exclusivity of subject and object, which focuses by contrast on Freud's theorization of *male* sexuality, see Michael Warner's "Homo-Narcissism; or, Heterosexuality," in *Engendering Men: The Question of Male Feminist Criticism,* eds. Joseph A. Boone and Michael Cadden (New York: Routledge, 1990), 190–206. Warner points out that the argument Freud offers to explain why a subject might choose one secondary identification over another is based entirely on recourse to the suspect notion of congenital predispositions: "Only the child's 'sexual disposition'—i.e., its 'masculine' or 'feminine' bent—will determine the relative *weight* of these identification axes" (196, emphasis mine).

18. Freud, *Group Psychology and the Analysis of the Ego* (1921), *Standard Edition,* 18:106.

19. See *Typography: Mimesis, Philosophy, Politics,* ed. Christopher Fynsk (Cambridge, MA: Harvard University Press, 1989), 114. Lacoue-Labarthe is one of the most astute readers of identification's inscription in the social field.

20. Sigmund Freud, *New Introductory Lectures,* 63.

21. Freud, *Group Psychology,* 107.

22. A simpler way to put this problem of desire slipping over and into identification is to say that it is possible to love someone so excessively and exclusively that one gradually becomes that person.

23. Kaja Silverman, "White Skin, Brown Masks: The Double Mimesis, or with Lawrence in Arabia," in *Differences: A Journal of Feminist Cultural Studies* 1:3 (Fall 1989): 25. Silverman helpfully suggests that we think of identification "not so much as the 'resolution' of desire as its perpetuation within another regime" (24).

24. Slavoj Žižek, *Looking Awry: An Introduction to Jacques Lacan Through Popular Culture* (Cambridge, MA: MIT Press, 1991), 92.

25. I am indebted to Alan Stoekl's identification of the Icarian complex, an "unconscious and pathological desire to fall," in the work of Georges Bataille. See Stoekl's introduction to Bataille's *Visions of Excess: Selected Writings, 1927–1939* (Minneapolis: University of Minnesota Press, 1985), xv.

26. Michèle Montreley, "Inquiry into Femininity," *m/f* 1 (1978): 83–102.

27. There can perhaps be no better, more playful, more mimetic response to such excessive parodies than more excess—a politics of mimesis. As recent work on camp, butch-femme, hermaphroditism, transvestism, and transsexualism has powerfully and performatively demonstrated, to be excessively excessive, to flaunt one's performance as performance, is to unmask all identity as drag. Central to each of these studies is Irigaray's distinction between "masquerade" and "mimicry" where the critical difference between them—between the "straight" imitation of a role and a parodic hyperbolisation of that role—depends on the degree and readability of its excess (see Chapter 5). But without the telltale signs of excess, encoded in the mimic's walk, speech, or dress, mimicry would be indistinguishable from masquerade and the political utility of mimesis would be neg-

ligible. Excess, in other words, is all that holds the two apart, for to fail in mimesis is usually to fail in being *excessive enough*. Currently, three of the most important works which attempt to theorize the problematics of excess in the politics of mimesis are Carole-Anne Tyler's *Female Impersonators* (New York: Routledge, 1996), Marjorie Garber's *Vested Interests: Cross-Dressing and Cultural Anxiety* (New York and London: Routledge, 1991), and Judith Butler's *Bodies That Matter* (New York and London: Routledge, 1994).

28. Mikkel Borch-Jacobsen, *The Freudian Subject,* trans. Catherine Porter (Stanford, CA: Stanford University Press, 1988), 47.

29. Sandor Ferenczi's 1909 "More About Homosexuality" contains one of the earliest suggestions in psychoanalysis that homosexuality may be the effect of an "excessively powerful heterosexuality." See Ferenczi's *Final Contributions to the Problems and Methods of Psychoanalysis,* ed. Michael Balint, trans. Eric Mosbacher (New York: Basic Books, 1955). Cited in Kenneth Lewes, *The Psychoanalytic Theory of Male Homosexuality* (New York: New American Library, 1988), 146.

30. For an excellent discussion of the differences between primary and secondary identification, see Mary Ann Doane's "Misrecognition and Identity" in *Explorations in Film Theory: Selected Essays from Ciné-Tracts,* ed. Ron Burnett (Bloomington and Indianapolis: Indiana University Press, 1991), 15–25. Regarding the problem of primary identification, Doane reasonably wonders: "Does it really define a moment which is neuter, which predates the establishment of sexual difference?" (21)

31. Lines like these, which suggest (on the part of the girl) a masculine object-choice in addition to a masculine identification, lead Judith Roof to conclude that Freud's theory of lesbianism amounts in the end to little more than a displaced analysis of *male* homosexuality. See Roof's "Freud Reads Lesbians."

32. Freud, *Interpretation of Dreams,* 305. One of Freud's most interesting readings of class conflict can be found in this analysis of a male patient's "sapphic dream" where "above" and "below" refer not only to sexual parts but to social positions as well. His patient's dream of laborious climbing reminds Freud of Alphonse Daudet's *Sappho,* a book that Freud understands as a powerful "warning to young men not to allow their affections to be seriously engaged by girls of humble origin and a dubious past" (286).

33. Jim Swan, "*Mater* and Nannie: Freud's Two Mothers and the Discovery of the Oedipus Complex," *American Imago* 31:1 (Spring 1974): 39. Swan hypothesizes that Freud's resistance to acknowledging publically his fear of a feminine identification has everything to do with his anxieties over homosexuality (27). Swan's essay remains one of the best and most suggestive readings of why Freud waited until shortly after the death of his mother in 1930 to "discover" the critical importance of preoedipality and the infant's primary erotic identification with the mother.

34. Mandy Merck asks: "In insisting upon a woman analyst isn't Freud acting precisely as he accuses his homosexual patient of doing?" (44). In "Russian Tactics," Mary Jacobus also provides a fascinating reading of Freud's feminine identifications, arguing that "even more than the woman doctor in whose favour Freud 'retires,' the lady turns out to be a rival authority on lesbian and bisexual matters." Both Merck and Jacobus provide particularly useful accounts of the case history's opening rhetoric of courtly love and its closing allusion to surgical sex change. I thank Mary Jacobus for generously sharing with me her work in progress.

35. I am indebted to Marcia Ian for seeing the implications of my reading of Freud here better than I did.

4

WHO WAS THAT GIRL?

~

John H. Gagnon

I take my title and the organizing impulse for these reflections from Neil Bartlett's *Who Was That Man? A Present for Mr. Oscar Wilde* (1988).[1] The title of Bartlett's work poses the crucial question: Is "homosexuality" at the core of Oscar Wilde's story? Was Oscar Wilde the ur-gay man, were his writings the genetic texts for camp, does Oscar Wilde deserve to be the most widely known "homosexual" of them all? Can the modern detective/historian/literary critic decipher from the body of Wilde's writings, from his and others' letters, from thickening layers of interpretive texts a "true" Oscar Wilde?

One of Bartlett's answers is:

> After 25 May 1895 ("Guilty") Wilde could no longer pass. Everyone knew that Oscar was a forgery, a fake. He was not what he appeared to be. It was no defense that he himself had never claimed to be anything other than both forger and forgery. ("The first duty in life is to be as artificial as possible.") *He was entirely lacking in wholeness and completeness of nature.* He wished, in fact, to be completely unnatural. He was a creator of copies, borrowing and reprocessing fragments of his own and other people's works. He assiduously composed his public life as father, husband, and moralist and he created a career for himself as a playwright whose plays are littered with the wrecks of fathers, husbands, and moralists, who are struggling to prove that they are who and what they say they are. His "private" homosexual life was an elaborate drama of deception, lies, and most of all, inspired invention. He could not, even in 1895, after concealment had failed, reveal his true nature. There was no real Oscar Wilde, if by real we mean homosexual. He did not, like us, have the alibi of "being like that," London in 1895 had no conception of a man being "naturally homosexual." A

man who loved other men could only be described as an invert, an inversion of something else, a pervert, an exotic, a disease, a victim, a variation. Wilde was an artist as well. He was entirely uninterested in authenticity. (pp. 163–164, emphasis in original)

I chose this paragraph to legitimate various forms of the question: Who was that girl who plays one of the two central roles (Freud plays the other) in the essay "The Psychogenesis of a Case of Homosexuality in a Woman." If we cannot be sure about the homosexuality of Mr. Oscar Wilde, there may be similar questions about the homosexuality of this young woman. What is it about this young woman that makes Freud so sure that this young woman is "homosexual"?

We are more restricted in answering this question about "the girl" than was Bartlett about Wilde. Wilde left behind volumes of works in his own hand, there are a vast number of commenting contemporaries, there are letters to and from a variety of others—even the streets of the city of London that Wilde frequented look much as they did then. One can slowly immerse oneself in Wilde and Wildeana until one has the illusion of being at one with the Other. Of course this metaphor for knowing is unlike the archaeological dig. Though both methods draw upon the romantic impulses of the nineteenth century, the latter requires an objective and scientific supervisor of the excavation. The exemplary searcher in Freud is the archaeologist. The mound on the plain contains the hidden ruins of the city; the diggers unearth pottery shards, figurines, sometimes a completed tomb that has escaped the grave robbers. The mound yields up its secrets to the prepared hand and mind. The layers that represent the ruined cities, one built upon the other, are obviously the layers of repressed materials, down through which the analyst sifts his or her way. The metaphor is too passive to be complete, for the active role of the analysand is missing—indeed it is the analysand, like the native digger, who unearths the psychic fragments for the analyst to evaluate and interpret.

What is left of the girl? All that we know is in the essay from which all of the identifying characteristics have been expunged. We know that we are in Vienna, a vast imperial city, now shorn from its territorial and cultural periphery by the vagaries of World War I. Left only with its German majority, this East Reich will welcome its inclusion in the Third Reich in 1938. In 1920 it is an impoverished city, seething with discontents and resentments and anti-Semitism. The girl is brought to Freud by her father, and she walks up the steps to the consulting room at Bergstrasse 19 for only a few months. The case report is published in 1920, so perhaps she was a patient during 1918 or 1919, perhaps born in 1900 or 1901. We are told that she is 18 and that she comes from still well-to-do parents, used to summering in resorts even during the War. These are the modest facts with which a detective might start. There are probably a few newspaper clippings about her suicide attempt that could lead us further in deciphering who the historical girl was and who she might have become.

Freud is now in his mid-60s. He too has been diminished by the end of Empire. His international reputation is growing, but the actual circumstances of daily life are problematic. His professorship counts for less than he paid for it, as does the medical establishment in which he works.[2] Indeed, psychoanalysis itself does not seem to have achieved its proper role in the sciences as Freud [1920] notes: "The low estimation in which psychoanalysis is so generally held in Vienna did not prevent him [the girl's father] from turning to it for help" (p. 149). Indeed, psychoanalysis was only the girl's father's penultimate alternative before a "speedy marriage [that] was to awaken the natural instincts of the girl and stifle her unnatural tendencies" (p. 149).

My desire to know more about the historical girl is dual. Knowing about the historical girl would answer questions about whether her "natural instincts" or "unnatural tendencies" triumphed during the course of the next decades. It is a crude test of whether Freud's analysis of her past would have predicted her future. Secondly, it might answer questions about Freud's reactions to her. The rejection by the girl of both psychoanalysis as science and Freud as analyst has resulted in a profoundly defensive response by Freud in the essay itself.[3] What were the attributes of the girl that allowed her to defend herself against the wishes of her natural father and his psychoanalytic surrogate? Perhaps we would learn nothing about "homosexuality" from this exercise in detective work, though we could learn something about Freud.

One important note. It is clear that unlike Wilde's London, Freud's Vienna does have a concept of the homosexual, perhaps not the "natural homosexual," but at least the "unnatural homosexual" or the pervert. Indeed, Freud is one the shapers of the category homosexual, both in explanations of its etiology and of its adult enactment. The theater, literature, and fine arts of *fin de siècle* Vienna were highly eroticized (an eroticization that is the context for Freud's own erotic works). The cross-cutting margins between ethnic groups and social classes, Jew and non-Jew, Austrian, Czech, Bohemian, and Hungarian, decaying aristocrats and rising bourgeoisie, employers and domestic servants are the fertile edges around which the erotic imagination and sexual practice flourished (Dabrowski and Leopold, 1997; Schorske, 1961; Werkner, 1994). It is hard to imagine Sigmund Freud *beginning* his work in late nineteenth-century London, although it is easy enough to find him near the end of his life in a Bloomsbury he helped create.

A Girl in Love

The narrative structure of this profoundly digressive and incoherent essay does not make the behavioral facts of the case very accessible. And as usual, the only voice that is heard in the writing is Freud's. The presenting conduct relevant to the classification of this "beautiful and clever girl" (p. 147) as homosexual appears in two widely separated sections of the essay. The first evidence is that the young woman has developed a passion (perhaps a "crush" in contemporary terms) for an attractive woman some 10 years older than she. The older woman, who is of high social origins (perhaps the upper bourgeoisie or aristocracy), has fallen upon economic hard times—perhaps because of the dire effects of World War I in dismembering the Austro-Hungarian empire. The older woman lives with a married woman (whether there is a husband present is unclear, as are all other characteristics of this third woman and her relation to the beloved) and is said to have sexual relations with a number of men in exchange for economic support. (Freud nowhere specifies whether this support is in the form of gifts, cash, or other resources). Freud uneasily describes this woman as a "*cocotte*" by which he means something more serious than a coquette, perhaps a prostitute or at least a woman of ill-repute.

The girl (given her age, why Freud refers to her as a woman is unclear; in current terms she is still a "teenager," but she may have become a "woman" because she resists his advances) is entirely open to Freud about her attachment to her older friend. In the period before the girl is brought to Freud for "treatment," she hung about various places where her beloved could be seen (outside the beloved's door and at tram stops), and the girl took every opportunity to spend time with her beloved (though she lied to her parents about her activities). Of particular concern to the parents was that the girl and her beloved walked (how often is unspecified) arm in arm in the crowded pedestrian districts of the city, sometimes near her father's offices.

One day while strolling together, the girl and her beloved met the girl's father, who gave them only an angry glance and passed on. When the girl told her beloved who that angry man was, the beloved told the girl that their relationship must end—whether because the father knew or because the father disapproved is not clear. Rejected by both her father and her beloved, the girl then threw herself into a suburban railway cutting in an unsuccessful attempt at suicide. The girl was rescued, and after a 6-month recovery at home once again began to see her beloved in a more open fashion than before. Her attempted suicide both made the girl's beloved take the girl's passion more seriously (or the beloved took the girl more seriously because she worried about the girl's self-destructive behavior[4]) and was the event that provoked the father to bring the girl to Freud.

Freud reports that these facts of the case are readily admitted by the girl. In addition, the girl reports other attachments to somewhat older women (often young mothers) in the girl's early teens (perhaps when she was 13 or 14). During one summer in this period, she also eagerly sought out the company of a film actress, though this attachment was curtailed by her father. Yet with all of these passions, even with this relationship to an older woman now lasting (perhaps) nearly 2 years, she has never had a physical sexual relationship with either a woman or a man. As far as one can tell from the text, not even passionate kissing has occurred (p. 153). She reports that she has rejected what she interpreted as homosexual advances from a young woman of her own age. The reason for this lack of physical sexual expression was that "[s]he was after all a well brought up and modest girl, who had avoided sexual adventures herself, and who regarded coarsely sensual satisfactions as unaesthetic" (p. 161). And, "[w]ith none of the objects of her adoration had the patient enjoyed beyond a few kisses and embraces; her genital chastity . . . had remained intact" (p. 153).

Are we to conclude from this interpreted evidence of what appear to be unconventional emotional attachments to women that the girl is "homosexual"? The evidence of attachments has clearly been selected and ordered first by the girl and then by Freud, and this is some species of interpretation. However, from the evidence, up until Freud terminates the sessions, the girl remains physically chaste. Further, Freud never says that girl labels herself as a homosexual or a lesbian (a word also well-known in Vienna). While she is articulate about the social aspects of sexual relationships, there is no evidence that she has had sex with either a woman or a man, nor that she is well-informed about the physical aspects of sex. Is evidence of such a "passion" by a "modest" girl, even one that includes a suicide attempt, sufficient evidence for inclusion in the category "homosexual"?

Clearly, just the fact that a woman has had or has not had sex with another woman is not enough to make any contemporary observer decide that a woman is a "homosexual" or lesbian. Even the psychoanalytic tradition has left spaces for acts without identity (the situational homosexual) or desires without action (the latent homosexual). Indeed, it is this issue that is at the heart of much of the recent discussion of the distinction between identity and behavior in gay and lesbian politics and studies. Similarly strong emotional attachments, even strong romantic attachments between men or between women, are not sufficient evidence of "homosexuality." From the evidence at hand, the girl only says "that she could not conceive of any other way of being in love" (p. 153).

Was This Girl a Boy?

> The beautiful and well made girl had, it is true, her father's tall figure, and her features were sharp rather than soft and girlish, traits which might be regarded as indicating a physical masculinity. Some of her intellectual attributes could also be connected with masculinity: for instance, her acuteness of comprehension and her lucid objectivity, in so far as she was not dominated by her passion. But these distinctions are conventional rather than scientific. (p. 154)

The girl is not a boy, at least in terms of "physical hermaphroditism," the ghost of nineteenth-century anatomic theories of the intersexes (see also p. 171) (Engelstein, 1989). Freud seems to consign these constitutional views of the origins of homosexuality to the realm of those who are "unversed in psycho-analysis" (p. 154). But biology remains prior to psychoanalysis in a tangled series of arguments that shift from "on the one hand" to "on the other hand":

> It is possible here to attribute to the impress of the operation of exter-
> nal influence in early life something which one would have liked to
> regard as a constitutional peculiarity. On the other hand, a part even of
> this acquired disposition (if it *was* really acquired) has to be ascribed to
> inborn constitution. (p. 169)

And therefore, "it is rather a case of congenital homosexuality which, as usual, became fixed and unmistakenly manifest in the period following puberty" (pp. 169–170). So the ghost of constitutionalism still lives.

But then what about the relation between masculinity and femininity (in mod-ern parlance, *gender identity* and *role*) and the gender of the sexual object-choice?

> A man with predominantly male characteristics and also masculine in
> his erotic life may still be inverted in his erotic life in respect to his
> object. . . . A man in whose character feminine attributes obviously
> predominate . . . may nevertheless be heterosexual. . . . The same is
> true of women; here also mental sexual character and object-choice do
> not necessarily coincide. (p. 170)[5]

This is the contemporary view, except among the biologists of sexual orientation. And yet the girl may be a boy, if only in her romantic style.

> What is certainly of greater importance is that in her behaviour
> toward her love-object she had throughout assumed the masculine
> part . . . the preference for being the lover rather than the beloved.
> She had thus not only chosen a feminine love-object, but had also
> developed a masculine attitude towards that object. (p. 160)

The girl behaves as a boy in love "even to the smallest details" (p. 160). Prior to finding her "*cocotte,*" the girl's desires were focused on women of marginal het-erosexual respectability ("coquettes in the ordinary sense of the word" [p. 161]), now she is bent on "'rescuing' her beloved from these ignoble circumstances" in which "she lived simply by giving her bodily favors" (p. 161). The girl, by playing the role conventionally taken by a young man (as in the question: "What is a nice girl like you doing in a place like this?") in seeking to rescue a fallen woman through the purity of her love, somehow becomes "homosexual."

Or perhaps the girl is a tomboy? She is "a spirited girl, always ready for romping and fighting" (p. 169), she has a "strongly marked 'masculinity complex' . . . She has developed a pronounced envy of the penis" (p. 169). It then follows that "[s]he was in fact a feminist; she felt it unjust that girls should not enjoy the same freedom as boys, and rebelled against the lot of women in general" (p. 169).

The girl's social "boyness" in her affectional styles of dealing with her beloved—that is, her gender role nonconformity—is central to Freud's decision to classify her as "homosexual," but a more critical theme is the girl's unwillingness to share "the lot of women in general "(p. 169), which for Freud is uniquely manifested in childbearing. During the girl's puberty her mother gave birth to a child, and Freud's interpretation is that at puberty, when the girl most strongly wished to have a male child by her father, her mother gave birth to her brother. Therefore, "[a]fter this first great reverse she forswore her womanhood and sought another goal for her libido" (p. 157). "[T]his girl had entirely repudiated her wish for a child, her love for men, and the feminine role in general" (p. 158). "She changed into a man and took her mother in place of her father as the object of her love" (p. 158). The first renunciation is the wish for the child, the second is the love of men, and the third is the feminine. If she is homosexual, she cannot be a woman.

A Journey Not Taken and a Suitor Rejected

Participation in psychoanalysis follows the pattern of all forms of romantic self-exploration during the nineteenth and twentieth centuries. It is a journey, either physical or psychical. But unlike the great solo journeys to other cultures and climes (here consider such examples as Byron to Greece, Gauguin to Tahiti, even Freud to Italy), the psychoanalytic journey into the land of the unconscious requires engaging a tour guide, the analyst. Only Freud has ever gone alone, and upon his return, he (like all great romantic explorers) wishes to make his journey available to others. The training of others in psychoanalysis creates a tour company similar to Thomas Cook's, and Freud's own writings become a Baedeker for the curious.

The role of the journey, particularly the train journey, was central to the development of psychoanalysis. It is on the train that Freud comes across those fertile slips of the tongue that are the empirical evidence for the unconscious. It is his own aborted train journeys to Rome that are central to his own personal history (Schorske, 1961). It is in "Psychogenesis" that Freud uses the metaphor of the train journey to characterize the two parts of the psychoanalytic journey:

> The first [part] comprises all the necessary preparations, today so complicated and hard to effect, before ticket in hand, one can at last go on to the platform and secure a seat on the train. One then has the

right, and the possibility, of traveling to a distant country; but after all these preliminary exertions one is not yet there—indeed, one is not a single mile nearer to one's goal. For this to happen one has to make the journey itself from one station to the other, and this second part of the performance may well be compared to the second phase of the analysis. (p. 152)[6]

The first part of the journey has been that period when the girl has told Freud all of the facts and Freud has shared with her the psychoanalytic explanations relevant to her condition. In Freud's words, "The analysis went forward almost without any signs of resistance, the patient participating actively with her intellect, though absolutely tranquil emotionally" (p. 163). The girl has willingly participated in the "necessary preparations, today so complicated and hard to effect," yet she is unwilling to get on the train and make the journey with this guide: "[E]verything that has been accomplished is subject to a mental reservation of doubt" (p. 163). Freud cannot accept that there has been no transference, yet the transference must have been insufficient. Faith has not repeated the history of its own origins. Freud then conceals his own individual failure by attributing it to a generalized hatred of men.

Freud has been rejected as a tour guide and as a theorist.

> Once when I expounded to her a specially important part of the theory, one touching her nearly, she replied in an inimitable tone, 'How very interesting,' as though she were a *grande dame* being taken over a museum and glancing through her lorgnon at objects to which she was completely indifferent. (p. 163)

The metaphor is rich with ambiguity. On Freud's desk are the antiquities (museum objects) that he has collected, signaling the end products of the archaeological dig, objects to which the girl is indifferent. The *grande dame* looks down from a higher social position on the servant-doctor, perhaps even on the old Jewish man.[7] The intellectual seduction has failed. Unable to persuade the girl to get on the train, Freud protects himself, and psychoanalysis, by terminating the journey.

An Unpredictable Future

Despite this rejection (or perhaps because of it) Freud is sure of his diagnosis; indeed, he tells us many times that he is very sure:

> "to trace its origin and development in the mind with complete certainty" (p. 147)
> "a full confirmation of my constructions" (p. 152)
> "It was established beyond all doubt." (p. 156)

"The analysis revealed beyond all shadow of doubt" (p. 156)
"This position on affairs . . . is not a product of my inventive powers. . . . I can claim objective validity for it." (p. 156)
"I was right." (p. 165)
"but surely in the case under consideration everything is simple
enough" (p. 165)
Except: "The amount of information about her seems meagre enough
nor can I guarantee that it is complete." (p. 155)

Even in the face of an analysis truncated by a contemptuous rejection—the
most important half of the analytic journey, during which new truths are assimilated, remains untaken—Freud has no doubts of his objective powers.

However, it is in his response to this case that Freud denies psychoanalysis a
capacity for prediction—a denial that casts the greatest doubt on psychoanalysis as
positive science. Consider this long quotation:

> So long as we trace the development from its final outcome back-
> wards, the chain of events appears continuous, and we feel that we
> have gained an insight that is completely satisfactory or even exhaus-
> tive. But if we proceed in the reverse way, if we start from the
> premises inferred from the analysis and try to follow these up to the
> final result, then we no longer get the impression of an inevitable
> sequence of events that could not have been otherwise determined.
> We notice at once that there might have been another result and that
> we might have just as well been able to understand and explain the
> latter. The synthesis is thus not so satisfactory as the analysis; in other
> words, from a knowledge of the premises we could not have foretold
> the nature of the result. (p. 167)

What then is psychoanalysis? Perhaps only a reinterpretation of the
analysand's story offering a new set of explanations for the set of facts. As such,
psychoanalysis is part of that archaeology of explanation in which one
hermeneutic interpretation is layered over another. In the first part of the ideal
analytic journey, the analysand tells her story and should place her faith in the
physician's healing powers (both as ideology and persona); in the second half of
the journey, the physician uses this faith to rewrite her interpretations.
However, this ideal analysis cannot predict the future. Even a satisfactory construction has no predictive power. While the girl may be a "homosexual" at 18,
what will she be in 1938 when she is 36? Depending on when in the patient's
life the analysis begins, perhaps another "exhaustive insight" might be produced.
What is important is not the actual life of the analysand, which is lived forward,
but the reconstructions of the analyst, in which the life of the analysand is interpreted backward.

Who Was That Man?

In the last analysis, there is no last analysis. Freud and each of his interpreters, as well as the interpreters of this specific essay (Appignanesi and Forrester, 1992; Merck, 1993; Jacobus, 1995), stand between us and the girl. Was she "actually" a homosexual girl of 18 in 1918 or 1919 in post-World War I Vienna? Does the answer to this question matter? Perhaps the debate about the girl is actually a debate about Freud and his authority to tell her story to us (Fuss, 1993).

The question is not, "Who was that girl?" but "Who was that man?" who stands between us and that girl, perhaps between us and all girls? The girl is pretext for avoiding the confrontation with Freud and Freudiana. This question brings us closer to Bartlett on Wilde. Perhaps a paraphrase of the opening quotation from Bartlett on Wilde may help:

> Freud was a creator of copies, borrowing and reprocessing fragments of his own and other people's lives. He assiduously composed his public life as father, husband, and moralist and he created a career for himself as a physician whose essays are littered with the wrecks of fathers, mothers, and children, who are struggling to prove that they are who and what they say they are. Freud's life was an elaborate drama of deception, lies, and most of all, inspired invention. There was no real Sigmund Freud. Freud was an artist as well. He was entirely uninterested in authenticity.[8]

And so the question might be reformulated one more time. The question is not who was that girl or even who was that man, but who are we and why are we still so interested in this girl and this man?

Notes

Support for the writing of this chapter has come from a Research Leave from the College of Arts and Sciences of the State University of New York at Stony Brook and a grant from the Ford Foundation.

1. Bartlett's subtitle is double—the work is a *gift*, a *present* to Mr. Oscar Wilde, but it is more than that, it offers Mr. Oscar Wilde a place in the *present*, a contemporaneousness that attempts to overwrite (it cannot erase) the layers of interpretation that have papered over his historicity.

2. "Paid for it" refers to Freud's decision to use personal influence to be given his much delayed professorship.

3. Indeed, there are moments of splenetic narcissism, when Freud is angry at the world and humanity (most of whom had never heard of him or his ideas) for not accepting his vision of the world and its purposes (or lack thereof): "I know, indeed, that the craving of mankind for mysticism is ineradicable, and that it makes ceaseless efforts to

win back for mysticism the territory that it has been deprived of by *The Interpretation of Dreams*" and "my astonishment that human beings can go through such great and important moments of their erotic life without noticing them much, sometimes even, indeed without having the faintest suspicion of their existence. . . . This happens not only under neurotic conditions, but also seems common enough in ordinary life" (p. 166). But even if they consciously noted these events they would not have the appropriate psychoanalytic explanations for them.

4. As evidence for this view, "the lady used to recommend [to] the girl every time they met to withdraw her affection from herself and from women in general, and she had persistently rejected the girl's advances up to the time of the attempted suicide" (p. 153). Given the girl's insistence on physical purity, it is difficult to know what these "advances" involved.

5. Here Freud shares with Kinsey the observation that there is no necessary relation between "obviousness" and gender preference in erotic relations. At the same time the "masculine in his erotic life" must refer to being a "top" or insertor rather than a bottom or insertee in sexual relations. Here styles of sexual activity become indicators of "masculinity" and "femininity."

6. It is difficult not to believe that the phrase "today so complicated and hard to effect" does not refer to the actual difficulties of travel in the early postwar period in contrast to the pleasures of Freud's many train journeys of the prewar period.

7. It would be interesting to know if the girl were Jewish or whether her distance from Freud was a combination of her superior economic situation and religious–ethnic difference.

8. Recall that Wilde (born 1854) and Freud (born 1856) were contemporaries and are equally guilty of helping to invent modernity. Freud lived 38 years longer than Wilde.

References

Appignanesi, L. & Forrester, J. (1992). *Freud's women: Family, patients, followers*. New York: Basic Books.

Bartlett, N. (1988). *Who was that man? A present for Mr. Oscar Wilde*. London: Serpent's Tail.

Dabrowski, M. & Leopold, R. (1997). *Egon Schiele: The Leopold collection, Vienna*. Museum exhibition catalogue. New York: The Museum of Modern Art, 1998.

Englestein, L. (1989). *Keys to happiness: Sex and the search for modernity in fin de siècle Russia*. Ithaca, NY: Cornell University Press.

Freud, S. (1953–1974). The psychogenesis of a case of homosexuality in a woman. In J. Strachey (Ed. and Trans.), *The standard edition of the complete psychological works of Sigmund Freud*. (Vol. 18, pp. 145–172). London: Hogarth. (Original work published 1920)

Fuss, D. (1993). Freud's fallen women: Identification, desire, and a case of homosexuality in a woman. *Yale Journal of Criticism, 6*(1), 1–23.

Jacobus, M. (1995). Russian tactics: Freud's "Case of homosexuality in a woman." *GLQ: A Journal of Gay and Lesbian Studies, 2*(1–2), 65–97.

Merck, M. (1993). *Perversions: Deviant readings*. London: Virago.

Schorske, C. (1961). *Fin de siècle Vienna: Politics and culture*. New York: Random House.

Werkner, P. (Ed.). (1994). *Egon Schiele: Art, sexuality, and Viennese modernism*. Palo Alto, CA: The Society for the Promotion of Science and Scholarship.

5

LYING DREAMS

~

Brenda Wineapple

I am not nor mean to be
The Daemon they made of me.
H.D., *Helen in Egypt*

In Dreams Begin Responsibilities

Dreams that lie: They deceive even the most perspicacious of interpreters. If their meaning seems intelligible, at least initially, they nonetheless divert, falsify, distort. And even more than ordinary dreams, themselves opaque, they are not what they appear. For they fulfill more than one intention of the dreamer and, perhaps, of the interpreter as well.

The dreamer, in this instance, is a young woman of 18, beautiful and clever, who dreamed the dreams that misled her analyst. Initially, he was credulous. These dreams, he decided, suggested his patient wanted to assist in her "cure."[1] But a short time later, suspecting mischief, he confronts her: "I told her one day that I did not believe these dreams, that I regarded them as false or hypocritical, and that she intended to deceive me just as she habitually deceived her father," he declares.

How did the young woman respond to the accusation? Did she protest? Weep? Laugh at the absurdity of an irate therapist who may have lost his composure as he imputed intentionality, and duplicity, to his patient's unconscious life? Or perhaps the patient remained aloof, exhibiting the "cool reserve" her therapist had already remarked upon (Freud, 1920, p. 164). Indeed, during much of her analysis, she had evinced a kind of indifference both to him and to his theories. "Tranquil emotionally," or so she was characterized by her analyst, who also recollected that

> when I expounded to her a specially important part of the theory, one touching her nearly, she replied in an inimitable tone, "How very interesting," as though she were a *grande dame* being taken over a museum and glancing through her lorgnon at objects to which she was completely indifferent. (p. 163)

The coolly patronizing young woman reminded her analyst that he served at her pleasure, not the reverse.

Perhaps, then, this young woman listened bemusedly when her therapist accused her of "lying dreams." But whatever her reaction, the analyst was pleased, for according to him, the offending dreams—that is, the dreams that had offended him—immediately ceased. Satisfied, he assumed his new interpretation of them correct and in retrospect also decided that these lying dreams may have been doubly deceptive: "an attempt to gain my interest and my good opinion—perhaps in order to disappoint me all the more thoroughly later on" (p. 165).

Sound like wounded pride? The analyst's response may well have been. Or, conceivably, the whole episode could be dismissed as a forgettable encounter, just another colloquy taking place in some dim room where two human beings happen to be talking. Doubtless, this would have been the situation had the analyst not been Sigmund Freud.

Ironically, however, Freud's response to this case, presented in the essay "The Psychogenesis of a Case of Homosexuality in a Woman," has been largely ignored, as has Freud's intricate, interesting narration of it.

Prologues to What Is Possible

To begin, Freud explains that a girl of 18 was brought to him by her parents. These parents, particularly the father, were distraught over their daughter's infatuation with a woman of poor reputation who was 28, or 10 years older than their daughter. And despite the father's objections and the mother's tolerance, the infatuation had persisted for some time—until, that is, the daughter, while accompanied by the older woman, one day happened to meet her father on the street. Seeing him glance furiously at her and her companion, she quickly ran off and flung herself onto a railway track.

Terrified by the suicide attempt, her parents did nothing further to upset their daughter. Six months passed. Then they knocked at Freud's door.

At the outset of the narrative, Freud is not anxious to treat the case. That the parents of the young woman, and not the girl herself, have sought his help makes treatment unlikely, he says—if not patently absurd. "As is well known," he explains, "the ideal situation for analysis is when someone who is otherwise master of himself is suffering from an inner conflict which he is unable to resolve alone, so that he brings his trouble to the analyst and begs for his help" (p. 150). In this particular case, the young woman suffers no inner conflict; she reports no regret, despondency, or guilt. Moreover, he adds, she is not ill. "Nor did she complain of her condition," he continues, which means "that the task to be carried out did not consist in resolving a neurotic conflict but in converting one variety of the genital organization of sexuality into the other" (p. 150–151). The best he feels he can therefore offer in such cases is a restoration of full "bisexual functions," for "[a]fter that it lay with themselves to choose whether they wished to abandon the other way that is banned by society" (p. 151).

In other words, Freud suggests, homosexuality is not a pathological condition, even though society certainly outlaws it, and society is a powerful adversary, which Freud, of all people, well knows. In fact, in his subtly textured narrative, Freud quickly establishes the social credentials of his new patient, noting that the young woman's parents belong to a "family of good standing" (p. 147); the object of the girl's affection, "in spite of her distinguished name, . . . was nothing but a *cocotte*," he sneers (p. 147). Of course, by invoking such hierarchical social divisions, Freud not only adumbrates the finely wrought class system in Viennese society but also implicitly elevates his own position within it, denigrating the young woman's paramour, not in terms of sexuality (at least not at this juncture) but in terms of social rank.

For like the "*cocotte*," by profession Freud himself lives in a border area—not the world of the *demi-mondaine,* to be sure, but decidely on the outskirts of the respectable bourgeoisie, where he too is an object of condescension. He acknowledges as much with wry humor, reporting that the girl's father was so distressed by his daughter's homosexuality, "he was determined to combat it with all the means in his power; the low estimation in which psychoanalysis is so generally held in Vienna did not prevent him from turning to it for help" (p. 149). Fully aware that the Viennese burgher regards psychoanalysis, and by extension Freud, as minimally more acceptable than homosexuality, Freud shrugs off the typical offense and decides—reluctantly, he insists—to treat the young woman regardless.

Postwar Vienna meant hardship and privation for Freud, who frequently mentions the impossibility of "feeding and keeping oneself" despite at least 9 hours of analytic work per day, or the sum of 5 sessions earning only 500 crowns.[2] No wonder he has taken this case, and no wonder he makes note of the frosty deportment of his analysand, which puts him in his place by reminding him of it. He imagines her a "*grande dame*" genteelly feigning interest in his pet theories.[3] And by way of explaining his reluctance to take on the case, he compares

himself ironically to the architect or artist commissioned by patrons superior to
him in class, if inferior in craft:

> Situations like that of a prospective house-owner who orders an
> architect to build him a villa according to his own tastes and require-
> ments, or of a pious donor who commissions an artist to paint a sacred
> picture in the corner of which is to be a portrait of himself in adora-
> tion, are at bottom incompatible with the conditions necessary for
> psycho-analysis. (p. 150)

Freud protests that the analyst cannot follow such orders; moreover, he argues,
the cure sought by someone on behalf of someone else may yield results little
anticipated, hardly welcome. "It is not a matter of indifference whether someone comes to analysis," Freud summarizes, "of his own accord or because he is
brought to it" (p. 150). Yet, despite—or through—such analogies, Freud recognizes his services are indeed for hire. And that being the case, he implicitly defends
himself against the charge that he will neither complete his work nor satisfy his
patron—which, by the time he wrote this narration, he knows he did not.

What's more, Freud himself is not without social prejudice. He condescends
to the so-called *cocotte,* whom he also patronizes, describing her as an aristocrat
"forced into her present position only by adverse family circumstances," a woman
who nonetheless preserves "in spite of her situation, much nobility of character"
(p. 153). Her nobility consists, not surprisingly, in her rejection of the girl's
advances, at least up until the time of the girl's suicide attempt, and also in her
admonishing the girl to renounce her attraction to women.

Which is another way of saying that the older woman's claim to gentility lies
in her willingness to tow the social line. But the social line is also the sexual line.
Having already admitted that "to undertake to convert a fully developed homosexual into a heterosexual is not much more promising than to do the reverse,
only that for good practical reasons the latter is never attempted," Freud decides
to treat the young woman. He says he "was prepared to study the girl carefully
for a few weeks or months, so as then to be able to pronounce how far a continuation of the analysis would be likely to influence her" (p. 152). But one can
easily speculate that those "good practical reasons," the cruel censure of society,
have influenced Freud in agreeing to this case despite (and perhaps because of)
his misgivings. Is he trying to separate himself, and his profession, from charges
of a social deviance that is also a sexual one, most especially in this situation?

Freud is a man of courage, to be sure, but not necessarily in the arena of
women's sexuality, where he clearly feels uncomfortable. And likely another
motive lurks here; perhaps Freud wants to avert an analytic failure occurring
along the lines of Dora, who had defected almost 20 years earlier. Interestingly,

"The Psychogenesis of a Case of Homosexuality in a Woman" is the only other full-dress case history of a woman, skimpy as it is, that Freud published after the Dora case.

The Theory: Henry's Bicycle

> "Never mention that," Bill said. "That's the sort of thing that can't be spoken of. That's what you ought to work up into a mystery. Like Henry's bicycle."
>
> Ernest Hemingway, *The Sun Also Rises*

Armchair psychoanalysis, especially the kind practiced in the 1920s, demands a fatal flaw or, at the very least, a significant psychic misstep altering the course of what one might otherwise suppose is an unswerving ascent toward fulfillment and pleasure. ("We could find the Achilles heel in everybody's psychic set-up," reminisced Margaret Anderson. "[T]he psychoanalysts were inferior sleuths compared to us. We stuck pins in people."[4]) Nowhere is this Achilles heel more keenly sought than in the area of sexuality: Until recently, Henry James' erotic life was explained, or explained away, by the "obscure hurt" rendering him impotent; so too has Emily Dickinson's famous withdrawal been attributed to a wound to the heart; and at the core of every biography is what Freud himself calls pathography.[5]

Inadvertent papa to these psychological parlor games, Freud also assumes some injury as key to his patient's homosexuality. In "A Case of Homosexuality in a Woman," this injury manifests itself as an intolerable disappointment in the father, whose child the 18-year-old unconsciously wished to have when—and because—her brother was born while she was said to be experiencing "the revival of her infantile Oedipus complex at puberty" (p. 157). Resentful she has lost her father's attention, she turns against him, defying him with her homosexuality. But this turning away is not of course a conscious act. Rather, according to Freud, the young woman's disappointment in her father helps rekindle her earlier preoedipal love for her mother. Thus, the young woman now turns toward her mother with the double aim of punishing her father while overcompensating hostility toward her mother. Since love for her mother also allows this "turn" to occur, attachments to women imply a revived, preoedipal attachment acted out with mother-substitutes.

But if we are to suppose—and it is a supposition—that the young woman is disappointed with her father, why not also assume she is equally disappointed in her mother? And why doesn't she turn away from her instead of him? Why not resent the father, who impregnated the mother? Or, if disappointed in the father, why not overcompensate for her hostility toward him with affection? The reader will ask just a few of the questions Freud's narrative does not entertain. Why does the girl have little "cause" for affection for her mother, as Freud insists? Does Freud's reading of the mother as crotchety and competitive come from the girl's estimation—or his own? Freud clearly prefers the father, whom he describes as an "earnest, worthy man, at bottom very tender-hearted" (p. 149). The mother, on the other hand, a woman "evidently unwilling to give up her own claims to attractiveness" is "neurotic" and "decidedly harsh toward her daughter,"(p. 149) even though Freud also concedes "it was not easy to ascertain anything more definite about her" (p. 149).

Doubtless alert to the leaps of logic presented in his case, Freud further contends that his analysand's development was determined by still other factors: For example, she evinces a strong "masculinity complex," with its requisite penis envy, demonstrated by her politics. "She was, in fact a feminist," Freud declares; "she felt it to be unjust that girls should not enjoy the same freedom of boys, and rebelled against the lot of woman in general" (p. 169). Freud knows that this young woman also rebels against him and his authority, although he will not—cannot, given his theory—consider that her dismissal of him results as much from political, cultural, and economic sources as from psychological sources. Notwithstanding, this young woman, whom Freud sees very little, must lie on the procrustean couch he's made for the female homosexual.

And therefore he can easily assume the analysand projects her resentment of her own father onto him. But if Freud truly believes as much, his response to this so-called transference is all the more peculiar. Why get so angry? Why retaliate? Why accuse her of those lying dreams?[6]

No-Name Woman

Dreams that lie are also dreams that tell the truth, for the truth itself is a kind of lie and a kind of dream. Freud's narrative is no exception; in the working out of several themes and a conjectural sexual theory, it reveals the artful evasions at the root of all narrative.[7] And it suggests Freud's reading of the female homosexual is less conclusive than it may first appear.

Freud seems cognizant of his reservations, reminding his reader at the outset of his essay that he can recount this single case "almost without a gap" (p. 147); yet he also says, in the very next sentence, that he will suppress "all the characteristic details" on which the forthcoming interpretation of this case will be based (out of a respect, he gallantly adds, for discretion). Indeed, he does not even give the young 18-year-old a name. A few pages later, he acknowledges frustration with his own narrative, explaining as if in apology that "linear presentation is not a very adequate means of describing mental processes" (p. 160)—his own, one assumes, as well as his subject's. By this time, of course, we know that the case itself contains a breach: Freud prematurely terminates the young woman's treatment. Thus, information about the young woman is per force meager in a case history purporting to recount "the origin and development" of homosexuality in women "with complete certainty" (p. 147).

Enter, then, lying dreams. They provide Freud with the excuse he needs, finds, or manufactures to break off treatment. The dreams the young girl brings to the analysis, says Freud, "could nevertheless be easily translated with certainty" (p. 165)—that is, until he began to doubt them, or her, or himself. "The Psychogenesis of a Case of Homosexuality in a Woman" is a study in doubt. Of what else, if not doubt, does Freud speak in his long introduction? Replete with disclaimers, pauses, reflections, contradictions, and detours, the narration of the case history is itself a lying dream in which the dreamer is as confounded as the interpreter.

For Freud, the young woman's dreams initially indicate to him her desire to participate in her analysis; soon afterward, they suggest to him that her analyst has become her father: "[S]he transferred to me the sweeping repudiation of men which had dominated her ever since the disappointment she had suffered from her father" (p. 164). As generic father, himself now without a name, the analyst ends the analysis.

But why does Freud bluntly end an analysis tentatively begun in the first place? Because of this negative transference? And, further, why does he then insist that despite his fragmentary knowledge about the girl, he can trace the psychogenesis of her homosexuality? In so doing, of course, he ironically composes a case that discusses female homosexuality by means of the same sort of hesitations and lapses that he attributes to erotic life: "It would seem that the information received by our consciousness about our erotic life is especially liable to be incomplete, full of gaps, or falsified" (p. 167).

This, of course, makes us consider yet again Freud's relation to the young woman under question. She is tall, "well-made," beautiful. Calling her clever, he notes that her comprehension is acute, her "objectivity" lucid—intellectual traits, he adds, conventionally but not scientifically associated with masculinity. He also likens her presumed superiority and detachment, as we have noted, to that of a *grande dame* at a museum. Evidently, however, the museum is Freud himself, who keeps on his desk and in his study a collection of ancient artifacts. And his fantasy of her indifferent inspection of them reveals, almost too patently, his own sense of rejection.

But in Freud's consulting room at 19 Bergasse, it is he who repudiates her. According to Freud, the girl's transference of negative feelings for her father onto Freud creates an impasse beyond which he cannot go. Why not? Even the loyal Lou Andreas-Salomé tactfully criticizes Freud: "Behind the negative transference to you there lay hidden no doubt the original positive transference to the father," she tells him. "Would not this original basis have come to light eventually through the *acting out* of the negative transference?"[8]

If we accept Freud's reading of this transference relation, Andreas-Salomé's is a good question. And even if we do not accept Freud's interpretation, we must still ask, with Andreas-Salomé, not only why he breaks off treatment, but why he then proposes that the young girl engage a woman analyst.

In fact, with this recommendation, it would appear that Freud, liberal geniality notwithstanding, takes cover in the same biological categories he is also willing, at other times, to contest. But his refusal to analyze his patient and his recommendation that she consult a woman analyst may illustrate Freud's incipient recognition that, as in the case of his inability to interpret or respect Dora's sexuality, he knows he will fail.

Toril Moi's shrewd interpretation of Freud's inadequacy with Dora is useful in this context:

> If Freud cannot solve Dora's riddle, the unconscious punishment for this failure will be castration. In this struggle for the possession of knowledge, a knowledge that is power, Dora reveals herself both as Freud's alter ego and as his rival. She possesses the secret Freud is trying to discover. At this point we must suspect Freud of countertransference to Dora: he identifies with the hysterical Dora in the search for information about sexual matters.[9]

Freud may also identify with his nameless young woman of 18, who keeps her own counsel and humors and manipulates him while seeking, like Freud himself, knowledge about sexual matters. Surely, he is beginning, in this case, to reinvestigate the matters of female sexuality that will preoccupy him for at least the next 10 years.[10] Yet, in the meantime, Freud writes of this case, "fathering" it—that is to say, trumping his own identification with the girl by becoming her father and duplicating his anger at her intractability.[11] In addition, he then dictates the course of the treatment by ending it. By hypothesizing that the girl has wished to have her father's child, Freud's identification with both the girl and her father allows him to "father" her child, which is ultimately *his* child—his case history.

In the fourth and final section of his essay, Freud launches into discussion of what caused the girl to pass from "the normal Oedipus attitude into that of homosexuality" (p. 167). As before, however, Freud hesitates. He warns his reader that "even supposing that we have a complete knowledge of the aetiological factors that decide a given result, nevertheless what we know about them is only their quality, and not their relative strength" (p. 168). Regardless, he then reintroduces the Oedipal model of (male) sexuality, suggesting by implication that he can use no other language for the female.[12]

But such language also suggests that for Freud female homosexuality still remains illegible, elusive, unknown and—hence—lying. Therefore, it cannot be represented. "Twenty years after his failure to synthesize the themes of transference and female homosexuality (bisexuality)," writes Suzanne Gearhart, "Freud once again presents himself as incapable of integrating the current of female homosexuality into the dynamic transference that would transcend its strictly negative phase."[13]

Broken treatment is itself a kind of gap—and a tacit confession of failure: You see me as your father, so I no longer want to see you; get thee to a woman analyst.

Fathers Are Depressing

> Mothers may not be cheering but they are not as depressing as fathers.
> Gertrude Stein, *Everybody's Autobiography*

In explaining his abrupt termination of the girl's analysis, Freud likens the circumstances to those he's encountered in cases of obsessional neurotics, where the neurotic engages in what he calls "Russian tactics":

> For a time, consequently, these cases yield the clearest results and permit a deep insight into the causation of the symptoms. But presently one begins to wonder how it is that such marked progress in analytic understanding can be unaccompanied by even the slightest change in the patient's compulsions and inhibitions, until at last one perceives that everything that has been accomplished is subject to a mental reservation of doubt. (p. 164)

Freud, however, represents doubt inadvertently in those lying dreams—the stuff out of which narrative is made.

From this point of view, we can say the analyst is himself enmeshed in a world of uncertainty and apprehension, the world identified by the hip literary critic as a world of interpretative possibility. But as a fine essayist, a propagandist for the sexually radical, and a good Victorian patriarch, Freud cannot leave his reader floating on a sea of doubt any more than he can fully condone the polymorphous implications of his own theory. So, in a clever rhetorical ploy, he anticpates his readers' skepticism: "'What!' they will exclaim, 'the unconscious . . . too can lie! Then how can we still build on the interpretations of analysis and the accuracy of our findings?'" (p. 165). He answers:

> A dream is not the "unconscious"; it is the form into which a thought left over from preconscious, or even from conscious, waking life, can,

> thanks to the favouring state of sleep, be recast. In the state of sleep
> this thought has been reinforced by unconscious wishful impulses and
> has thus experienced distortion through the dreamwork, which is
> determined by the mechanisms prevailing in the unconscious. (p.
> 166)

By Freud's own logic, then, language can be understood to be form in which a
thought from preconscious or conscious wakefulness can be recast, even though
it is impelled by unconscious wishful impulses and distorted through language
itself. Language is a form of lying dream, slippery and fanciful and problematic:

> There is something in the material itself which takes charge of one
> and diverts one from one's first intentions. Even such a trivial
> achievement as the arrangement of a familiar piece of material is not
> entirely subject to an author's own choice; it takes what line it likes
> and all one can do is ask oneself why it has happened in this way and
> no other.[14]

Freud, no less than the young woman of 18 whom he attempts to analyze, is
the subject of his narrative. For Freud is the storyteller supreme, modulating tales
told him by others with those he tells of himself and his own dream life. And
Freud the storyteller endeavors to weave the strands of social mores, sexual ideology, conjecture, insight, presumption, and wish into a coherent theory—a task
that he tacitly concedes is impossible.[15] He thus concludes the portion of his essay
devoted to lying dreams, which he calls a digression, with another detour, as if
to discover by analogy and metaphor what he wants to say.

In this detour, Freud speaks of love and its bewilderments, meditating on the
ways we happily deceive ourselves. "It must be admitted," he writes, "that poets
are right in liking to portray people who are in love without knowing it, or
uncertain whether they do love, or who think that they hate when in reality
they love" (p. 167). Indeed. Perhaps Freud, in accusing the patient of lying
dreams, discloses the depths of his own disappointment—with the girl to conform to his theory, with the girl herself, with himself. And perhaps his aside is
an admission that he, too, is unaware of the feelings that motivates his taking,
and breaking with, this patient.

But then, as if to retract his admission while still asking for the reader's for-
bearance, he concludes this section of his essay with a convoluted, perplexing,
and self-contradictory assertion, as if he now must straighten his tie and
rearrange his desk. "Needless to say, in this discussion I have not omitted to
allow for the part played by subsequent failures of memory" (p. 167). Oddly
bumbling, the master of language asserts mastery over his case.

Mothers

Over time, Freud's teleological theory of female development, with its biological emphasis on castration, sublimated penis envy, and the desire to have children, has been reviewed, revised, and criticized by analysts, writers, literary critics, biographers, and psychologists; presently, these critics are now reevaluating Freudian readings of heterosexuality, homosexuality, and female desire. Still quiet, however, are most of Freud's female patients, who speak to us only through the master.

The poet H.D. (Hilda Doolittle) is a notable exception. In 1933, she went to Vienna to be analyzed by Freud, whom she saw 5 days a week for about 4 months; after a pause in treatment, she returned to analysis in October 1934. A writer suffering from a creative block, she had consulted analysts before, but it is this "midwife to the soul" whom she would honor in her evocative memoir, *Tribute to Freud*.[16]

At the time of her analysis, however, Freud did not want H.D. to write in her journal about their sessions, which he considered a form of homework inhibiting to free association. Notwithstanding, H.D. did keep notes that, although lost, are the source for another recollection, "Advent." In it and *Tribute*, Freud speaks through H.D. and reveals his reservations, provocatively telling her, for example, "about the growth of psychoanalysis and how mistakes were made in the beginning, as it was not sufficiently understood that the girl did not invariably transfer her emotions to her father."[17] It is, of course, tantalizing but ultimately fruitless to speculate on Freud's meaning here, for H.D.'s memoir is full of its own evasions, especially with regard to H.D.'s bisexuality and her lesbian relationship with Bryher (Winifred Ellerman). But we do learn that H.D. saw Freud as both father and mother at various times.

Freud, however, admits to H.D. that

> "I do *not* like to be the mother in transference—it always surprises and shocks me a little. I feel so very masculine." I asked him if others had what he called this mother-transference on him. He said ironically and I thought a little wistfully, "O, *very* many."[18]

Could it be, then, that Freud's 1920 analysand, the young woman of 18, did not see him as a father but as something else, someone else, someone who made Freud uncomfortable? And, with that in mind, we can again ask why he assumed that the so-called lying dreams were designed to fool and belittle him, as father? Couldn't they have been directed elsewhere—at a tolerant mother figure, perhaps, whom she was trying to please? Sensing this, would Freud then be motivated to take up the father's role all the more insolently?

Perhaps the lying dreams were the reason as well as the excuse Freud needed to remove himself from a transference he little understood or welcomed.[19] Whatever the possibilities, the lying dreams do in fact represent more than one intention of the dreamer, but they also represent more than one intention of the interpreter as well. And that is why, overall, the loosely threaded case is itself Freud's lying dream.

Tentative Conclusions

A biographer reading Freud's "Psychogenesis of a Case of Homosexuality in a Woman" cannot tarry with the case itself. It's too vague, elliptical, contradictory. And like any testimony proffered by a biographical subject, it is suspect; for although its theory can be tested, refuted, argued—and will be—the theory is inseparable from the man who produces it.

To place the case within the life, we need to understand more fully why Freud took it: whether, for instance, finances played an even more important role than we already suspected. We need to know how much he was paid and whether the crowns he receive in wages themselves helped foster a sense of incompletion, or regret, motivating him to write his case history: or how other factors leavened his decision. Surely, he intended the case as part of his ongoing project for psychoanalytic theory. "Homosexuality in women, which is certainly not less common than in men . . . has also been neglected by psychoanalytic research" (p. 147), he stentoriously begins his paper. Surely, his obstreperousness grew from his wish to lay claim to an area, that of female sexuality, in which he was just beginning to test his hypotheses publically. For psychoanalytic research, Freud well knew, meant more than practitioners engaged in analysis; it involved their writing, legitimizing, defending and promoting their views, as well as competing with one another. Since Karl Abraham was working on a paper on the castration complex in women when Freud was writing "Psychogenesis," neither Abraham nor his paper could be incidental to Freud's own. Nor was his daughter Anna, whom Freud might have been preparing to analyze just at this time.[20]

If the circumstances—and there are many more—surrounding this case provide its necessary setting, the case affords its own special kind of insight into Freud and so-called "Freudianism," or that fetishizing of the man and his theory. Gertrude Stein once remarked that psychoanalysis—Freud—was something one had to get in, and out, of one's system.[21] Perhaps we can begin by recognizing that a case history is inevitably a lying dream, fulfilling more than one intention of, in this case, a very astute, wily dreamer—a man as blind and as clairvoyant as dreamers invariably are.

Notes

1. Sigmund Freud, "The Psychogenesis of a Case of Homosexuality in a Woman" (1953–1974). In J. Strachey (Ed. and Trans.), *The Standard Edition of the Complete Psychological Works of Sigmund Freud* (Vol. 18, p. 165). (London: Hogarth; original work published 1920); hereafter citations to this case will appear parenthetically in the text and to the *Standard Edition* as *SE*.

2. Hilda C. Abraham and Ernst L. Freud, editors. *A Psychoanalytic Dialogue: The Letters of Sigmund Freud and Karl Abraham* (New York: Basic Books, 1965), p. 291.

On the economic relation between patient and analyst in Freud's "Fragment of an Analysis of a Case of Hysteria," see Diana Fuss (1993), "Freud's Fallen Women: Identification, Desire and 'A Case of Homosexuality in a Woman,'" *The Yale Journal of Criticism,* 6(1), 17–18; Jane Gallup (1982), *The Daughter's Seduction: Feminism and Psychoanalysis* (Ithaca, NY: Cornell University Press, 1982), pp. 132–150; and Janet Malcolm, "Reflections: J'appelle un chat un chat," in Charles Bernheimer and Claire Kahane (Ed.), *In Dora's Case: Freud—Hysteria—Feminism* (New York: Columbia University Press, 1990), pp. 310–314.

3. See also Marjorie Garber's (1993) astute comment on Freud's fantasy in *Vested Interests* (New York: Routledge, 1993), p. 154: "A lorgnon is not a monocle, but a pair of spectacles on a stick, the 'feminized' version of the peering instrument. It is perhaps significant that Freud imagines her *not* as cross-dressed but as coldly ladylike, *not* as masculine but as feminine. But—or and—we should note that the monocle—and, indeed, the lorgnon—is a preeminently detachable part."

4. Margaret Anderson, *My Thirty Years' War* (New York: Horizon Press, 1969), p. 186.

5. Freud uses this term in "Leonardo da Vinci and a Memory of His Childhood" (1910) *SE,* vol. 11, p. 130: "It would be futile to blind ourselves to the fact that readers today find all pathography unpalatable." Joyce Carol Oates, a reader who does find "pathography" unpalatable, has been wrongly attributed with coining the term. Her definition of pathography as "hagiography's diminished and often prurient twin" is condemning. Freud obviously is not. See Joyce Carol Oates, "Adventures in Abandonment," *The New York Times Book Review* (August 28, 1988), p. 3.

6. See Nina Auerbach, "Magi and Maidens: The Romance of the Victorian Freud," in Elizabeth Abel (Ed.), *Writing and Sexual Differences* (Chicago: University of Chicago Press, 1982), p. 123: "Freud's skepticism toward virtually all the assertions of his female patients . . . [leads to] his characteristic professional stance" which "is to translate their helpless deceit into his own impregnable truth."

7. For a good overview of Freud's sexual theory, as presented in this case, and a well-argued, informed analysis of the contradictions therein, see Mandy Merck, "The Train of Thought in Freud's 'Case of Homosexuality in a Woman,'" *m/f* 11:12 (1986): 35–46 and, more recently, Teresa de Lauretis, *The Practice of Love: Lesbian Sexuality and Perverse Desire* (Bloomington: Indiana University Press, 1994), pp. 29–54.

8. Ernst Pfeiffer, ed. *Sigmund Freud and Lou Andreas-Salomé: Letters* (New York: Harcourt Brace Jovanovich, Inc., 1996), p. 102.

9. Toril Moi, "Representation of Patriarchy: Sexuality and Epistemology in Freud's Dora," in Charles Bernheimer and Claire Kahane, ed., *In Dora's Case: Freud—Hysteria—Feminism,* p. 195.

10. See Lisa Appignanesi and John Forrester, *Freud's Women* (New York: Basic Books, 1992), pp. 184–185.

11. See Lisa Appignanesi and John Forrester, *Freud's Women,* p. 187.

12. See Elizabeth Grosz "Experimental Desire: Rethinking Queer Subjectivity," in Jean Copjes, (Ed.) *Supposing the Subject* (London: Verse 1994), p. 149: "Clearly, lesbianism remains the site of the greatest and most threatening challenge to the phallocentricism that subsumes the female under the generic produced by the male in so far as it evidences the existence of a female sexuality and sexual pleasure outside male pleasure and control." Also, Noreen O'Connor and Joanna Ryan *Wild Desires & Mistaken Identities* (New York: Columbia University Press, 1993), p. 31, ascribe Freud's not giving his patient a name to a "widespread difficulty psychoanalysts have had in approaching this subject."

See also Judith Butler, *Gender Trouble. Feminism and the Subversion of Identity* (New York: Routledge, 1990), especially chapters 1 and 2, on the relation between identity politics, gender, theory, and representation.

13. Suzanne Gearhart, "The Scene of Psychoanalysis: The Unanswered Questions of Dora," in Charles Bernheimer and Claire Kahane, (Ed.), *In Dora's Case: Freud—Hysteria—Feminism,* p. 118.

14. Quoted in *Literature and Psychoanalysis: The Question of Reading: Otherwise,* ed. Shoshana Felman (Baltimore: Johns Hopkins University Press, 1982), pp. 307–308.

Or, moving in the opposite direction to a similar point, Lacan advises "to remind yourself that the dream has the structure of a sentence, or, rather, to stick to the letter of the work, of a rebus; that is to say, it has the structure of a form of writing . . . which, in the adult, reproduces the simultaneously phonetic and symbolic use of signifying elements, which can also be found both in the hieroglyphs of ancient Egypt and in the characters still used in China," Jacques Lacan, *The Language of the Self,* trans. Anthony Wilden (Baltimore: Johns Hopkins University Press, 1968), p. 30.

15. See Teresa de Lauretis, *The Practice of Love: Lesbian Sexuality and Perverse Desire* (Bloomington: Indiana University Press, 1994), p. 44.

16. H.D. (Hilda Doolittle), *Tribute to Freud* (Boston: David R. Godine, 1974) p. 116. This volume contains "Writing on the Wall" and "Advent." Elegant and provocative analyses of H.D.'s analysis and writing can be found in Susan Stanford Friedman's *Psyche Reborn* (Bloomington: Indiana University Press, 1981) and *Penelope's Web: Gender, Modernity, H.D.'s Fiction* (Cambridge: Cambridge University Press, 1990).

17. H.D. (Hilda Doolittle), *Tribute to Freud,* p. 175.

18. Ibid, p. 146.

19. Diana Fuss "Freud's Fallen Women: Identification, Desire and 'A Case of Homosexuality in a Woman,'" p. 18, speculates that Freud's masculine identification "makes a deeper, more disturbing feminine identification with the mother who 'enjoyed her daughter's confidence concerning her passion.'"

20. Neither Ernest Jones, in his three volumes on Freud's life, nor Freud's more recent biographer, Peter Gay, discuss these relations, but Elizabeth Young-Breuhl, in her biography of Anna Freud, raised such questions. See Elizabeth Young-Breuhl, *Anna Freud* (New York: Summit Books, 1998), pp. 91–104.

21. Edward. M. Burns and Ulla E. Dydo, *The Letters of Gertrude Stein and Thornton Wilder* (New Haven: Yale University Press, 1996), p. 58.

6

THE FAILURE OF LIBERALISM

David Woolwine

Inevitably, therefore, Freud opened the way to a series of emphases which saw homosexuality in men and women as a failure to achieve normality. . . . Freud's accounts of the genesis of homosexuality read today as unfortunately opprobrious and moralistic. But if psychoanalysis is to have any contemporary significance the real lesson that needs to be learnt is that both heterosexuality and homosexuality are peculiar compromises, partial organisations of the flux of sexual desires which are shaped, in complex ways by the cultural organisation of sexual difference, and the centrality assigned to heterosexuality.

Freud was a liberal of his time in his attitude toward homosexuality. He favored law reform, and his attitude toward his young lesbian patient was cautiously sympathetic. He affirmed that "the girl was not in any way ill," and he accepted her passionate statement that "she could not conceive of any other way of being in love." But inevitably, there are certain normalising assumptions in his attitudes.

The difficulty with Freud (especially for someone who wants to use his *critical insights* [emphasis added]) was that in the end he did believe that a heterosexual genital organisation of sexuality was a *cultural* [emphasis added] necessity, so that although he could readily concede that all of us have "seeds" of perversion, a healthy development demanded their subordination to the norm.[1]

Jeffrey Weeks is known as a strong "constructionist" in the study of human sexuality, meaning that he emphasizes the nonuniversal nature of sexual categories and desires. He emphasizes the ways in which our sexual and gender categories, manners of conceptualizing sexual identity (and the very notions of a sexual "identity" or of "sexuality"), as well as the ways in which individuals in various cultures understand, label, and experience their "desires," are all "socially constructed," that is, contingent on particular historical and social factors that have created habits of mind and emotions. The history of the study of sexuality, especially the so-called "scientific" study of human sexuality in the West is, for Weeks, not a history of the progression of knowledge but rather a history of reconceptualizations, usually with a social or political or ideological end in mind. Constructionism for Weeks, as a "queer theorist," is especially useful, since much of the history of the understanding of sex and sexuality in the West can be read as an attempt to "expertly" establish same-sex desires and behavior as deviant and in need of regulation and control by those who claim heterosexual privilege. Constructionism not only allows us to critique this history and to see how claims to knowledge are in fact power moves, but, since so much of (or all of) sex and sexuality are "constructed," it also allows us to point to the fact that same-sex desires and behaviors have been constructed differently in different cultures. Finally it allows us, ideologically and with a power interest of our own (which is permitted since there is no place free from such interests), to point to the possibility that our own culture might be able to move to a new and more tolerant position on same-sex desires and behaviors, precisely by seeing such desires and behaviors as some among other equally socially constructed ones.

Social constructionism in queer theory moves easily from description (largely a correct one in my view, at least of the history and sociology of sexology) to prescription. (The prescriptions are ones with which I largely agree.) Biology, however, takes on a peculiar and centrally problematic role in such constructionist accounts, for biology may come to represent that which is "universal" and, therefore, not constructed. Now the advocates of the biological in the study of human sexuality have, historically, often deployed it in that universalizing way and have also adopted the position of biological determinism. It is my own view that the role of the biological in sex and sexuality, as it is further explicated, is highly unlikely to support a deterministic position; in other words, I believe that there will always be a role for the cultural and historical in our understanding of sex and sexuality. But it is also my view that the biological remains problematic for constructionists, especially queer theorists, in that they do not acknowledge sufficiently that the body, as a material entity, is somewhat (and possibly in important ways) outside of discourse and offers a restriction on what might be said. In other words, the body is resistant to speech at some level and to some degree. Determinism by discourse is also to be avoided. Biology is a problem for Freud as well as for queer theorists such as Weeks. It is here that the connections for this essay may be made. Weeks chooses to appropriate Freud to his own constructionist project by interpreting Freud as "critical" and as a "liberal." Weeks does this by ignoring the role of the biological in Freud's texts. We often avoid confronting what is most problematic for us, as Freud himself would no doubt like to tell us. This essay takes up that particular question.

So the question with which this essay will be concerned is whether the "liberal" and "critical" Freud, encapsulated in Weeks quotations at the beginning of this essay, is the dominant Freud found within the text under consideration. The advantage of a close reading, and of one of the few Freud texts on the subject of homosexuality, is that one can subject such orthodoxy to a critical test. The orthodoxy here is that of the "left" school of Freudian interpreters, representatives of which can be easily identified by their ongoing desire to preserve something of the master and his doctrine, although—or perhaps because—he has been already so thoroughly deconstructed. They believe that Freud must still be rescued and his critical insights taken to the heart of a gay constructionist understanding of sex and sexuality or of a feminist or postmodernist psychology.

I will assume, and Weeks' quotations bear this out, that the most important critical insights of Freud for gay or queer constructionist theorists are the doctrines of polymorphous perversity and the "essential bisexuality" of all humans. It is only because of the original polymorphous perversity out of which springs the universal bisexual stage of all humans that one can speak of a "compromise" that both heterosexuals and homosexuals must make. These two closely related doctrines allow one to believe in the possibility of an original plasticity of desire and "orientation" in all humans, and they point to the need, or perhaps unfortunate role, of cultural or social organizing (i.e., "repression"—we seem to be unable to escape the repressive hypothesis), which produces, specifically, "heterosexuality." We will return to these doctrines later in this essay, but let us take a diversion into and through the text at hand.

Let me say up front that the Freud of this text is, for me, the Freud of power, the man who is always willing to subordinate any "liberal" inclinations he might have to a desire for professional power and who, to do so, must in the last analysis be the handmaiden of the "normal," (i.e., of the heterosexual regime). He is the failed liberal whose failure is implicit and present from the beginning in his "liberal" agenda. The only thing that makes this particular text pleasurable to read is that ultimately, Freud is shown, despite his own attempt to have it otherwise, to be unsuccessful in his assertion of power (via his claims to knowledge and professional standing) over an unruly object (lesbianism) and an unruly subject (a young woman).

Despite Weeks' assertions, Freud does not mention—in this text at any rate—the role of culture in forming sexuality. It is hard to consider the family constellation and the "Oedipal" interaction as culture, and Freud does not here treat it as such. For Freud believes the Oedipus complex to be universal (with, if any, only minor cultural modifications). Freud only mentions cultural and social influences explicitly when he writes about why homosexuals would seek to cure themselves of the disorder. In the section referred to by Weeks, Freud states, rather unsympathetically, of the girl:

> Further unfavorable features in the present case were the facts that the girl was not in any way ill—she did not suffer from anything in herself, nor did she complain of her condition—and that the task to be carried out did not consist in resolving a neurotic conflict but in converting one variety of the genital organization of sexuality into the other. The removal of the genital inversion of homosexuality is in my experience never an easy matter. On the contrary, I have found success possible only under specially favorable circumstances, and even then the success essentially consisted in being able to open to those who are restricted homosexually the way to the opposite sex, which had been till then barred, thus restoring to them full bisexual functions. After that it lay with themselves to choose whether they wished to abandon the other way that is banned by society, and in individual cases they have done so. One must remember that normal sexuality also depends upon a restriction in the choice of object; in general, to undertake to convert a fully developed homosexual into a heterosexual is not much more promising than to do the reverse, only for good practical reasons the latter is never attempted.

And:

> If he [the homosexual] comes to be treated at all, it is mostly through the pressure of external motives, such as the social disadvantages and dangers attaching to his choice of object, and such components of the instinct of self-preservation prove themselves too weak in the struggle against the sexual impulses. . . . It is only where the homosexual fixation has not yet become strong enough, or where there are considerable rudiments and vestiges of a heterosexual choice of object, i.e., in a still oscillating or in a definitely bisexual organization, that one can make a more favorable prognosis for psychoanalytic therapy.

But we see here no talk of cultural or societal "causes" of homosexuality—only a discussion of why one would seek a "cure" and how a cure or conversion (for homosexuality and, in theory, heterosexuality) might be assisted. The doctrine of the "essential" or perhaps "partial" bisexuality of all, including the "normal" heterosexual, is present, but it is not used by Freud to argue that it is only, or primarily, cultural forces that change such bisexuality, even in the case of the heterosexual, into one object-choice. No, Freud will not locate the construction of sexuality in the larger social or cultural realm. Rather, he will do what we have always known him to do: produce his real insights.[2] Freud's "insights" are primarily the creation of a system of signs, a linguistic realm that prior to Freud had not really existed, namely, the "psychoanalytic," a place for the interplay of internal "drives" and external influences, but with the special condition that the external is almost entirely the sexual drama of the family—a familial drama that, as was pointed out earlier, is in no meaningful way located by Freud within a larger social or cultural context. Freud does not need to place the family drama in a larger context, for he connects the psychoanalytic with the biological. This connection happens first in the theory of drives, which is always present throughout and which here supports the discussion of the Oedipus complex. The connection of the psychoanalytic to the biological (a near reductionism here) is also less subtly present in Freud's discussion of the nonsocial and noncultural basis of gender. Finally, least subtly of all, it is present in the final horrifying paragraph of the case study, when Freud dismisses the use of surgery to correct homosexuality in a woman on mere practical grounds.

What is the "cause," or "causes," of homosexuality laid out in this particular text? There are several causes presented—homosexuality is nothing if not overdetermined. At the end of the study, Freud returns to the issue of the biological, but the core explanation, or rather the one he is most interested in, is the psychoanalytic, and it can be briefly summarized here. During puberty, the young woman experiences the revival of the infantile Oedipus complex and desires to have a male child by her father but must confront the fact that her young mother has the male child instead. The young woman becomes homosexual out of "furious" resentment and embitterment; turning away from her father and all men, she "changes" into a man, taking her mother (described earlier as a "hated rival") instead of her father as her love-object, and retires from the field of battle in favor of the mother. Ultimately the young woman realizes how she could "wound her father and take revenge on him" and, therefore, remains homosexual "out of defiance against" him. It should be obvious to all that by this masterful story Freud has produced an interpretation of lesbianism that displaces the female from the center and places there, instead, the male—both the father and the male child. If one were a Freudian, one might read this as a cultural and personal projection of the male psychoanalyst's greatest fears—the displacement of the father and his authority and the discontinuation of his progeny (psychoanalysis) by the unruly and unrepentant female, who by refusing treatment refuses to assist in the perpetuation of the Freudian line. Freud's own restrained, but real, fury breaks through when he writes (in what is my favorite passage of the text because despite himself, Freud reveals so much of the young girl's personality), "Once when I expounded to her a specially important part of the theory, one touching her nearly, she replied in an inim-

itable tone, 'How very interesting', as though she were a *grande dame* being
taken over a museum and glancing through her lorgnon at objects to which she
were completely indifferent." One also senses here Freud's insecurities, which
must make the languid refusal of treatment all the more galling since this refusal
does not allow for the complete exercise of power over the young woman. This
woman does not submit in any sense. She is willful, she produces "lying
dreams," she will not believe sufficiently to be cured, she is haughty, she cannot be overpowered. One is left with no other course but to create another
world, the world of this particular text, a case study in which she can be at least
partially controlled by being dissected and analyzed.

The part played by the psychodynamic, familial, or Oedipal element in creating
this case of homosexuality in a woman has here been laid out. Ultimately, it is
revenge against the father for not supplying a male child. What of the biological?
At this level Freud may be treated with more sympathy. He refuses, unlike some
today, to accept the binaries of biology and culture. But is his formulation a "liberal" and "critical" one and one that can be of use to a constructionist argument
concerning sexuality? Let us see. Freud begins by acknowledging the obvious, that
not every young girl who experiences the birth of a brother at the particular point
when she is also undergoing the revival of the Oedipus complex becomes a lesbian: "On the contrary, other kinds of reaction are probably commoner." This
young woman had indicated what we would today call predispositions toward
homosexuality (perhaps not entirely biological, however, since biological predispositions cannot, of course, be a major "cause"—if they were, there would be no
need for psychoanalysis). Episodes pointed out by Freud earlier in the text—
episodes which otherwise might not fit into his account of the role of the revived
Oedipus crisis—are now neatly incorporated as evidence of other psychodynamic
factors: schoolgirl crushes, interest in "young mothers" (convenient evidence of
both pre-lesbianism and a desire to be a mother and to have the male child—
namely, of normal female heterosexuality). It appears that the young woman's
libido has been twofold from the beginning—homosexual on the surface and heterosexual at depth. The "deeper heterosexual libido-stream was deflected into the
manifest homosexual one" at the time of the crisis. So she is not a homosexual on
the deeper level. Yet she has also suffered from a "masculinity complex in her childhood"; she was "spirited . . . always ready to fight . . . not at all prepared to be
second to her slightly older brother"; she suffered from penis envy (here an indi-
cation of "masculinity," in other works a necessary stage for the female in her rejection of her attraction to the inferior mother and her substitution of an appropriate
male libido-object, namely the father). She was "in fact a feminist; she felt it to be
unjust that girls should not enjoy the same freedom as boys, she rebelled against the
lot of women in general . . . the idea of pregnancy and child-birth was disagree-

able to her." But, Freud states, these characteristics are not biologically grounded and, in fact, are what would be expected of a girl with a strong mother-fixation combined with an indifferent mother and penis envy and so are, as noted earlier, psychodynamically caused. By being relegated to mere psychodynamic predispositions that are not sufficient in themselves to "cause" homosexuality, such factors do not displace the father in this drama. The later revived Oedipal crisis is the "true" psychodynamic cause. Not only is psychoanalysis preserved by these means, but the form that remains is firmly centered on the male.

But again what of the biological in all this? Another way of phrasing this is to ask why Freud brings up the biological at all. With all this psychodynamic drama, why is there a need for that particular discussion? Part of the answer to this question must consist in Freud's desire to *appropriate,* by approximation or by simply laying one term next to the other in the text, the biological to the psychoanalytic. See, there is a relationship, the exact nature of which I cannot determine, but the terms can appear together here. But in this particular text the biological is used in another way as well, one that is relatively rare with Freud—namely, to set the limits of the psychoanalytic and by that means supply another excuse for his failure to cure. The unwillingness on the part of the young woman to be "cured" is not enough. Freud no doubt believed that he *should* have been able to overcome that in the "normal" state of affairs; no, something deeper was at work here. (The third reason given by Freud for failure—the lack of sufficient bisexuality on the part of some homosexuals—will be discussed later). Toward the end of the case study Freud writes:

> It is not for psychoanalysis to solve that problem of homosexuality. It must rest content with disclosing the psychical mechanism which resulted in determination of the object-choice and with tracing the paths leading from them to the instinctual basis of the disposition. There its work ends, and it leaves the rest to biological research, which has recently brought to light . . . such very important results concerning the influence of the first factor mentioned [the "physical sexual characteristics—physical hermaphroditism"] . . . on the second [the "mental sexual characteristics—masculine, or feminine, attitude"] and third ["kind of object-choice"].

And:

> When one compares the extent to which we can influence it ["altering inversion"] with the remarkable transformations which Steinach has effected in some cases by his operations, it [psychoanalysis] does not make a very imposing impression. Thus it would be premature, or a harmful exaggeration, if at this stage we were to indulge in hopes of a "therapy" of inversion that could be generally used.

Now, it is true that Freud also says that Steinach's cures by operation have worked only on cases of "very patent physical 'hermaphroditism'" and that analogous treatment of lesbians is "at present quite obscure." The fact, however, that he goes on further to say that he believes that such a "cure" would consist in removing "hermaphroditic ovaries" and implanting those which would be "of a single sex," (a prospect ruled out on the practical grounds that women, including lesbians, would resist it since it would mean renouncing motherhood), indicates the extent to which he is open to the seriousness of a biological etiology of homosexuality. In the case of such ovaries, or other yet-to-be-disclosed physiological causes, what is psychoanalysis to do? Can psychoanalysis "cure" homosexuality in such instances? The conditions for a cure seem increasingly rare: The patient must want to be cured and must cooperate, must not have too strong a physiological predisposition to homosexuality, and must present a case "where the homosexual fixation has not yet become strong enough, or where there are considerable rudiments and vestiges of a heterosexual choice of object, i.e., in a still oscillating or in a definitely bisexual organization, that one can make a more favorable prognosis for psychoanalytic therapy." The first two conditions listed are ones over which psychoanalysis—and more importantly, the psychoanalyst—cannot be reasonably expected to have control. One must also ask how such insights, which give so much away to biology, can be of much use to a social constructionist view of sexuality.

And what of the last condition for cure—why are some individuals not bisexual enough? To ask this question is to bring us back again to the issue of the "essential" bisexuality—or as Freud calls it, in his only direct connection between psychoanalysis and biology, the "original" bisexuality of all humans. He writes, "Psychoanalysis has a common basis with biology, in that it presupposes an original bisexuality in human beings (as in animals)." Whatever the reason or reasons for this failure to be bisexual enough, this losing of the original nature—this first fall from the state of grace and nature on the part of some (most?) homosexuals (and one must speculate if it is the case for some or most heterosexuals as well)—reduces such an original state and essential nature to an empty category as far as its power to explain the cause of homosexuality. One is, nonetheless, forced to ask if it was some early psychical drama that established the orientation of these homosexuals so that they cannot act on their original bisexuality. If that is so, what is the role of the latter psychic dramas discussed by Freud in this case study, and why has the earlier drama not been discussed at least as much as the Oedipal ones since the earlier ones have had such a significant effect? Perhaps Freud would like to hold that some individuals are not bisexual enough for "instinctual" (read "biological") reasons. If this is so, then it brings into question the notion of an original bisexuality. It would appear from this analysis that although all may be indeed universally polymorphously perverse (another notion that might be deconstructed at a later time) at some very early stage, it does not follow that all are originally bisexual as well. Bisexuality appears then to be too much like an "orientation"—it must be arrived at or activated; it seems to exist in degrees; and, as has been said, some possess so little of it that it has no discernible effect at all. The young woman in this case is both. She is described by Freud as having both heterosexual and homosexual orientations simultaneously—that is, she appears to be "bisexual" (if that is what the term means), but she cannot be cured. She is not sufficiently bisexual. Bisexuality is used in this text to set up a conflict: to explain, in part, her homosexuality and her inability to be cured—hardly a liberal or critical use of the concept and certainly not a consistent one.

The truth is that original and universal bisexuality in Freud is, like most other concepts, useful for his own ad hoc arguments, although the concept of original bisexuality is one that Freud—for whatever personal, historical, sociological or intellectual reasons—particularly liked. Perhaps he was fond of it for no other reason than the one given in the text—that he believes it links his method more closely to biology. I find it strange that constructionism would find such a concept "critical" since, biologically grounded or not, consistently articulated or not, it is nonetheless presented as a characteristic of a universal and original human nature.

None of the arguments here are meant to deny that bisexuality exists in the same way that other "sexual orientations" exist. All "sexual orientations," I would argue, are culturally accepted shorthands for collections of desires. These notions are "fuzzy," that is, the exact meanings are impossible to determine. What falls into the categories varies from individual experience to individual experience and even within individual experience; it does not point to an "original bisexuality." "Original bisexuality" is one notion we use, thanks to Freud, to make sense of this unruliness of experience. The fuzziness of the categories does not make them any less useful for day-to-day speech or perhaps even, surrounded by enough caveats and qualifiers, for use in the so-called "social sciences." In that sense, "bisexuality" most surely exists in the same way "heterosexuality" and "homosexuality" exist, and anyone moving in relatively liberal or progressive circles in a city like New York is bound to encounter more than a few individuals who take such an identity. Such an identity or label is a social choice determined by one's experience of desire and by the available linguistic codes and social categories of one's milieu. But Freud's category is fuzzier that most; he uses it to cover girlhood or boyhood crushes, the elements of certain same-sex heterosexual friendships, an early universal stage in sexual development among humans and animals, and some forms of fully expressed adult human sexual behavior. Also, "original bisexuality" (again to use the pragmatic maxim) is not a useful notion, for it is too easily reduced to inconsistent nonsense and it cannot be integrated with Freud's fuller explanation of homosexuality without considerably more work than he is willing to do. Finally, and most importantly, since the concept universalizes and since it supports an unexamined and uncritical biology of sexuality, it is a reactionary and ultimately normalizing concept—it does not serve us, or the constructionist position, in the long run.

What are the critical insights of this text, other than the critical insights into Freud's methods and attitudes? They reside, as has been noted earlier, in the presentation of a young woman—in some sense "immortalized" in the text as a heroine (if we are still allowed to speak of such) to "gay men," "lesbians," and even "bisexuals" at this late date. She shines through as a remarkable resistor to authority and to what has come to be called patriarchy. Secondly, in this account, beyond the young woman herself, there also seems to lie—albeit in dimmer tones—something like a "gay" and "lesbian," or "bisexual," world represented by the "friend" to whom the young women was attracted—the distinguished lady who was also a *cocotte* and about whom Freud writes, "[S]he lived with a married woman as her friend, having intimate relations with her, while at the same time she carried on promiscuous affairs with a number of men." That such people existed in the everyday life of that time is a useful and critical historical insight, and we owe Freud a debt of gratitude for producing this historical evidence. (We know this from other sources as well, but I think that evidence presented in the form of "personalities" seems to us more moving.) These individuals, inasmuch as they lived before the general acceptance of Freudianism, did not need Freudian insights to produce their resistance to anti-gay culture and, in fact, it was precisely such insights that the young woman in this case was resisting.

Finally, if we give up the possibility of critical insights from Freud on the issue of homosexuality, what is constructionism in sexuality to do? Constructionism has had its own insights, admittedly often overstated, about the historical construction of sexual categories and the medicalization of sexuality. It continues to play a critical role in our attempts to understand the resistant and unruly subject of sexuality. Because of constructionism, no sociologist any longer believes that the categories we use today in this area are truly universal; we are all nominalists now. Constructionism does not need the notion of a universal plasticity of desire, of "original bisexuality" or any other similar universalizing notions rescued from the Freudian corpus to produce its accounts. What it requires are the standard insights of sociology, anthropology, history, and deconstruction and a postmodern sensibility applied to a variable and unruly subject (which it seems to have in sex and sexuality) to prevent (for the foreseeable future, at any rate) the rise of another totalizing scientific discourse on this topic. What it also needs, and this may take some time to develop, is a new encounter with biology, one that is both nonscientifistic and nonreductionist. This requires recognizing a few other points as well. One, as stated, is that the Freudian understanding of biology, especially the universalizing conception of a "essential" bisexuality of all humans, must be seen to be inconsistently used within the Freudian corpus and to be inconsistent with the "strongest" or most radical constructionist position. Secondly, it means to recognize that as constructionists, we have no way of knowing in advance what biological arguments about human sexuality will make reasonable claims for incorporation in some modified constructionist account. But to refuse to engage in a dialogue with biologists and to cling to the critical insights of a nineteenth-century master ensures that we, as sociological constructionists, are bound to simply repeat our earliest positions ad nauseam.

To engage in a renewed dialogue with the biologists is to "acknowledge sufficiently that the body, as a material entity, is somewhat, and possibly in important ways, outside of discourse and offers a restriction on what might be said. In other words the body is resistant to speech at some level and to some degree." This is not to ignore constructionist treatments of the "body" or the "social body," nor is it to ignore the insights of the sociology of science, including those of Michael Mulkay, who has argued that the world and the word are intertwined in ways which we cannot entirely decipher.[3] (This is an issue I have addressed elsewhere.[4]) It means, rather, to recognize that this is a period in which the dilemma of the exact relationship of the world to the word is philosophically insoluble. In other words, the insights and discoveries concerning the social construction of reality shared by the various forms of constructionism are reasonable and, in fact, unavoidable, but, on the other hand, a conclusion drawn from those principles that the world is reducible to the word (in this case, that the body does not exist in some fashion outside of discourse) also appears unreasonable, and the feeling that such a conclusion is unreasonable is itself unavoidable. Given that this philosophical or intellectual problem is insoluble at this time leads me to believe that the best thing is to encourage this renewed dialogue with a hope that new insights and accounts will come out of such a dialogue and out of cooperative work across the great divide between constructionists and biologists.

Notes

1. Jeffrey Weeks. (1985.) *Sexuality and its discontents: Meanings, myths & modern sexualities.* New York: Routledge, pp. 154–155.

2. Albeit ones that the constructionists will find hard to deal with and that I also find impossible to credit—for they are, on one hand, impossible to prove or disprove in any sense if one wishes to be a positivist, and, on the other, they stand as merely one possible—once interesting but by now rather tired—interpretation, one way of organizing

as well as creating, a system of signs, and not, at this stage in our collective experience, any better than many others on the issue at hand—if one wishes to take a deconstructivist view of the master.

3. Michael Mulkay. (1985). *The word and the world: Explorations in the form of sociological analysis*. London: Allen & Unwin.

4. David E. Woolwine. (1992). Reading science as text. In R. Wuthnow (Ed.), *Vocabularies of public life: Empirical essays in symbolic structure*. New York: Routledge.

Part III

~

CONTRIBUTIONS FROM PSYCHOANALYSTS

7

DESIGNING THE LESBIAN SUBJECT
Looking Backwards, Looking Forwards

Ann D'Ercole

Can the subject of lesbianism be rescued from a perplexing body of psychoanalytic thought on gender and sexuality? This liberation is not easy. Women in same-sex relationships have had to endure psychoanalysis's tendency to ignore their unique individual experiences and to catalogue them clinically as "female homosexuals." Consequently, Foucault (1989), in his wisdom, accused psychoanalysis of systematically forming the objects it considers. Are lesbians really the creation of these theories? My aim is to argue that Freud's (1920) psychoanalytic depiction of his lesbian patient is built on the sands of cultural change.

It is a story constructed from myth disguised as science. Within this elemental case, Freud's "female homosexual" is represented with a specific voice. But a careful reading reveals two voices: one that has been incorporated into the psychoanalytic theory and another that has been left out. Revisiting this case study provides an opportunity to rescue same-sex love from the theoretical grip of myths and from the burden of Freud's own voice, to discuss current attempts to escape from these myths, and, finally, to conceptualize desire in a way that more accurately reflects and enhances the lives of all people. My hope is to identify the myths in Freud's constructs and to generate a psychoanalytic discourse that captures the diversity of life experience. This can best be accomplished by directing our attention to the future, while at the same time being mindful of the past so as not to repeat earlier mistakes.

A Brief Review of Freud's Case

Freud's patient is 18 years old and the only girl among 3 brothers. The father, Freud tells us, is "an earnest, worthy man, at bottom very tender-hearted" (p. 149), but stern toward his children, for whom he has little time. Freud describes the mother as a woman who suffers from some neurotic troubles and treats her only daughter harshly while catering to her sons. Interestingly, the mother is less angry than her husband about her daughter's romantic behavior since she enjoys sharing her daughter's secrets. Both parents are worried that their daughter "would be seen in bad company" and are offended by the fact that she will not hide her affection from the public. At times, they appear to be more offended by her openness than they are by her romance. She refuses to offer excuses, lies, or deceptions to cover up her feelings. While her mother holds a less punitive, "don't ask, don't tell" attitude, the father's reaction has been much harsher. On learning of his daughter's romance with another woman, he flew into a rage, and he continually tries to stop her with various threats. He considers her vicious, degenerate or as mentally ill. Deeply bitter, he is determined to change her. If the reparative analysis with Freud fails, he plans to arrange a speedy marriage in the hopes of stimulating her "natural instincts."

The parents describe their daughter as an active young child and then as a beautiful and intelligent young woman. The woman with whom she falls in love is older, 28 years old, and "lived with a friend, a married woman, and had intimate relations with her, while at the same time she carried on promiscuous affairs with a number of men." Freud reports that the patient showers her love with flowers and waits for her for hours outside her door, seizing every opportunity to be with her. Freud enters the scene after a dramatic turn, an attempted suicide. One afternoon while the two young women were out together, the patient's father walked by and cast them an angry glance. The daughter rushed off and flung herself over a wall; this action led to her being confined to her bed for a time. The gesture brought some short-term rewards and ended with the parents coming to Freud for help.

Freud interprets his patient's dreams as expressions of joy over the possible cure of her "inversion" and, further, as a confession of her longing for a man's love and for children. He does not describe the dreams to the reader, offering only his interpretations.

He reports that the patient has a normal attitude toward the Oedipus complex and that she has substituted a slightly older brother for her father. He notes that she compared her genitals with her brother's with no lasting impression and that the birth of a second brother also had no impact on her development. From his talks with the patient, Freud learns that during puberty, she became acquainted with the facts of sex and that at age 13–14 she showed strong feelings for a 3-year-old boy and made friends with his parents.

This becomes the critical junction in Freud's theory. He finds that the patient's interest in the young child was simultaneous with her first interest in young mothers and that the trauma was sealed at the age of 16 when her third brother was born.

Freud's Lesbian Subject

Freud concludes that the patient's love for a woman is a love for a mother substitute. To support this argument, he cites the reports of the patient's attachment to young mothers whom she befriended during family vacations and holidays. He notes that these attachments provided a source of attention that the patient's mother was unable or unwilling to give. In addition to the mother substitution hypothesis, Freud finds it important that the patient resembles her brother; the combination of slender figure, severe beauty, and straightforward manner blends her feminine and masculine ideal. To Freud, this represents a "combination of the homosexual tendency with the heterosexual one." His Oedipal interpretation describes the patient as yearning for a gentler, kinder mother and also wanting to have her father's baby. He presents as evidence of this wish her interest in her younger brother. He generalizes this formulation to all daughters, concluding that they yearn for their father's love and substitute the wish for a penis with the wish for a baby.

Freud describes the patient as resentful and embittered. He attributes her hostility to the fact that it is her mother, not her, who gave birth to the father's baby and concludes that because of this disloyalty she turns away from her father and men altogether. Here cultural myths are embedded in the language of science and theory; Freud reasons, that in extreme cases like this one if a woman is betrayed by a man, she may become a man hater.

The myths disguised as science and theory continue. For Freud, lesbian love also includes an act of defiance against fathers: "Since you have betrayed me you must put up with my betraying you." Here again we find another myth, that of lesbians seeking revenge. In this theory, not only is the father–daughter relationship problematized, but so is the mother–daughter relationship. Freud assumes that the patient withdrew from competition with her mother, leaving the men to her mother and turning instead to women for satisfaction. Stretching this idea, he calls her suicide attempt a fulfillment of a punishment (self-punishment) and the fulfillment of a wish: the wish to have a child by her father. Freud believes that the patient's conscious thoughts are about her rejection by the woman she admires but that her unconscious thoughts are about her father's rejection of her. That is, he uses the heterosexual model of relationships to understand how his patient is feeling. He believes that is supported by the fact that there has been no genital contact in this romance and that the object of the young woman's affection does not return her interest.

Today, we know much more about the difficult journey involved for a woman moving toward loving another woman in a culture that derides that love with psychological, legal, and religious sanctions. However, Freud simply perpetuates the heterosexual myth of his time (and ours) that women cannot really be sexual in the absence of a man. The heterosexist position is that the woman who loves a woman is really a man. Historically, even before Freud, the mannish lesbian was offered as a way to explain love between women (Kiersky, 1996).

Rewriting Myths

How do we rescue same-sex love from myth? Freud's approach to the question of homosexuality is to ask the two key questions: "Did this homosexual girl show physical characteristics plainly belonging to the opposite sex, and second, did the case prove to be one of congenital, innate or acquired (late onset) homosexuality" (p. 153)? The myth interwoven in his questions and throughout his culture is that at the heart of female same-sex desire is "the soul of a man trapped inside a woman's body" and vice versa (Sedgwick, 1993). Kiersky (in press), looking back over the history of psychoanalysis and lesbians, suggests that the problem of the lesbian subject began in Freud's 1905 *Three Essays on the Theory of Sexuality* with the notion that "little girls are really little boys until a certain age." The idea that male precedes female is cited and repeated in Freud's theory of both female development and female homosexuality. This hierarchy is reflected in the manner in which Freud approaches the question of homosexuality in this case. He notes that appearances can be deceptive and suggests that the choice of sexual object, sexual characteristics, and sexual attitudes do not necessarily coincide. Here he does not take for granted differences between the sexes but is simply curious about the relationship between prevailing conceptions of sex, sexuality, and social norms. However, he conceptualizes sexual desire for a woman as being innately masculine and thus reinstates a psychological homunculus that is never fully eliminated. While his questions boldly outline the topic, they limit the possibilities for exploring new possibilities. This delimiting the topic leads Kiersky (in press) to argue that the way Freud frames his questions limits in significant ways what can be discovered. It underscores how science is a social construct and how Freud's theory is a product of culture. Freud's questions also impose his voice, his preconceived idea of the subject.

On Hearing Another Voice

I previously alluded to two voices coexisting in this case: the one that speaks loudly about psychoanalytic theory and the one that is singularly absent—that of the patient. Imagine the excitement this 18-year-old woman must feel as she catches sight of the possibilities of life lived with a freedom her own mother never enjoyed. This case takes place in Austria as the buds of feminism are bursting into full bloom in England and the United States and are opening up new possibilities for women to relate to other women. Do the seeds of that new wave of cultural thought influence this young woman? She tells Freud that she cannot imagine any other way of being in love! She feels "she could easily have sex with a man and a woman." This is not a voice that makes its way into psychoanalytic theory. This is a passion that is unconstrained by gender. Her words suggest a determination and confidence, a sense of agency and action, that is minimized in Freud's psychoanalytic story. She reports having been consciously aware of her feelings since puberty, including her crushes on teachers and young mothers. She describes her love as bringing her "bliss" with each encounter and kiss of the hand, despite the fact that her love is not returned. She takes pleasure from the possibilities of love between women. She rejects the advances of other women her own age. This is a woman who is delighting in being recognized and seen. She is not a ghostly lesbian hidden and denied, but a real-life woman coming eye to eye with another woman.

Her analyst does not hear or acknowledge the power of this meeting. Rather, he offers various interpretations to explain away what his young patient tells him; the patient holds her ground with comments like, "how very interesting." He thinks she is behaving like a man, overvaluing the object of her desire and preferring to be the lover rather than the beloved. The myth that women are passive receptors and men the possessors of agency dominate his thinking. He is unaware of the contradiction inherent in his admission that he feels treated like an object in a museum because the patient pays him little attention. He retaliates, denigrating her, calling her a "feminist." He presents as evidence her comments that she feels it "unjust that girls should not enjoy the same freedom as boys," and that she "rebelled against the lot of women in general" (p. 169). These are clearly feminist attitudes.

Freud confuses the voice in his own head for that of the patient's. The voice he thinks he hears he incorporates into his psychoanalytic theory. He leaves out the voice of his patient who proclaims that she cannot imagine any other way of being in love. He cannot imagine why a woman would love a woman. He cannot imagine a feminist love in which women are valued for who they are, rather than for who they are not. For Freud, an independent and autonomous woman is synonymous with sexual deviance (Castle, 1993).

While I am aware that the act of listening always involves claiming and rejecting different elements of a narrative, my attention is drawn to the passionate pursuit involved in this romance, the choice of this particular woman to love, as well as the erotic possibilities involved in the relationship. I wonder, is the woman who wins this young girl's heart beautiful, smart, exciting? I am drawn to the conflict present in this case, the patient's wish to pursue her own desires without disappointing her parents, resulting in her willingness to undergo treatment. Examining this conflict opens the door to a discussion of feelings generated by a culture terrified by same-sex love.

The patient in this case presents the clinical picture of a young woman who wants to make a choice that will placate her family, poised as she is on the threshold of separation. However, the analyst's aim is to cure her of her homosexuality, despite his assertion that a goal of cure is futile. Both aims are troublesome. It is no surprise that a struggle ensues. Freud becomes angry when he discovers that the patient never really intends to give up her desires. The patient tries to comfort her parents (and Freud) by playing along with their solution. But she always maintains her ground, brushing aside Freud's laborious interpretations. The encounter fails to confront the pain in both their experiences. Freud feels rejected and inadequate, and he blames the patient. She leaves unaffirmed and unheard, dismissed to a woman analyst.

Freud's use of heterosexuality as normative ultimately subjugates all issues of the patient's identity to their function within the Oedipal scenario. Her idealization and identification with her mother-substitutes are labeled as defensive attempts to resolve conflicted feelings of jealousy and hatred for her mother. Idealization and identification, of course, could have their own developmental authority; for example, Magid (1993) suggests that they serve self-development and the preservation of self-object ties in the face of familial disruption.

Several analytic questions worthy of exploration appear in this material. How is a woman affected by her resolve to be different from her mother and from her cultural prescriptions, to be a woman who loves another woman? Can she challenge those values, those social attitudes and even ideas about motherhood without feelings of shame, guilt, and uncertainty? Guilt and shame are certainly part of this story, but they are feelings developed within a social context. They are conditioned by the correspondence of societal values with internalized values that the individual has taken over from her parents.

The Politics of Shame and Guilt

The psychoanalytic theory of guilt has been deeply wedded to Freud's model, where guilt is seen as the result of conflict between intent and moral stricture

(Summers, 1996). Guilt in this case may be a complexly derived feeling of self betrayal and a courage to be separate. This is quite different from Modell's (1965, 1971) preoedipal separation from mother guilt or from a guilt equated simply with dangerous wishes (Summers, 1996). This patient may have suffered a guilt of recognition, brought on by looking into the eyes of another woman and having that gaze returned. It provokes a feeling both exciting and powerful. This experience also comes with a dark side, the burden of guilt. According to Rank, the burden of guilt presents itself to creative individuals who are most instrumental in the building of culture (Menaker, 1995).

Castle (1993) describes how virtually every distinguished woman suspected of loving another woman has had her biography sanitized in the interest of order and public safety. Lesbian contributions to culture have been regularly repressed or ignored. They have been ghosted, vaporized right before our eyes! At the same time, these same-sex attachments have haunted Western literature and culture since the eighteenth century (Castle, 1993). Can psychoanalysis account for these acts of hide-and-seek in a culture that imbues the players with guilt and shame?

Perhaps the American cultural school of psychoanalysis and self-psychology's intersubjectivity offer a way to deal with these feelings. Unlike Freud and queer theory revisionist Butler (1992), Sullivan's (1953) approach does not focus on loss and sites of melancholy, but on barriers to growth. Self-psychology places its emphasis on self-object failures and nonattunement (Kohut, 1971). These theories call attention to interpersonal situations, focusing as they do on areas that generate anxiety or shame and that obstruct human connections and affections. Their models provide a wider range of possibilities and include the patient's own relational needs. For me, they provide a more plausible explanation of why Freud's patient chose this particular woman to love. By choosing someone unavailable, the patient protects herself from having to face a stronger social rejection, a rejection that might result from fully bringing someone into her life. This strategy both pushes the limits of the social milieu while simultaneously staying within it. It is an approach influenced by shame and guilt—not a guilt of autonomy but one of compliance.

This path is still prevalent among some lesbians today as a clinical anecdote reveals: A patient, Susan, tearfully acknowledges that "if she tells her mother she is gay, it will kill her." On the other hand, she is certain her mother already knows. Is it really a secret, and why will this knowledge kill Susan's mother? Does separating from mother by embracing another woman feel murderous to both Susan and Freud's patient? Or is it the compliance, the pull to stay connected and abandon oneself, that troubles each of these women? Staying close to the clinical material can be clarifying. Susan's parents encourage her achievements, and unlike Freud's young patient, she derives much satisfaction at work,

including economic prosperity and social status. Despite these gains she continues to have ongoing difficulty in her attempts to find a partner to integrate fully
into her life. Like her cultural contemporaries, Susan is comfortable playing with
gender. In fact, her words confirm an idea of gender as performance (Butler,
1993b). She speaks of enjoying being a woman and also takes pleasure from
playing the "man." She characterizes herself as chivalrous, aggressive, and nurturing. She feels androgynous, feminine and masculine. Her identifications are
multiple and entwined. Her construction of the role of gender and desire at
times de-emphasizes gender and at other times interprets gender without the
material body.

Despite these contemporary views of gender and sexuality, Susan keeps her
romantic life secret from her colleagues at work and from her family. She har-
bors a fear of losing everything she values if people come to really know her,
while simultaneously she yearns to be known. There is an aspect of her that
remains paralyzed. She dreams of "carrying a heart packed in ice to a transplant
center." In the dream, she is at the airport. Her task is to transport a heart to the
waiting recipient. She feels her own heart is on ice, stranded between her desire
to please—be a good girl—and her desire to have the girl. Her struggle to stay
connected to her family and culture while creating her own life is courageous.
She works at having a life that neither conforms to the conventional norms nor
ruptures the bonds she holds dear. Her fears of loss are not irrational. Discrimination and sometimes even persecution are part of the social fabric of contemporary gay life. For Susan, her fears have become a hiding place for her
conflicts, and they drive a wedge between her desire for autonomy and her
longing for nurturing.

In both clinical cases, the women have mothers who once enjoyed their
daughters' confidences and even encouraged them, until the time came when
they crossed the social barrier and chose women with whom to fall in love. This
crossing aroused considerable anxiety, positioning the daughter in a land of
divided loyalties and leading to a discrepancy between self and social situation.
It may have begun years before, when the daughter expressed her longing, her
desire and love for her mother. But conceptualizing "mother" in this way, with
an unwavering and exclusive presence and a concreteness in our formulation of
gender, as O'Connor and Ryan (1993) point out, leads us back into essentialist
terrain. To gain a nonessentialist footing can we give up the question of who
the Other is in lesbian eroticism? Can Wittig's (1992) observation that "the
refusal to become (or to remain) heterosexual always meant to refuse to become
a man or a woman, consciously or not" (p. 13), be of help? For a lesbian, she
suggests, this goes beyond the refusal of the *role* woman: "It is the refusal of the
economic, ideological, and political power of a man" (p. 13). This is symbolic

emasculation that Western society demands of its female members. Is a lesbian a woman who refuses to be mutilated by society's conventions? And if that is so, how is the analyst to approach the patient's refusal?

Lynd (1958), writing with the injustices of racism in mind, makes an important point about people who feel a discrepancy between themselves and the social situation:

> If a person were wholly independent of the demands and conventions of his society, he might not feel shame, but the feeling of shame for the values of one's society, and the transcending of personal shame would seem to depend upon having some perspective, some standards of significance, against which one can call into question the codes of one's immediate culture. (p. 36)

She calls for an examination of human desires, decencies, and values and of the variety and richness of human values that may be appealed to beyond those that are shaped by particular societies or particular cultural traditions. The term "transcultural values"—those values that include the selective identification with different aspects of one's culture—adds significantly to psychoanalytic theory. It is the individual combining of these selected aspects into new forms, as well as identifications with wider values beyond those of one's immediate culture, that allows for change. This process involves the distinction between feeling shame for things that one believes are truly shameful and feeling ashamed of the feeling of shame because one does not accept the standards on which the emotion is based. The experience of guilt and shame are critical ingredients involved in the process of integrating what is outside the self. Can psychoanalytic theory hold onto Fuss' (1995) definition of identification: "the detour through the other that defines a self" (p. 12) without resorting to a gender rigidity? Fuss describes how, in our attempts to become a man or woman, we incorporate an "Other," man or woman, who then lives inside, in place of what was longed for. In her model there is no original self; rather, the self is an interpersonal, socially constructed creation.

This view fosters a human sexuality that is extremely flexible and nonspecific with regard to sexual objects. It allows the possibility for feelings to be catalogued and organized into open behavior and lifelong identities that are dependent on a variety of social and cultural dynamics (Menaker, 1995). In this theory, sexual life is seen as being grafted onto, or emerging from, relational life. It encompasses a relief from loneliness and a yearning for affection and love, and it is constructed through interpersonal relations and culture. In thinking this way, we are always plagued by the question of who the doer of the action is.

While these ideas do not preclude psychic agency, the answer to the identity of the doer may remain forever existential.

As contemporary revisionists build the lesbian experience on social constructions, gender is seen as being performed in fluid and multiple ways (Butler, 1993a; Dimen, 1995). This performance can be conscious or unconscious depending on social contexts (i.e., prohibitions and supports). Moving forward, the lesbian subject is redesigned and reconfigured, shifting from a focus on the biological substance of identity to the psychological matter of self in relationship. Sexuality then is not a steady categorical state—homosexual, heterosexual—but rather sexuality follows desire; feelings are influenced by a myriad of factors.

What connections exist between the lesbian voice of the past and contemporary notions of sexuality? The Darwinian psychoanalysis promoted by Freud (Dimen, 1995) both captured and released the feelings and fears prevalent at that time about human behavior. Female same-sex relationships were brought into a cold, somewhat tolerant world. Faderman (1981) describes how the romantic attachments of the past were, after Freud, negatively labeled and how the identity "lesbian" solidified. Not until postmodernism, with its downplay of ideology and its use of a vocabulary with associated insights, has there been help in disclosing these clinical categories of "homosexual" and "heterosexual" as scientifically unfounded, noncoherent, and politically biased formulations (Lesser, 1996; Schoenberg, 1995).

As a result, a postmodern psychoanalysis has emerged, freeing the ends of sexuality from the traditional belief in its singular procreative purpose. This leaves us without gender as the quintessential path to understanding sexuality. Rather than traits derived from fixed developmental stages, the fluid constructs of gender and sexuality have become a variable wardrobe of postures and poses, worn and rejected as the fashion and context change.

In this interpersonal and interactive arena, relational acts are performed in contexts and are connected to subjective experience more than objective reality. Clinical psychoanalytic practice reveals that some patients can be seen rigidly clinging to labels like "lesbian," "gay," or "straight" as a way to hold their identities together. This rigidity is understandable in a world that neither recognizes nor tolerates difference. Other patients may abandon labels altogether, feeling that none of the labels fit. Finding the words to explain this elusive experience is difficult. I have suggested elsewhere (D'Ercole, 1996) that density and performance may be ways to think of this confluence of subjectivity and experience.

Toward a Conception of Density

Fluid self-representations vary in quantity and quality depending on the setting (D'Ercole, 1996). For example, sometimes our self-representations are thick, as if all the different aspects of experience have been packed into a moment. Yet at other times self-representations seem thin and shallow, reflecting only a fragment of our subjective experience. This concept is helpful in describing the closeness of the constituent parts of subjective experience. It is a way of drawing attention to how variable experience can be and how dependent it is on context and social rules. An example of this experience is represented in a session with a patient who asks a therapist if he or she is gay. This question may require the therapist to focus on an aspect of self that is not dominant during the session, just as thinking of oneself as Catholic or Jewish or as a mother remains in the background until for some reason you are called to categorize yourself in these ways. These categories construct aspects of identities that can be meaningful or not. Butler (1993a) has been enormously helpful in her descriptions of how we perform or put these aspects of identities into play rather than being them. But even this dialogue leaves us inside the psychoanalytic canon struggling to reconfigure preconceptions of same-sex desire rather than finding our way out.

Despite these advances, women in same-sex relationships remain outside of psychoanalytic language and continue to be represented clinically as "female homosexuals." As O'Connor and Ryan (1993) have pointed out, no lesbian would use this term to describe herself. Instead, protesting absence from language, lesbians sometimes use the terms "dyke," "queer," "fem," and "butch" as self-proclaimed inventions of an identity continually denied by culture. These self-representations encompass sexuality and gender, partly in parody, partly in play, and certainly in resistance. They are discernible throughout today's culture and in our clinical practices. Unfortunately for some therapists and patients, these self-representations are misheard as organizing elements of identity rather than as fluid concepts composed of various interpersonal and cultural configurations.

Postmodern Wisdoms and Warnings

The postmodern notion that everything is ideological has been used effectively by scholars like Butler (1993a) who examine inscriptions of difference and social inequality. However, if we adhere too closely to the text and interpret Freud on the basis of his assumptions, we will remain locked inside the walls of classical psychoanalysis and outside the scope of psychoanalytic theory that is being rewritten by contemporary interpersonal, relational, and self psychoanalysts. For these analysts, the point of convergence is emotional connection, not developmental stages. Their focus is on those experiences and meanings that are shaping or constricting the individual's capacity to experience life in a more fully human way, rather than on blocked affects or identifications resulting from blind drives.

Not all theories have carried us in the same direction with regard to same-sex relationships. In Drescher's (1996) view, both Winnicott and Sullivan provide a more respectful approach to same-sex relationships, consistent with his clinical experience and those of other contemporary psychoanalysts (D'Ercole, 1996; Domenici & Lesser, 1995; Glassgold & Iasenza, 1995; Kiersky, 1996; O'Connor & Ryan, 1993; Orange, 1996). For me, the clinical and theoretical efforts within this paradigm shift exceed the scope of queer theorists like Butler (1993) who, while providing new and provocative ideas, adheres too closely to Freudian text, as if it were the only psychoanalytic canon worth exploring.

This blind adherence to Freud can lead to a contortion of the postmodern, so that the words persist but the ideological meanings fail to be fully developed. For example, using postmodern language in a classical interpretive psychoanalytic scheme, Gerson (1996) confronts a lesbian patient who appears one day for a session wearing a t-shirt with the words "whore, slut, tramp, bitch" (p. 353) printed on it. He explains to her that her wearing the shirt is both a rejection of the use of the feminine body to excite male desire and one that paradoxically designates her as that which she ridicules. While his plan is to show that discourse influences how bodies, gender, and desire are named and known, the dialogue presented is steeped in the traditional attitudes it tries to escape. For example, the therapist voices his concern that talking about sexual feelings with the patient may change her sexual orientation and thereby disrupt her entire social network and identity. He reports, "My fears centered on how changes in her sexual orientation would affect her life, one which was publicly and deeply involved in lesbian culture and politics" (p. 354). He acknowledges to her that he knows she is concerned that he may try to "rehabilitate" her into a heterosexual life but vows that this is not his agenda. The use of postmodern rhetoric obscures the essentialist attitudes embedded in the work—a kind of knowing the words but not the music. In this work only the patient's sexuality is literally assumed to be totally unstable. How else can we understand the extreme position the therapist takes by assuming that even his suggesting a divergence from her lesbian identity may toss her into chaos? He offers a conventional explanation to the patient that her desires for involvement with her absent father were beginning to appear in relation to him. But the patient argues, "No, I do not want the father in you to love me, I want the lesbian in you to love me" (p. 353). The therapist misses what the patient is talking about. He does not seem to be able to imagine what being a lesbian would be like. Instead, he feels excluded and anxious. He wonders how can he be with her. It is as if he were saying that since she is a lesbian she can't have tender, affectionate, erotic feelings for him because he is a man! This is, of course, a reification of male and female, with universal assumptions about the relations between men and women—assumptions he disclaims.

The idea of questioning why it is important to distinguish between sexes does not appear in this case. Rather, it perpetuates the very myths it struggles to be free from. Perhaps this is what Domenici (1997) would call "bad faith." As he explains it:

> [B]ad faith is not a "state" one is in, rather it is a commitment to a way of being, usually supported by a world view. Typically acts, feelings, or emotions that cause the conflict inherent in bad faith to emerge are at best not sufficiently attended to or typically dismissed as themselves a lie or due to the aggression on the part of the other. (p. 225)

The second warning about the postmodern comes from clinicians who suggest that abandoning identities that are already fragile and inconsistent and embarking on what may be a deconstructive journey to nihilism can be dangerous to patients (Flax, 1993). With these cautions in mind, I submit that it is ultimately in the abandonment of identities that are fragile, rigid, and confining that a space is provided for the formulation of better and expanded possibilities.

Conclusion

I agree with Kilcooley (1994) that the interpretation of Freud's case over time has perpetuated a blindness and, I would add, a deafness by leaving out the actual spoken words and subjectivity of the patient. It has also designed a lesbian subject concretized in biologized, psychic metaphors. Yet there are revolutionary configurations of gender and sexuality within psychoanalysis that both extend and depart from Freud's initial inquiries. There is a forward-looking psychoanalysis, including gay and lesbian psychoanalysts who struggle to break away from the myths contained in early psychoanalytic discourse. Our challenge is to be inclusive of the many feelings we own and disown both in our dreams, visions, and desires. Ultimately, we need to develop a theory of sexuality devoid of gender and sex that is based on *feelings,* erotic and otherwise—feelings that are sustained and transformed in our ongoing relationships throughout our lives.

References

Butler, J. (1992). The lesbian phallus and the morphological imaginary. *Differences: A Journal of Feminist Cultural Studies, 4,* 141.

Butler, J. (1993a). *Bodies that matter: On the discursive limits of sex.* New York: Routledge.

Butler, J. (1993b). Imitation and gender insubordination. In H. Abelove, M. Barale, & D. Halperin (Eds.), *The lesbian and gay studies reader.* (pp. 307–316). New York: Routledge.

Castle, T. (1993). *The apparitional lesbian: Female homosexuality and modern culture.* New York: Columbia University Press.

D'Ercole, A. (1996). Postmodern ideas about gender and sexuality: The lesbian woman redundancy. *Psychoanalysis and Psychotherapy 13* (2), 142–152.

Dimen, M. (1995). On "our nature": Prolegomenon to a relational theory of sexuality. In T. Domenici & R. Lesser (Eds.), *Disorienting sexuality: Psychoanalytic reappraisals of sexual identities.* (pp. 129–152). New York: Routledge.

Domenici, T. (1997). Antihomosexuality, bad faith, and psychoanalysis: Response to commentaries. *Gender and Psychoanalysis: An Interdisciplinary Journal 2* (2), 225–239.

Domenici, T. & Lesser, R. (Eds.) (1995). *Disorienting sexuality: Psychoanalytic reappraisals of sexual identities.* Routledge: New York.

Drescher, J. (1996). Across the great divide: Gender panic in the analytic dyad. *Psychoanalysis and Psychotherapy 13* (2), 174–186.

Drescher, J. (in press). *Psychoanalytic therapy and the gay man.* New York: Analytic Press.

Faderman, L. (1981). *Surpassing the love of men: Romantic friendship and love between women from the Renaissance to the present.* New York: William Morrow.

Flax, J. (1993). *Disputed subjects: Essays on psychoanalysis, politics and philosophy.* New York: Routledge.

Foucault, M. (1989). *The archaeology of knowledge.* London: Routledge.

Fuss, D. (1995). *Identification papers.* New York: Routledge.

Freud, S. (1953–1974). The psychogenesis of a case of homosexuality in a woman. In J. Strachey (Ed. and Trans.), *The standard edition of the complete psychological works of Sigmund Freud.* (Vol. 18, pp. 145–172). London: Hogarth. (Original work published 1920)

Freud, S. (1953–1974). Three essays on the theory of sexuality. In J. Strachey (Ed. and Trans.), *The standard edition of the complete psychological works of Sigmund Freud.* (Vol. 7, pp. 123–243). London: Hogarth. (Original work published 1905)

Gerson, S. (1996). Shared body of language. *Gender and Psychoanalysis: An Interdisciplinary Journal 1* (3), 345–360.

Glassgold, J. & Iasenza, S. (1995). *Lesbians and psychoanalysis: Revolutions in theory and practice.* New York: Free Press.

Kiersky, S. (1996). Exiled desire: The problem of reality in psychoanalysis and lesbian experience. *Psychoanalysis and Psychotherapy 13* (2), 130–141.

Kiersky, S. (in press). *Exiled desire: Essays on psychoanalysis and lesbians.* New York: Analytic Press.

Kilcooley, A. (1994). Lesbians who as yet have no name. *Feminism & Psychology 4* (3), 487–492.

Kohut, H. (1971). The analysis of the self. *Monograph series of the psychoanalytic study of the child, 4.* New York: International Universities Press.

Lesser, R. (1996). "All that's solid melts into air": Deconstructing some psychoanalytic facts. *Contemporary Psychoanalysis, 32,* 5–23.

Lynd, H. M. (1958). *On shame and the search for identity.* New York: Science Editions.

Magid, B. (1993). A young woman's homosexuality reconsidered: Freud's "The psychogenesis of a case of homosexuality in a woman." *Journal of the American Academy of Psychoanalysis, 21,* 421–432.

Menaker, E. (1995). *The freedom to inquire: Self psychological perspectives on women's issues, masochism, and the therapeutic relationship.* Hillsdale, NJ: Jason Aronson Publications.

Modell, A. (1965). On having the right to a life: An aspect of the superego's development. *International Journal of Psychoanalysis, 46*, 323–331.

Modell, A. (1971). The origin of certain forms of preoedipal guilt and the implications for a psychoanalytic theory of affects. *International Journal of Psychoanalysis, 52*, 337–346.

O'Connor, N. & Ryan, J. (1993). *Wild desires and mistaken identities: Lesbianism and psychoanalysis.* New York: Columbia University Press.

Orange, D. (1996). A philosophical inquiry into the concept of desire in psychoanalysis. *Psychoanalysis and Psychotherapy 13* (2), 122–129.

Schoenberg, E. (1995). Psychoanalytic theories of lesbian desire. In T. Domenici & R. Lesser (Eds.), *Disorienting sexuality: Psychoanalytic reappraisals of sexual identities.* (pp. 203–226). New York: Routledge.

Sedgwick, E. (1993). Epistemology of the closet. In H. Abelove, M. Barole, & D. Halperin (Eds.), *The lesbian and gay studies reader.* New York: Routledge.

Sullivan, H. (1953). *The interpersonal theory of psychiatry.* New York: Norton.

Summers, F. (1996). Existential guilt: An object relations concept. *Contemporary Psychoanalysis, 32*, 43–63.

Wittig, M. (1992). *The straight mind and other essays.* Boston, MA: Beacon Press.

8

LAS MUJERES
Women Speak to the Word
of the Father

RoseMarie Pérez Foster

Each contributor to this volume has been moved in his or her own way by Freud's (1920) story of the father who falls into an agitated despair when his daughter begins to love a woman. What is additionally intriguing about this story is how the daughter's cool and dismissive attitudes toward Freud's therapeutic interventions cause the analyst himself to despair in transferential allegiance to the family drama and in sheer mystification at such atypical presentation in a young woman. It is the extreme autocentric reaction of these fathers that moves me to write this essay and to explore how deeply lesbian love threatens the patriarchal order. My interest is in the young woman's will, her insistence to love how and whom she wants, and her refusal to forswear her womanhood in the name of her father's wishes.

Preoccupied only with the object of her desire, the young patient in Freud's tract manages in fact to instigate a revolution in the symbolic order of her nineteenth-century world. She boldly opts to pursue someone who bears no obvious likeness to the father figure she has been socially primed to court and engage. Struggling with the deep personal issues of her own life, she inadvertently rattles the social scaffold that configures erotic love in a male–female dyad embedded within male privilege. So stymied are father and Freud, the writers of her narrative, that their various attempts at historical/psychodynamic understanding of her behavior all eventually fall sway to the resonating shock that she neither desires nor heeds the likes of them.

Unfortunately, the girl is brought to Freud at an untimely juncture in his theoretical career. When Freud is presented in 1920 with this optimal opportunity to explore intimate connection and eroticism in a female dyad, he has already given up his exciting early foray into the interactive anatomic and psychic fungability of gender that he briefly entertained in his *Three Essays on Sexuality* in 1905. Had he pursued this line of thinking and fully integrated it with his discoveries of unconscious determinism and the uncoupling of object from aim (Harris, 1991), he might have been led to the road subsequently taken by numerous contemporary psychoanalytic thinkers: that sexual object-choice evolves as the complex product of multivariate identificatory and passionate aims and not as the prescribed outcome of biological script (Burch, 1993; Harris, 1991; McDougall, 1986). In 1920, however, Freud is heavily submerged in the traditional waters of his sociohistorical milieu. He is deeply identified with the father's narcissistic injury and unable to understand his patient's complex gendered experience and object relation outside the parameters defined by the cultural patriarchy and biological zeitgeist that informs his clinical work. His therapeutic recommendation is stunningly simple: The girl is not to dally with the love of a woman; she is simply to return to her father.

In this contemporary North American era, we have assumed the power both to use theoretical canon and to stand in sober discrimination of the voice(s) it represents. This, in fact, is the new propelling zeitgeist behind a volume such as this. In the social sciences, feminist thought, postmodernism, social constructivist epistemology, and now multiculturalism are the sounding rods we have been using thus far to pursue this task. However, as a psychologist/psychoanalyst trained in this North American academic culture, I am also trained in another culture where Freudian patriarchs still exert an intoxicating influence on both word and action. As a Latin American woman, I have grown up with men whose subjective sense of hegemony over the women in their lives is as sure as the sun rises. I am essentially describing here what Lacan (1997) and the postmodernists (Butler, 1990; Flax, 1990; Irigaray, 1985) would call "the word of the father," and the power of that word through large segments of ethnohistory—and early psychoanalysis—to have defined both the symbolic parameters of the human experience and the gendered contours of the psychic self. In the Latin American culture of my origins, the "word" maintains mythical proportions still and serves as the ethnocultural fulcrum around which gendered self-experience is ordered, structured, and realized. As a contemporary analyst, I tend to view much of development through the bifocal lens of object relational operations and sociocultural dynamics. I see gendered self-experience as embedded within internalized relational matrices; and these structures are honed from individualized family dynamics steeped in sociocultural beliefs.

I would like to describe some aspects of female gender identity development in native Latin American culture for 2 reasons: (1) its fresh, present-day similarity to the sociocultural milieu through which Freud understood and misunderstood his patient and (2) its critical representation of the woman's struggle to define her gendered self-structure outside the purview of male patriarchy. These dynamics represent both the current gendered lives of many native Hispanic women who live in the United States today, as well as the academic foci of gender dialogues in contemporary psychoanalytic thought. They will provide a rich field of information for answering the questions posed for me by Freud's young lesbian patient: Within the deeply embedded matrix of patriarchal law, how have women gone about the business of reconfiguring and reorganizing their gendered self-experiences and erotic relationships?

Using the refreshing context of this multidisciplinary volume, I will take some departure from the traditional illustrative case presentations of clinical texts and include instead a personal/family description of gender life in the Latin American world. From this subjective perspective I hope to illuminate how a group of women from a particular segment of ethnohistory went about the same task assumed by Freud's patient: saying no to the "word of the father."

The Latin American Gender System—*Sin Ilusión*

Genderedness is very serious business in Latin American culture.

For the purpose of this essay I have defined Latin American culture as those broad ethnocultural features common to the 18 Spanish- and 1 Portuguese-speaking countries of the Americas. Each of these countries has a distinct history, national culture, class distribution, and unique blend of Indian, African, and European intermixture. However, they share as their common history conquest by Europeans, and by virtue of this, a near-common Spanish language and religious Catholic ethic that permeates individual, family, and institutional life.

Like the sociocultural markers displayed in Freud's piece, the gender construction system in Latin America is deeply entrenched in the reproductive distinctions between women and men. This is a system that offers no respite from the reified bifurcations of physical anatomy and the specified array of human activities and experiences that are assigned to each gender by culture. As aptly described by Dimen (1991), culture has used anatomical difference as a "force field" of sorts for the psychic self: tagging, magnetizing, and parsing human attributes into oppositional poles demarcated by male and female, dominant and submissive, active and passive. Thus, the gender construction project is pursued relentlessly in most Latin American homes. Female and male genderedness, respectively, tightly configures, prescribes, and packages a large spectrum of distinct affective, imaginal, cognitive, and behavioral self-experiences and actions. There is very little self that is left nongendered in this kind of culture.

As dramatically illuminated in Freud's historical piece, men in the Latin American culture are likewise the sanctioned gatekeepers of the strict gender bifurcation system. As the guardians of both their gender's agency and that of the female's, Latin men stand square in the middle of a gender politic that is based on relationship domination (Flax, 1990). In addition, special social and historical influences (which are not unique to Latin culture) have in fact elevated the "word of the father" into a social cult. This is *machismo*—the cult of the man, which throughout Latin America is firmly rooted in patriarchal law and male privilege over women. Within the purview of this cult lie male agency, dominance, a subjective sense of invulnerability, and sexual prowess. Goldwert (1985) has conjectured that the vehemence behind Latin American male dominance of women is a projected displacement or enactment of the subjugation he himself suffered at the hands of the European conquistador.

At the opposite extreme lies the cult of the woman that prevails throughout Catholic Latin America. *Marianismo* is the cult of one who submits. Symbolized by the virgin mother Mary, this cult encourages an idealized identification with a female self who roundly accepts her socially impotent status, possesses no sexual or aggressive agency, and furthers her self-development only by nurturing others. Formidable social rewards are garnered by women for the attentive care of children and for their overt resilience after repeated trauma. In an interesting double bind, they are also rewarded for overt displays of sexual coquettishness that must be devoid, however, of real sexual desire. While contemporary feminist trends have made inroads into countries such as Colombia, Argentina, and Cuba, the dominant gender system in most Latin American countries still remains firmly rooted in male hegemony (Rich & Arguelles, 1985).

These are clearly generalized social norms; however, like all group-specific ethnocultural constructions, they provide a scaffold around which self-experiences are organized and interpersonal operations are negotiated and eventually internalized as object relational structures. I understand ethnocultural influences as systems of common understanding shared by a group of people about their internal selves, external worlds, and connection to others. The manifest Latin system of understanding gender identity and object-choice, like the system in which the young lesbian woman finds herself is one tightly yoked to biological taxonomy. However, Latinos seem to have further sealed their gender fates through the ideals of gender cults, elaborating the meaning of gender role expectation to tremendous proportions. In this emotionally measured essay, it is difficult to express the intense sense of gendered entrapment for Latin women, who in their own countries aim to expand the definition of self through voice, worldly movement, or sexual expression. The multiple sets of meanings that strangle such aims encompass sin, deep cultural betrayal, nonwomanliness, and psychic murder of the family. In speaking of gender in parts of Latin America, Almaguer (1993), an anthropologist, points to how deeply the "psychic cartography" is etched in the "physical (anatomical) landscape." This is not dissimilar to Harris' contemporary analytic position that anatomical definitions of gender leave precious little space for creating new meaning, new interpretation, or new ventures into self-experience. These are gender systems *sin ilusión* without hope of becoming anything more.

Caribbean Gender Training—a Personal Family Journey

The following is a vignette from my own early life that takes place in the Caribbean of the 1960s. Its similarity to the middle-class sociofamilial milieu of Freud's young patient is strikingly similar.

During my summers as a child, I was sent to my immigrant parents' Caribbean country to become acculturated in formal Latin American ways and particular gender habits. This was a place where "girls were girls" and "boys were boys." The compelling cultural significance of these gendered concepts was reflected in often-used colloquial expressions that referred to a young woman or man who had satisfactorily evolved through her or his gender training: *una mujer hecha y derecha* (a correctly behaving and properly formed woman) and *un macho hecho y derecho* (a correctly behaving and properly formed man). In the evenings after supper, the adults would congregate on porch rockers. In practiced gestures, the women cooled themselves with Spanish fans, and the men fumed over politics and cigars. If you were a *señorita* (having had your first period), you could no longer ride bikes or play ball on the sidewalk. You could, however, stroll around the church square with your girlfriends, who were often *amigas intimas*—intimate female friends with whom you shared deep affection and confidence (Hidalgo & Christensen, 1977). Permission to take these walks, however, and the standard blessing offered on departure (*la bendición*) was given by whatever paternal figure was in residence. I once asked my mother why this was necessary, and she told me that a man in the house needed to be on the alert in case a girl ever strayed or needed to be rescued.

It was in the square that some of the girls engaged in a ritual—they coquetted with boys. Those girls who were interested, willing, and well-initiated in the rules had dressed seductively for the boys and learned jokes for them. If you were going to school in North America like me, you were supposed to speak English for them. One thing was clear: You did not emerge with a social position or value in the church square culture of budding *mujeres* and *machos* unless a boy had found you worthwhile to engage in conversation. Intelligence, outside of interpersonal social craft, was never even a playing card in this game except as a cloddish, nonfeminine quality. Those girls with no interest in this ritual were relegated to a marginal social group in this ruthlessly segregated culture. No accepted social space existed, of course, for a girl to love another girl. The venue that had developed for *amigas intimas* was firmly closed to any acceptable adolescent exploration once the *machos* had entered the social scene. At least in the hetero-dominant milieu of the Caribbean 1960s, lesbianism and male homosexuality were naively seen as an American-European peculiarity, not something that was borne from our people (*no nace de nosotros*). Thus, for young girls, the game of heterosexual coquette was the only act accepted in town. And it was a contrived one at that, because at least in the middle class, real sexual exploration could dangerously lead to a serious fall from the *marianismo* ideal. My adolescent rebellion eventually took the form of refusing to attend this yearly Caribbean gender-training camp and of engaging in as much risk-taking as the North American 1960s had to offer!

My mother had come from a family of six boys and three girls. What is of interest here is that the girls all emigrated to the United States. The boys stayed behind on native land to pursue the family business: the overthrow of a despotic dictator on the island. I was told that the women had emigrated to North America for political safety, and indeed, several brothers were subsequently killed or disappeared in attempted coups. However, as I grew up in the more balanced gender panorama of New York City, I came to understand that the women had in fact come to the United States to claim their womanhoods, for each in her own way had been deeply moved, molded, or maddened by the regimes of the family's own patriarchal dictatorship. These women subsequently had daughters, and as a group we essentially comprised a female collective dedicated to one common task: restructuring the definition of how to be female. For the women in this family, the migration to North America provided both the real and psychic catapult for undertaking the formidable task of engaging the internalized representations of our gendered selves. From our vantage point, these were selves that had been shaped, envisioned, and willed upon us by our fathers.

Is There Life after the Male Imaginary?

Luce Irigaray (1985) has essentially posed the question (as have other postmodern feminist writers): Is there life after complete immersion in the male imaginary? Can we construct our female lives outside the symbolic system constructed for us by the Latin male hegemony? After heavy training in an arch form of female masquerade (Butler, 1990), can we ever stop performing to consider the meaning of what we are doing?

As I have worked with people from varied cultures (Pérez Foster, 1992; 1993; 1996a, b, c; 1998), I have learned that all immigrants share a common feature apart from the separation anxieties and narcissistic issues that tend to dominate initial clinical presentation. Immigrants are all actively immersed in the creative developmental process of constructing new meanings in their symbolic worlds. The wish to redefine both the parameters of the self and the systems of meaning that explain human acts is the driving force behind many voluntary migrations. The immigrant who has planned her move has also spent long hours conjuring herself in new spaces, contexts, and relationships. This is certainly the case in point for the women of my family who saw the United States as both open territory for creating new definitions of their gender and transitional space for rewriting the forced heterosexual scripts mandated by their culture.

This has been a tremendous process for all of us who—through varying levels of life experience, partnership experiments, education, psychoanalysis, new identifications, and sheer will—have managed to create lives far from the performances in the church square. We are extremely diverse in character, age, sexual preference, lifestyle, and spheres of interests; however, we all share a habit of asserting our voices in our respective professions or social/community groups. This is jokingly referred to as the female form of rebellion against the Caribbean dictator, but the interpretation is apt, for it embodies the dynamics recently elaborated by Benjamin (1988) in her expansion of the traditional Freudian views on gender development. In speaking of women, Benjamin underscores the tragedy of sociocultural traditions that have permitted the girl's identification with female figures but no more connection to the father/man than as his sexual object. But what of her attraction to the father/man's agency and mastery in the world? Sadly, for many women these latter human qualities have heretofore been relegated to the male sector of the gender force field (Dimen, 1991). As we know, in large sections of the Western world, these gender constructs have thankfully begun to shift in the last few decades. However, for many women of the Latin *machista* cultures, it is only in the neutralized territory of a foreign country—far away from the patriarch's seductive and inhibiting gaze—that they have permitted themselves, and been permitted, identification with his agency, worldly inquisitiveness, sexual expression, and public voice. This is to say that as women, they have expanded the imaginal and living configuration permitted to female gender in Latin American life, but have done so with caution, when they were far away and subjectively out of harm's way. The migratory distance seems to serve a dual function, a compromise formation, as it were: It provides fertile space for new self-growth, as well as a safe distance from the source of conflict.

Fear and anxiety can thus be familiar companions in this gender expansion project, as the migratory respite from life in the patriarchal regime often gives way to early self-states and the unconscious tropisms of psychic transference. We optimistically view these symptoms as auspicious signs of the collapse of reified gender forms. However, we are watching closely and are taking great care and action with our next generation of daughters, offering them models of being human and being women that hopefully span far beyond the cultural norms of our early upbringing.

As for the domain of intimate relationships, it is in this arena that our emigrated family of women is more individually complex and comparatively diverse. It is here that in varying degrees and forms we expose the deep tracks of the patriarchally ordered bifurcations we are trying to eschew. Psychoanalytic clinicians have pointed out that human connections are always formed on an exciting edge, hovering between the bright hope of creating new relational experiences and the dim assumption of finding past disappointments in the present (Fairbairn, 1952; Seinfeld, 1995). Thus, we shift and slide between psychically old and expectantly new object connections, transferring our complex aims to the women and men of our partnered lives.

The varied relationships in our family of women are far more easily described through power dynamics than sexual preference. There are some whose female potency in the external world, for example, belies a home life characterized by deferral to a dominant partner. Dulce, a hospital administrator, feels loved and protected by her lesbian partner. Dulce is especially demonstrative in her nurturing style and also shows her partner the *respeto*—quiet deference to an esteemed authority—that a traditional Latin wife would show a husband. Patricia, who employs several people in her own successful business, is married to a man who consistently mismanages finances at home and in his workplace. However, Patricia is unable to offer him constructive suggestions, much less assume financial control, since she feels that directly exposing his vulnerability would shame him as a man.

While Dulce and Patricia have undoubtedly deconstructed some of the gender expectations of their early training, they still hold fast to what Flax (1990) would call culturally sanctioned systems that offer meaning and organization to their relationships. Psychoanalysts would view these interactions as reflective of the varied and fluctuating unconscious transferences and self-other internalizations that come to life in the intimate presence of another. Dulce consciously emigrated to the United States to form a relational life on her own terms outside the forced heterosexuality (Rich, 1990) of her native culture. Patricia used the freer social/economic enterprise of North America to exercise creative aspects of self that would have never been permitted expression at home. However, both women imbue their significant other with a power that serves as the pivot around which they consciously or unconsciously organize many of their relational actions and submissions. Whether one views this dynamic as a variant mode of human relational contact deconstructed of gender meaning, or as an example of psychic bisexuality (McDougall, 1986) or as a parodic imitation of fluid versus fixed gendered identification (Butler, 1990), I believe this connection to be based on a deeply grooved (across culture and time) patriarchal transference. Notwithstanding its potential associations with maternally transferred vicissitudes, this dynamic represents a formidable legacy from the male dominance hegemony of male–female dyads.

But then there are other women from the extended family group—those who have created a type of male or female partnership where power distributions and gender-associated habits shift, collapse, and interact, easily heeding the exigencies of immediate needs or external practical demands, rather than the protocols of social script. These are selves in relationships who operate in what Dimen (1991) would consider deconstructed gender fields. However, it is of interest to note that these women have all formed these partnerships with someone who is not from their own Caribbean background. It is only with a "foreigner," so to speak, someone from a different part of Latin America or the non-Spanish-speaking world, that they are able to live outside the early gender training program. On the one hand this is easily explained by the women's exposure to the multicultural environment of North America and by their assumption of North American social values (Pérez Foster, 1996a). Most of us would label ourselves "bicultural": Latin American and North American in varying degrees. To this explanation, we would also add the subjective impression that a native Caribbean who is not wedded to some form of the domination hegemony is hard to find! All manifestly true. But the well-known secret among us is that we also use the "Other" to disguise what still remains of an unresolved anxiety about saying no to the "word of the father," which would mean turning to the familiar Caribbean face and stating in a clear voice how we have shaped our own agency and privilege. Whether we assess our relationship choices on the external face of female oppression in patriarchal Latin American lifestyle or on the internal face of psychic internalization and conflict, there is anguish for all of us in realizing that we seem to have traded self-development for living in the diaspora.

Is There Life beyond the Gendered Imaginary?

Freud's young patient was more courageous than we. Ensconced within the rigid social perimeter of her bourgeoisie Viennese world, she nevertheless protested her confinement and squarely faced her father and eventually his surrogate. Having felt strong-armed by the dominant majority and unable to live the contrived heterosexual life that her father would coerce her into, this girl—

who expressed no emotional complaints other than wanting to pursue romantic love—had made an attempt on her life.

Attempted suicide, leaving one's country of origin, involuntary submission to another—these are monumental acts. They are extreme responses and rebellions to the gender mandate, to maintenance of the deeply grooved cultural definitions of male and femaleness, and to the day-to-day lives that must follow from such relationship arrangements. In her essay "Toward a Critical Relational Theory of Gender," Goldner (1991) argues not only that gender identity and conformity are culturally mandated normative ideals, but also that they require the aggressive activation of pathogenic mechanisms for their maintenance. She points out that gendered self-construction necessitates the suppression, splitting off, and denial of human self-attributes that do not conform to the gender requirement of the particular environment. This phenomenon is what I hope to have illuminated in the vignette of "Carribean gender training," along with the tenacity of this training's influence on a subsequent generation of women.

My particular response to Freud's essay on his treatment of a young lesbian woman emerged from a specific focus: her crisis over heeding or discarding her father's vision for her life. From my own very personal worldview, I have explored some ways in which a group of immigrant women have also said "no" to this paternal vision. I am well aware that shifting the cultural meaning systems that configure the female gendered self must move far beyond single acts of rejecting the male imaginary to volitional, self-propelled constructions of experience and action. Beyond these gendered constructions, cultural systems—as interpreted by family systems, as internalized by individual psyches—may very well move toward the construction of a multifaceted and variegated human self that is beyond any gendered imaginary at all.

References

Almaguer, T. (1993). Chicano men: A cartography of homosexual identity and behavior. In H. Abelove, M. Barale, & D. Halperin, (Eds.) *The lesbian and gay studies reader.* New York: Routledge.

Benjamin, J. (1988). *The bonds of love.* New York: Pantheon Books.

Burch, B. (1993). Gender identities, lesbianism, and potential space. *Psychoanalytic Psychology, 10,* 359–375.

Butler, J. (1990). *Gender trouble: Feminism and the subversion of identity.* New York: Routledge.

Dimen, M. (1991). Deconstructing difference: Gender, splitting and transitional space. *Psychoanalytic Dialogues, 1,* 335–352.

Fairbairn, W. R. (1952). *Psychoanalytic studies of personality.* London: Tavistock Publications.

Flax, J. (1990). *Thinking fragments.* Berkeley: University of California Press.

Freud, S. (1953–1974). The psychogenesis of a case of homosexuality in a woman. In J. Strachey (Ed. and Trans.), *The standard edition of the complete psychological works of Sigmund Freud*. (Vol. 18, pp. 145–172). London: Hogarth. (Original work published 1920)

Freud, S. (1953–1974). Three essays on the theory of sexuality. In J. Strachey (Ed. and Trans.), *The standard edition of the complete psychological works of Sigmund Freud*. (Vol. 7, pp. 123–243). London: Hogarth. (Original work published 1905)

Goldner, V. (1991). Toward a critical theory of gender. *Psychoanalytic Dialogues, 1,* 249–272.

Goldwert, M. (1985). Mexican machismo: The flight from femininity. *Psychoanalytic Review, 72,* 161–169.

Harris, A. (1991). Gender as contradiction. *Psychoanalytic Dialogues, 1,* 197–224.

Hidalgo, H. & Christensen, E. (1977). The Puerto Rican lesbian and the Puerto Rican community. *Journal of Homosexuality, 2,* 109–121.

Irigaray, L. (1985). *This sex which is not one*. Ithaca, NY: Cornell University Press.

Lacan, J. (1977). *Écrits*. New York: Norton & Co.

McDougall, J. (1986). Eve's reflection: On the homosexual components of female homosexuality. In H. Myers (Ed.), *Between analyst and patient: New dimensions in countertransference and transference*. (pp. 213–228). Hillsdale, NJ: The Analytic Press.

Perez, E. (1994). Irigaray's female symbolic in the making of Chicana lesbian "sitios y lenguas" (sites and discourses). In L. Doan (Ed.), *The Lesbian Postmodern*. (pp. 104–117). New York: Columbia University Press.

Pérez Foster, R. (1992). Psychoanalysis and the bilingual patient: Some observations of the influence of language choice on the transference. *Psychoanalytic Psychology, 9,* 61–75.

Pérez Foster, R. (1993). The social politics of psychoanalysis: Commentary on Altman's "Psychoanalysis and the urban poor." *Psychoanalytic Dialogues, 3,* 69–84.

Pérez Foster, R. (1996a). The bilingual self: Duet in two voices. *Psychoanalytic Dialogues, 6,* 99–121.

Pérez Foster, R. (1996b). What is a multicultural perspective for psychoanalysis? In R. Pérez Foster, M. Moskowitz, & R. A. Javier (Eds.), *Reaching across boundaries of culture and class: Widening the scope of psychotherapy*. (pp. 3–20). Hillsdale, NJ: Jason Aronson Publishers.

Pérez Foster, R. (1996c). Assessing the psychodynamic function of language in the bilingual speaker. In R. Pérez Foster, M. Moskowitz, & R. A. Javier (Eds.), *Reaching across boundaries of culture and class: Widening the scope of psychotherapy*. (pp. 243–264). Hillsdale, NJ: Jason Aronson Publishers.

Pérez Foster, R. (1998). *The power of language in the clinical process: Assessing and treating the bilingual person*. Hillsdale, NJ: Jason Aronson Publishers.

Rich, A. (1980). Compulsory heterosexuality and lesbian existence. *Signs, 5,* 631–660.

Rich, B. R. & Arguelles, L. (1985). Homosexuality, homophobia and revolution: Notes toward an understanding of the Cuban lesbian and gay male experience, part II. *Signs: Journal of Woman in Culture and Society, 11,* 120–136.

Seinfeld, J. (1995). *The bad object*. Hillsdale, NJ: Jason Aronson Publishers.

9

CONDUCT UNBECOMING
Female Inversion and Social Disorder

~

Carolyn C. Grey

Reading Freud's (1920) "The Psychogenesis of a Case of Homosexuality in a Woman" recalled a crucial bit of advice imparted to my freshman college class of 1961 on the eve of women's liberation. Our dean, or some other representative of the social order, fearful for our safety and reputations and doubting the strength of our characters, enjoined us to repulse untoward invitations from boys and other miscreants with the firmly indignant assertion that "I am a Wellesley girl, and, I hope, a lady!"

Like Christian crosses thrust at vampires, that deceptively naive statement invoked the scathing force of a moral order, defined for us by social class and gender imperatives, where Right was Right, and Wrong was virtually unthinkable. In this order, principles of morality, mental hygiene, and propriety were seamlessly fused into an apparently impenetrable shield against the forces of evil, insanity, and bad manners. These principles shaped our deepest fears and desires, the guiding images for our lives and our will to pursue them.

We knew what was expected of us: Having turned 18 (like Freud's young lady), and having been accepted into this bastion of the enlightened upper middle class, we had the responsibility to ensure that our conduct was "becoming"—fitted to our privileged social position and to our status as Wellesley girls and ladies. Make no mistake: We were not to be doormats or bimbos. It was assumed we would develop our intellects and commit them to worthy personal and social causes. But come what may, we would be well-bred, well-rounded, and refined.

141

Some of us snickered at the proffered advice and what we considered the hopelessly prissy, obsolete pretensions and inhibitions it implied. Some of us would, within a few years, begin raising our consciousnesses about gender and thinking of ourselves as neither "girls" nor "ladies" but women. In the meantime, we rebelled in our own ideologically unguided and unimaginative ways by breaking as many rules as possible about curfews, domestic neatness, smoking, drinking, dress codes, bad language, and boys (sex).

No doubt our parents would have been horrified had they been aware of our shenanigans. (Thirty years later, my own parents have not forgiven Wellesley for the unfeminine Anglo-Saxon vulgarities they think I learned there.) But for the most part, they were blessedly ignorant, principally because, however daring, subversive, or avant-garde we thought we were, we committed no major public transgressions against the moral and aesthetic imperatives of our elite social world. We had our little rebellions to establish our right to individuality, and then, only partly aware, we fell into line. We upheld the honor code, took seriously our noblesse oblige, pursued high culture in the form of operas, concerts, plays, and art museums, and practiced with feminine reticence the sports appropriate to our station (fencing, crew, sailing, tennis, horseback riding). We could be relied on at critical junctures to display impeccable grooming and manners, to know the correct use of eating utensils, to chew with our mouths closed, to send thank you notes for gifts and invitations, and to wear basic black dresses with pearls to mixers and blind dates. Our sexual practices, to the extent that we had them, were timid and conventional. We gossiped avidly about one girl who boldly declared she "had to have it" as she signed out overnight with forged permission from home. We were shocked (titillated? revolted?) to learn about oral sex. And, none of us even knew a homosexual (whatever that was!). Probably most important, whatever our intellectual achievements, we were prepared to abandon all independent aspirations when opportunities arose for falling in love, marrying, and having offspring. Every junior I knew dreamed of becoming one of those serene seniors who proudly sported tasteful diamond engagement rings and who could postpone indefinitely planning autonomous lives.

Not one of us had come to Wellesley without significant intellectual achievements and proven other interests (the well-roundedness criterion). So each of us was clearly strong-willed and ambitious in having pursued the opportunities conceivable in our limited imaginations and supported by our social worlds. We were also definite individuals with idiosyncratic characters and life experiences. But notwithstanding our differences, most of us arrived at post-college adulthood with unclear images of what we could be other than wives and only vague yearnings for something more than love and marriage.

My own precollege life prepared me well to reach adulthood confused and adrift. It had become clear to me in my adolescent social group that girls should be careful about displaying untoward intelligence, ambition, or sexuality lest they be seen as unfeminine and undesirable by suitable middle-class boys. My parents were pleased by my academic competence, yet they seemed less interested in my intellectual development than in my brother's or in my future as mate to some socially desirable, ambitious man. They did their best to instruct me in a variety of social graces like bridge, golf, and cooking for company, all of which would be necessary were I to play hostess to my husband's business associates and their similarly equipped wives. They policed my sexual virtue and reputation by imposing curfews and haranguing me with "What will the neighbors think?" when I spent more than two minutes saying goodnight to my dates in the driveway. And they did their best to protect me by encouraging me to get a teaching certificate "to fall back on" in the cataclysmic event that I ended up without a man.

I was painfully sensitive to the messages from peers—not so sensitive as to give up my intellectual ambitions, but sensitive enough to hide them behind an ambivalent nonchalance. Meanwhile, my parents bore the brunt of my confusion about what I wanted for myself and of my resentment about the requirement that I shape myself to someone else's idea of desirable femininity. Their attempts at guidance were met with sullen annoyance, partly because I hated being consigned to a subsidiary role in life and partly because my parents' relation to each other and to me, while responsible, was also critical and angry. In any case, I horrified them by blatantly conveying my contempt for their conformist lives, reading Jack Kerouac, dressing in torn jeans and black turtlenecks, drinking, smoking, and refusing to learn the graces they saw as necessary to sustain a lady-like upper-middle-class life.

But after college, I succumbed to a failure of nerve and imagination. I floundered for six months as a $75/week clerk typist in a prestigious, stuffy publishing house in New York where all the editors were men and the head secretary was a middle-aged Radcliffe graduate. With her fate as an omen of my future, I fled into marriage to escape the suffocating glass ceiling, daunting financial poverty, and mouse-sized roaches in my tiny West Village basement apartment. It took several years of discouraged drifting and angry reliving of my mother's life to find my way to an independent sense of purpose. In the meantime, like Freud's young lady, I submitted myself to a Freudian analyst who for years on end talked penis envy and transference while my disastrous marriage deteriorated and I failed to develop an alternative life.

This, then, is the personal history I bring to bear in reading Freud's case. Clearly I responded to what he must have regarded as incidental details of his narrative rather than his insights about homosexuality. In fact, from the outset I rejected his formulation of his patient's difficulty. It is at best questionable whether sex of any variety was an important factor in this young woman's story. After all, she seemed to be lacking in sexual interest and experience with partners of both sexes. Further, she did not identify herself as homosexual, did not acknowledge specifically sexual fantasies or attractions to same sex partners, had not engaged in homosexual actions "beyond a few kisses and embraces" (Freud, 1920, p. 153), chose heterosexual women as the objects of her devotion, and turned down an opportunity for sex with a female friend her own age. She even declared that her love was "pure" and that she found the idea of intercourse repellant (p. 153). Even when we take account of unconscious motivation, surely life as lived merits some recognition. But Freud, committed to confirming his libido theory, seems to have confused obsessive adulation with sexuality and to have assumed, in keeping with his culture, that homosexuality was, whatever his disclaimers, a pathological state worthy of therapeutic intervention.

I, on the other hand, was struck by the middle-class gender story and the surprising and disturbing continuity between Freud's patient's social-psychological life and my own adolescence and early adulthood. In both cases, intimate, individual family life, as well as life in the local community, offered limited legitimate versions of female identity, and these, while legitimate, were also devalued. Both her analyst and mine saw idiosyncratic pathologies where I see common struggles with the problems of gendered life for educated middle-class women in Europe and America, at least through the 1960s. Finally, the analysts in both cases played the role of conventional gender enforcers, using masculine authority to confirm devalued, underdeveloped identities and the legitimacy of entrapment in unsatisfying lives.

Were I to retell Freud's story with these observations in mind, it would not be a narrative about the sexual currents of his patient's life. Rather, it would be a story, much like my own, of how a "spirited" (p. 169) energetic, intelligent, and attractive girl grew up in a well-to-do, privileged, respected family with the gifts of education and leisure. Her own qualities—strength of will and "acuteness of comprehension" (p. 154), as well as the advantages conferred by class, might have offered opportunities for developing independent aspirations and competencies and for creating independent sources of meaning, interest, and self-valuation. Nonetheless, she arrived at 18 in a state of confusion and desperation, unable to conduct her life in a meaningful, purposeful way. Instead, she attached herself to a woman who offered her neither love nor guidance, nor a capacity for fidelity. The mystery is not what happened to her sexuality. It is what aborted the development of her resources for living and her judgment about her own and her lady's worthiness for love.

One strand of this story, like mine, must have to do with her family life—its emotional climate, its potential for confirmation, comfort, and guidance, and its encouragement of growth. In spite of their excellent social credentials, the parents seem to have conveyed an attitude of indifference and even hostility to their daughter, while at the same time they indulged and favored her brothers. The father was stern with all his children, though apparently he was more reserved and despotic with his daughter. The mother was capable at times of attending to her daughter's feelings but more often was apt to be harsh and competitive with her. The mother also "limited her independence as much as possible"(p. 157). From the age of 16, the daughter seems to have begun looking outside the family for the parental love and guidance she could not rely on at home.

Another strand to this story involves the confluence of cultural and familial expectations and valuations related to this young woman's gender development. At 18 years of age, she found herself in a familial and cultural milieu where, having attained near-adulthood of the female variety, she was expected to focus her energies on grooming herself and being available for marriage, regardless of her own inclinations, reservations, and anxieties. For her, there was no other legitimate purpose to her life than being some proper man's proper wife. She was also expected to submit to parental—mostly paternal—authority and to protect her own and her family's reputations and social standing through conduct becoming to her status as upper-middle-class young lady.

In this same cultural and familial situation, she as a girl was less valued than her brothers, received less attention and consideration than they, and had less freedom of action and ambition. All of this was particularly galling to a girl gifted with spirit and intelligence who had grown up romping and fighting. She envied her brothers and rebelled against the lot of women (p. 169). Thus, at the same time that she was lonely, dependent, and starved for affection, she was also angry and questing for alternatives to an adult femininity that meant submission and loss. These two seemingly disparate strands of character converged in her falling in love with an older woman who seemed both strong and noble, an idealized maternal substitute who was also an ideal goad to her family by virtue of her gender and reputation as a "*cocotte*." The girl's offense was compounded by making a public spectacle of her love, deceiving her parents, and publicly attempting suicide.

Notwithstanding her apparent rebelliousness in the realm of love, Freud's patient seems very much bound by convention and need for her family's attention and approval. She cared enough for her father's rejection that she attempted suicide after his angry glance and then submitted herself, however ambivalently, to analysis with Freud. She also promised to give up the lady at the end of her aborted treatment (p. 164). Her routine social behavior was also conforming.

Freud himself described her approvingly as "well brought up and modest" (p. 161) and "by no means lacking in a sense of decency and propriety" (p. 147).

Even her deception, manipulation, and self-destructive behavior seem predictably feminine to the extent that dependent and devalued people often do not feel themselves to have the option of direct, forthright challenges to those on whose good will they depend. Her unconscious, too, was apparently conventional. Though Freud later recanted, he initially interpreted her dreams as confessing "her longing for a man's love and children" and "her joy over the prospects . . . that would be opened before her if she were cured of her inversion "(p. 165).

In addition, the girl's choice of a female object for her affection was not as daring as it appears. First, notwithstanding sometimes hostile reactions from adults, particularly male authorities in both public and private realms (especially educators and scientists), at least in England and the United States in the late nineteenth and early twentieth centuries, the kind of adolescent crush on an older woman exhibited in this case was quite common. This was particularly true in middle-class girls' circles where these relationships were dubbed "romantic friendships" (see Vincinus, 1989). That Freud's patient's friends and even her mother were not at first shocked by her crush suggests that she was not defying custom. Also, perhaps more to the point, the form her attachment took—of an obsessive quest for romantic love, which required abandoning her rebellious spirit, intellectual gifts, her education, and her life with friends—conforms perfectly to the still operative gender imperative for women to live lives of "relatedness as purpose" (Grey, 1991). Far from becoming a man as Freud claimed, she remained every inch a stereotypical woman in yielding her will, and even her life, to another's acceptance and approval.

Half a century later, researchers from the 1970s to the present have documented the pervasiveness of women's orientation to connection. This orientation manifests itself in the realm of moral values (Gilligan, 1982; Kohlberg, 1981), academic and professional life (Alper, 1974; Horner, 1972), friendship patterns (Rubin, 1985), and desire for intimacy (Bartholomew & Horowitz, 1991). Archer (1996) summarizes these studies, which confirm women's focus on "communion" versus men's orientation toward "agency." Miller (1986) concludes, "[W]omen tend to find satisfaction, pleasure, effectiveness, and a sense of worth if they experience their life activities as arising from and leading back into a sense of connection with others" (cited in Mann, 1991). For women in our time and Freud's, this has meant negating and crippling the female self through concealing or dissociating significant aspects of identity or desire, denying competence, and failing to pursue goals that might threaten the harmonies of gendered social life (Grey, 1991). Ambition, intelligence, competitiveness, and conflict exist within a male-only preserve qualities to be extirpated or at least buried under a pleasingly feminine appearance. The power of this female orientation is demonstrated in the ideas of even some current feminist gender theorists who celebrate women's presumed innate relational capacities without noting the unfounded essentialism of their own theories and without taking account of the negative characteristics and consequences that accompany exaggerated dependency on others (see Cixous, 1975; Gilligan, 1982; Irigaray, 1977; Miller, 1986 [cited in Mann, 1991]). As Frosh (1989) points out, this line of thinking "risks absorption in a romantic image of womanhood which characterizes some of the crudest sexist discourses" (p. 171).

Freud's "homosexual" patient was not alone in her own time. Her familial/cultural and psychological dilemmas were echoed by the cast of women in *Studies in Hysteria* (Freud, 1895). The self-destructive illnesses endured by these women testify poignantly to the double binds that women lived, and to the failure of Freud's sexualized intrapsychic theory to help them find their way. The intelligence, energy, and independent strivings, casually noted by Freud himself as asides to his sexual theorizing, were paralyzed by the force of social expectations and by the women's equally strong inner imperatives to maintain their place in their communal and familial worlds by living gendered lives.

The 21-year-old Anna O., treated by Breuer from 1880–1882, was well educated and had "great poetic and imaginative gifts," "penetrating intuition," "a powerful intellect," and "sharp and critical common sense." She was also a woman of "energetic" and "tenacious" willpower (Freud, 1895, p. 21). Yet energy and intelligence were stifled by the constraints of living a "monotonous life" with her "puritanical family," in which she devoted herself to nursing her sick and dying father. The lack of opportunity and of sanction for developing her own purposes and talents were manifested in and reproduced by her feminine character—a "sympathetic kindness" that led her to "look after a number of poor sick people" (p. 21). No thanks to Breuer, she emerged in the 1890s as Bertha Pappenheim, pioneer social worker, feminist, Jewish, activist, and writer, a "tireless fighter against injustice" (Appignanesi & Forrester, 1992, p. 78).

Emmy Von N., a 40-year-old widow, was also described by Freud (1920) as having had an unusual degree of education and intelligence (p. 49), "moral seriousness . . . and energy" (p. 103). But the "natural helplessness of a woman" (p. 102) combined with her identity as a "true lady" ensured the sacrifice of these resources to "her benevolent care for . . . all her dependents, her humility of mind, and refinement of manners" (pp. 103–104). Freud, her analyst, clearly approved her self-effacing character, without recognizing the personal cost it entailed.

Elizabeth Von R., another highly intelligent young woman, "was indignant at the idea of having to sacrifice her inclinations and freedom of judgement by marriage" (Freud, 1920, p. 140). Freud disapprovingly describes her as "too positive in her judgements . . . [and] regardlessly telling people the truth" (p. 140). Yet she too was paralyzed—caught between her loyalty to her family, her own need to find her worth in being a caretaker, and her urge to satisfy her independent affectional and achievement needs. She too fell into line, nursing others yet suffering great guilt for her fantasized transgressions of the moral (gender) order.

And, of course, there was Dora (Freud, 1905 [1901]), a spiritual twin of our anonymous putative lesbian, another young woman who was intellectually precocious, gifted, independent of judgment, and bored with her feminine life. Dora, too, had a mother who offered her little nurturance and who obviously preferred Dora's brother (the *coup de grace* to her daughter's value as woman). She too sought maternal substitutes who failed her. And she too despaired to the point of threatening suicide. As in the other case, her parents turned her over to Freud ostensibly out of concern for her welfare but clearly also because her behavior was disrupting their lives. And, as in the other case, Freud assumed the role of paternal authority and social role enforcer, indoctrinating her in the sexual etiology of her unhappiness and letting her go when she rebelled against his tender ministrations.

Overall, the picture that emerges of these cases is one of women (and girls) who had considerable personal resources but who lacked any acceptable model for how to use them and who were dependent on familial relationships in which they were neglected, devalued, or exploited. Given their families' and society's valuation of girls and women, they had little sense of self-worth and no vision of or hope for constructive change. In fact, they were caught not only between their private desires and personal and social gender imperatives but also between being bad (nonconforming)—and hence devalued—and being good (conforming)—and hence a woman and hence devalued. Further, it seems that some of these women had been valued as children for their intelligence and independence (Dora, Anna O., Elizabeth Von R.), but the passage to adult femininity required them to deny or disown these valued traits. (See Broverman, Broverman, Clarkson, Rosenkrantz, & Vogel, 1970, and Brown & Gilligan, 1992, for contemporary equivalents to these dilemmas.)

Hysteria (or romantic obsession) became a way out for these women, a solution that maintained connection through disavowing conflict and difference. The women's anger, self-assertion, and despair converged and emerged distorted in socially accepted illness, at once a communication of distress and a rebellion against social and familial tyranny (much as bulimia and anorexia have become the language of simultaneous rebellion and submission for contemporary young women).

There was something to be gained for all the participants. For the women, as Smith-Rosenberg (1985b) points out: "[N]o longer did she devote herself to the needs of others, acting as self-sacrificing wife, mother or daughter: through her hysteria she could . . . force others to assume those functions. . . . Through her illness, the . . . woman came to dominate her family" (p. 208). She could maintain her status as proper woman while simultaneously extorting caretaking and dispensing revenge.

For the masculine establishment, the benefits of the hysterical solution were even clearer. While individual husbands or fathers might be inconvenienced and burdened, they did not have to examine the moral implications of their own and their sons' privileged positions in relation to the women they presumably loved. And, more important for both male and female constituents of the social order, no radical change was necessary if the women could be written off as sick from unsatisfied sexuality. As Appignanesi and Forrester (1992) point out, "The label 'hysteric' [and homosexual] legitimized the increasingly endangered status quo in a period of rising demands for equality and independence" (p. 68).

Freud himself was probably unaware of the social and political meanings and consequences of his psychoanalysis or the ways in which he acted as an agent of social control. He saw himself as a theorist of biological science and a practitioner of scientific medicine. Basing his psychology on the physical reality of the body—specifically its innate sexual drives—legitimized its scientific status and was in keeping with work by influential thinkers of his day. As Foucault (1990) demonstrates, in nineteenth-century medicine, psychiatry, and pedagogy, sex was regarded as "a cause of any and everything." In fact, "there was scarcely a malady or physical disturbance to which the nineteenth century did not impute at least some degree of sexual etiology" (Foucault, p. 65). Given Freud's theory, his mission with his patients was clear: to reconstruct the sexual currents of their lives, to observe the reliving of that history in the transference, and to overcome the patient's resistance to insight about the infantile sexual origins of their troubles (1920, p. 152).

In all of this talk about sex, Freud (and other sexologists like Kraft-Ebbing and Havelock Ellis) took an explicitly moral stand. His goal was to liberate sexuality from the prudery and hypocrisy of bourgeois morality, to gain acceptance for the multiplicity of sexual desires that being human entails, and to understand these desires through scientific study. But as liberator, his mission was limited in scope. While he wrote a great deal about the normality of sexual feelings of every sort, particularly in polymorphously perverse childhood, he did not suggest that it is normal, healthy, or acceptable for adults to live unconventional sex lives. This is particularly true in "Psychogenesis," where the "considerable measure of . . . homosexuality . . . in normal people" is rel-

egated to the "latent or unconscious" (p. 171), where consummated homosexual loving is at best "irregularity," "a misfortune like any other" (p. 149),
and where "the homosexual" is portrayed by implication as pleasure-driven,
weak, and devious (p. 151). While he condemns society for its prudery about
sexuality in the abstract and while he notes the "social disadvantages and dangers attaching to [their] choice of object" (p. 151), Freud does not recommend
that society should change its attitude toward or treatment of homosexuals.
"Favorable" outcome from psychoanalysis is not self-acceptance but conversion to heterosexuality (p. 151).

Freud's essential ambivalence toward his emancipatory moral project is
nowhere more obvious that in the constant oscillation between words like
"normal," "natural," "intelligible," "common" (pp. 149, 151, 154, 155, 157,
158, 159, 167, 168, 171) and words like "disorder," "sexual impulsion," "inversion," "abnormality," "victim to homosexuality" (pp. 140, 151, 152, 157, 154,
168) used to describe the same phenomenon. At the end of the case history,
Freud the conservative moralist seems to seize victory over Dr. Freud the liberator. He offers hope for a solution to the bind he has written his way into by
suggesting that a cure for female homosexuality might one day be available
through operations similar to those "remarkable transformations that Steinach
has effected" by replacing "what are probably hermaphroditic ovaries" (p. 172)
with properly feminine ones.

As with homosexuality, also with gender issues. Again we have Freud the scientist whose moral message is disguised as scientific realism. He suggests that we
are all a mixture of masculine and feminine qualities and that there is no necessary link between gender traits and homosexuality. Further, he acknowledges
that masculine and feminine are conventional distinctions, not scientific categories. These observations would seem to open the door to a culturally con-
textualized theory and to a tolerance for diverse ways of living male and female.
Indeed, when he describes the women in his case histories as intelligent or spirited, it is often in terms that suggest admiration (see earlier). And he seems to
have accepted many of his female colleagues as worthy intellects with independent lives. Nonetheless, he clearly reserves his highest praise for masculine men
and for women who show conventional inclination toward caretaking and self-
effacement (see *Studies in Hysteria*). In "Psychogenesis," Freud ends in the
anomalous position of disputing the scientific basis of the masculine/feminine
distinction (p. 154) while at the same time saying that psychoanalysis takes this
same distinction as its basis (p. 171). Thereby he legitimizes the gender order
that he has just, however inadvertently, called into question. Had he thought
further, he might have seen a compelling link between that order and the illnesses he sought to treat.

In fact, one can read the case histories as inadvertent commentaries on the upper-middle-class good life, including, but not limited to, its gender and sexual arrangements. Freud slips from the role of cool objective scientist into the role of purveyor of bourgeois social practices and arbiter of values—an early twentieth-century cross between Amy Vanderbilt on manners and Dr. Spock on childrearing. Assuming consensus with his reader, in "Psychogenesis" he adjudicates the actors' worthiness of their social class and gender, the adequacy of their social role performance, the normality (social acceptability) of their motives and deeds. The family is introduced approvingly as being "of good standing" (p. 147), the father as "earnest and worthy . . . at bottom very tender hearted," although too "stern" toward his children and too "considerate" of his wife (p. 149). The mother, on the other hand, is described as inadequate as a woman and mother because of her harsh and competitive attitude toward her daughter and, significantly, her inability to renounce her own "claims to attractiveness" (p. 149), which presumably mature women must do.

The girl's would-be lover is described approvingly as having a "distinguished name" (p. 147), "good birth," and perhaps "much nobility of character" (p. 153). The latter judgment is granted on the basis of her advice to the girl to give up women as love-objects. On the other hand, her own sexual activity—outside of wedlock, with multiple partners, including a woman and numerous men—is roundly condemned by the labels "*cocotte*" (p. 147) and "*demi-mondaine*" (p. 153).

As for Freud's patient, her beauty, cleverness, modesty, sense of decency, and propriety are all applauded (pp. 147, 161) and her yearning for a tender mother is understood (p. 157). But the public display of her love ("neglect of her reputation") and her "deceitfulness" (p. 148) are disapproved. We learn from Freud that a good girl at 18 years of age obeys her parents, cares for her reputation, attends to educational studies, "social functions," and "girlish pleasures," is interested in young men, and maintains decorum. The only new twist to these suggestions is that she is allowed sexual curiosity (p. 155) and murderous hostility toward loved ones (p. 163), since Freud has judged these emotions, when not acted on, to be normal.

Perhaps most striking is the strength of Freud's reaction to what he sees as the girl's angry defiance, repudiation of men, and challenge to masculine authority, particularly his own (see pp. 158–169). Once on this track, he interprets her motivation as essentially hostile, including her dreams (p. 165). He ignores all evidence of her needs for tenderness, approval, or guidance, dismisses her as a "feminist" (p. 169), and in short order aborts the treatment with the rationalization that she needs a female doctor.

Freud was not the only theorist who reacted with thinly disguised rage to challenges to masculine authority and prerogative. The sexologists of his day saved their most scathing scientific condemnation for women who were non-conforming in even trivial ways. One egregious example is Krafft-Ebing, who, as Smith-Rosenberg (1985a) points out, focused on "social behavior and physical appearance" as clues to homosexuality. His own now astonishing list of telltale signs included having short hair, wearing masculine dress, pursuing masculine sports and pastimes, competing with boys, "preferring the rocking horse, playing at soldiers, etc., to dolls and other girlish occupations," and complaining of being "barred from a military career" or "deprived of the gay college life . . ." (Krafft-Ebing, 1908, cited in Smith-Rosenberg, 1985a, pp. 269–270). Thus, "women's rejection of traditional gender roles and their demands for social and economic equality" were linked to "cross dressing, sexual perversion, and borderline her-maphroditism" (Smith-Rosenberg, p. 270).

It is easy to deplore Freud's ignorance of historical contingency and of the ideological value-laden character of his theories and practice and to condemn the particular moral stand he took. But lest we become too satisfied with our-selves, we should note that morality still masquerades as science and that big-otry is alive and well on the current psychoanalytic scene. One has only to read the case discussion of Trop and Stolorow (1993) and the debate that followed about views of homosexuality in current analytic theory (Blechner, 1993; Lesser, 1993; Schwartz, 1993) to see how the best-intentioned and most sophisticated theorists and practitioners slip unaware into assumptions about the pathology of nonconforming lives. Hirsch's (1993) case and Shapiro's (1993) reply reveal the same problems in relation to gender stereotyping (see also Grey, 1991, 1993).

Gender continuity between Freud's time and ours demonstrates Fukuyama's (1995) observation that changes in cultural "habits" of feeling and action are far slower to occur than changes in ideas (p. 40). Nineteenth-century European and American middle-class culture had already produced the economic and social conditions whence a nascent feminist ideology could arise. Middle-class women, no longer bound in domestic servitude, had the money, leisure, and education to become restive in their stereotypical roles. Some women were able to use feminism to reinvent themselves. Anna O.'s transformation to the activist Bertha Pappenheim demonstrates that possibility. But there were many more women who were touched only slightly—enough to stir dissatisfaction but not to generate purposeful change. Freud accused his rebellious patient in "Psychogenesis" of being a feminist, but as Harris (1991) says, "If she was, in fact, a feminist, she was . . . quite without the support of feminism" (p. 198). She, as well as Freud's hysterics and, indeed, most other women, lacked mod-els, consensual value positions, and supportive institutions that could have helped shape confusion, resentment, and undefined longings into a coherent struggle for new identities, both personal and political. Without these supports, they remained captive to the same taken-for-granted truths (Fukuyama's [1995] "ethical habits") that Freud and his colleagues, as well as European and American middle-class society, espoused and lived. The women could not believe in the justice of their own unease and thus were caught between the choices of knuckling under or falling ill.

My generation was more fortunate in that by the 1970s, consensual habits of feeling and acting had to some extent been transformed through further changes in social institutions and economic conditions. The ideological frame of feminism and the gradual widening of its influence in the educated middle class gave women justification and will to fight more purposefully against our own dependency, self-devaluation, and fear, and to fight more purposefully for the right to define ourselves in terms of our competencies and desires, in addition to our relatedness to other people. Gay and lesbian awareness and action have followed a similar path. Neither the internal nor the external battles are won, but it is possible, in this time and place, to engage the issues in the discourse of positive aspirations rather than the discourse of medical science and illness.

Conclusion

What can psychoanalysis learn from Freud's brief encounter with the young woman in "The Psychogenesis of a Case of Homosexuality in a Woman"? We can observe at a safe distance Freud's embeddedness in the values of one segment of early twentieth-century bourgeois Viennese culture. We can discern his representation of these values as scientific knowledge in his theory of human psychology. And we can see him enact these values in his relationship with his patient as he claims authority to judge and dismiss her. But the most valuable lesson we can learn is that we ourselves are mired in the same epistemological problems as Freud. That is, my acceptance of the legitimacy of same-sex sexual love is as much a product of my zeitgeist as Freud's pathologizing is of his. The same is true of my view of what women's lives can and should be. And my collaborative model for analytic practice is also as dependent on history as Freud's authoritarian model. To speak in the discourse of medical science about psychological health and disorder or disease is simply to disguise this reality, not to alter it. However, our recognition of historical/cultural contingency can leave us with the valuable tools of constructivist skepticism and humility. These habits of mind can keep us honest about what we cannot know and keep us open to alternative visions of what constitutes a good life and how to achieve it. We can also weigh, both in psychological science and analytic practice, the personal and social consequences of these visions for particular people within particular human contexts.

References

Alper, T. (1974). Achievement motivation in college women: A now-you-see-it-now-you-don't phenomenon. *American Psychologist, 23,* 194–203.

Appignanesi, L., & Forrester, J. (1992). *Freud's women.* New York: Basic Books.

Archer, J. (1996). Sex differences in social behavior. *American Psychologist, 51*(9), 909–917.

Bartholomew, K. & Horowitz, L. M. (1991). Attachment styles among young adults: A test of a four-category model. *Journal of Personality & Social Psychology, 61,* 226–244.

Blechner, M. J. (1993). Homophobia in psychoanalytic writing and practice. *Psychoanalytic Dialogues, 3*(4), 627–638.

Broverman, I. K., Broverman, D. M., Clarkson, F. E., Rosenkrantz, P. S., & Vogel, S. R. (1970). Sex role stereotypes and clinical judgments of mental health. *Journal of Consulting and Clinical Psychology, 34,* 1–7.

Brown, L. M. & Gilligan, C. (1992). *Meeting at the crossroads: Women's psychology and girls' development.* Cambridge, MA: Harvard University Press.

Cixous, H. (1975). Sorties. In H. Cixous & C. Clement (Eds.), *The newly born woman.* (pp. 63–132). Manchester, England: Manchester University Press.

Foucault, M. (1990). *The history of sexuality, volume I: An introduction.* New York: Vintage Books. Original work published 1976.

Freud, S. (1953–1974). Studies in hysteria. In J. Strachey (Ed. and Trans.), *The standard edition of the complete psychological works of Sigmund Freud.* (Vol. 2, pp. 3–181). London: Hogarth. (Original work published 1893–1895)

Freud, S. (1953–1974). Fragment of an analysis of a case of hysteria. In J. Strachey (Ed. and Trans.) *The standard edition of the complete psychological works of Sigmund Freud.* (Vol. 7, pp. 3–122). London: Hogarth. (Original work published 1905)

Freud, S. (1953–1974). The psychoanalysis of a case of homosexuality in a woman. In J. Strachey (Ed. and Trans.), *The standard edition of the complete psychological works of Sigmund Freud.* (Vol. 18, pp. 145–172). London: Hogarth. (Original work published 1920)

Frosh, S. (1989). *Psychoanalysis and psychology.* New York: New York University Press.

Fukuyama, F. (1995). *Trust: The social virtues and the creation of prosperity.* New York: Simon & Schuster.

Gilligan, C. (1982). *In a different voice.* Cambridge, MA: Harvard University Press.

Grey, C. (1991). Relatedness as purpose: A psychoanalytic inquiry into gender imperatives for women. *Contemporary Psychoanalysis, 27*(4), 661–680.

Grey, C. (1993). Culture, character, and the analytical engagement: Toward a subversive psychoanalysis. *Contemporary Psychoanalysis, 29*(3), 487–502.

Harris, A. (1991). Gender as contradiction. *Psychoanalytic Dialogues, 1*(2), 197–224.

Hirsch, I. (1993). Countertransference enactments and some issues related to external factors in the analyst's life. *Psychoanalytic Dialogues, 3*(3), 343–366.

Horner, M. (1972) Toward an understanding of achievement-related conflicts in women, *Journal of Social Issues, 28*: 157–176.

Irigaray, L. (1977). *The sex which is not one.* Ithaca, NY: Cornell University Press.

Kohlberg, L. (1981). *The philosophy of moral development.* San Francisco: Harper and Row.

Lesser, R. C. (1993). A reconsideration of homosexual themes. *Psychoanalytic Dialogues, 3*(4), 639–641.

Mann, C. (1991). Anatomy is destiny? A new look at an old controversy. In C. Grey (Ed.), *The psychoanalyst: The interplay of work and identity.* (pp. 42–53). White Plains, NY: The Westchester Center for the Study of Psychoanalysis and Psychotherapy.

Rubin, L. (1985). *Just friends: The role of friendship in our lives.* New York: Harper and Row.

Schwartz, D. (1993). Heterophilia—the love that dare not speak its aim. *Psychoanalytic Dialogues, 3*(4), 643–652.

Shapiro, S.A. (1993). Gender role stereotypes and clinical process. *Psychoanalytic Dialogues, 3*(3), 371–387.

Smith-Rosenberg, C. (1985a). Discourses of sexuality and subjectivity: The new woman, 1870–1936. In M. Duberman, M. Vicinus, & G. Chauncey, Jr. (Eds.), *Hidden from history: Reclaiming the gay & lesbian past.* (pp. 264–280). New York: New American Library.

Smith-Rosenberg, C. (1985b). The hysterical woman: Sex roles and role conflict in nineteenth-century America. In C. Smith-Rosenberg (Ed.), *Disorderly conduct: Visions of gender in Victorian America.* (pp. 197–216). New York: Knopf. (Original work published 1972)

Trop, J. L., & Stolorow, R. D. (1993). Defense analysis in Self Psychology: A developmental view. *Psychoanalytic Dialogues, 2*(4), 427–442.

Vincinus, M. (1989). Distance and desire: English boarding school friendships, 1870–1920. In M. Duberman, M. Vicinus, & G. Chauncey, Jr. (Eds.), *Hidden from history: Reclaiming the gay & lesbian past.* (pp. 212–229). New York: New American Library. (Original work published 1984)

10

GENDER AS CONTRADICTION

~

Adrienne Harris

Gender is one of the most contested concepts in contemporary social thought and social life. Gender has provided an organizing principle for social movements and critical analyses. In some contexts, it has been seen as an inalienable fact of life and biology. Gender has also been viewed as a troublesome set of shackles, best broken off and discarded. In the last two decades, our understanding of gender experience has undergone profound critique and reframing within psychoanalytic thought and practice (Benjamin, 1988; Chodorow, 1976; Dinnerstein, 1976; Mitchell, 1975).

This article makes a contribution to these ongoing debates by considering gender as a point of paradox. Gender can be as core and coherent an experience as any structure of self and subjectivity. But gender can also mutate, dissolve, and prove irrelevant or insubstantial. In short, gender can be as fragile, as unreliable, or as tenacious as any structure of defense or layer of the self.

I begin this consideration of gender and contradiction through an extended discussion of Freud's (1920) essay on the case of homosexuality in a woman. A critique of the case, using contemporary clinical examples, is the launching point for an analysis of gender dilemmas. The aim is to challenge monolithic models of gender and to argue that a paradoxical model of gender as simultaneously tenacious and evanescent is faithful to Freud's radical vision of sexuality.

"She Was in Fact a Feminist"

This is Freud's summary judgment of a young girl sent to him by her father. The father is determined to disrupt the passionate attachment formed by his daughter for an older, disreputable woman. But this young girl is not ill, has no

156

symptoms, and has no noticeable motivation to give up her lover. She has, however, in the throes of conflict with her father and the older woman, made a serious suicide attempt.

Rounding up the usual suspects, Freud summarizes his patient's "masculinity complex":

> A spirited girl, always ready for romping and fighting, she was not at all prepared to be second to her slightly older brother; after inspecting his genital organs she had developed a pronounced envy of the penis and the thoughts derived from this envy still continued to fill her mind. She was in fact a feminist. (p. 169)

If "she was in fact a feminist," she was a feminist quite without the protection and support of feminism. Through recent work in psychoanalytic feminism, the widening theory of transference and countertransference (inherent in relational perspectives), and a semiotics-based mode of reading psychoanalytic narratives, I want to recuperate and position the woman in this case. For she is not positioned. Strikingly, the woman Freud treated and mistreated in this case has been almost completely effaced. Eclipsed under the generic terms given in the title (a "Case of Homosexuality in a Woman"), she is denied her real name on the grounds of medical discretion, but also, inexplicably, denied a metaphoric displacement into pseudonym. Without even the luxury of disguise, this woman is relegated to object status. Introduced descriptively as "a beautiful and clever girl of 18," she remains throughout the essay nameless and virtually speechless. In the course of an extended discussion of sexual object-choice, the patient loses not only her name, but even her gender in the slippage, midparagraph, to the masculine pronoun:

> Further unfavorable features in the present case were the facts that the girl herself was not in any way ill—she did not suffer from anything in herself . . . thus restoring *his* bisexuality. After that it lay with *him* to choose whether *he* wished to abandon the path that is banned by society and in some cases *he* has done so. [(pp. 150–151) italics added.]

If we cannot encounter her subjectivity, can we come closer to her desire? Again, Freud's language relegates this desire to the margins. The particular love object of our nameless, subjectless heroine is also barred from subjectivity by Freud's language. The lover is variously described by Freud as *cocotte* or *demi-mondaine* or, contemptuously, "society lady." Freud uses these quotation marks as a kind of linguistic semaphore signaling instructions on how to read this term, so that we get its ironic twist. This lady, who is no lady, is Other who slips perversely in a degraded circuit of sexuality—with men, with women, in a social space outside the realm of bourgeois security and family. Like Dora's governess, or the beautiful white body of Frau K, this is a love outside legitimacy. The sexual woman, the object of homosexual desire and the subject of bisexual sexuality, is marginal and degraded. Even the young girl's longings for this woman are rendered in another language: *"Che poco spera e nulla chiede"* (p. 160). The *cocotte* embodies an illicit, free-ranging desire. A woman's desire is presented paradoxically as exotic, dangerous, and degraded.

In this reading of Freud, I want to set contradiction center stage. Published in 1920, the essay depends on the core ideas of the *Three Essays* (Freud, 1905a), glances laterally though enigmatically at *The Interpretation of Dreams* (Freud, 1900), and prefigures the later essays on femininity and female sexuality. It has a crucial and underestimated place in the development of Freud's thought and holds some of the subtlest writing on sexuality and identity that exists in Freud's canon. There are, of course, a number of different strategies for reading Freud's theory of sexuality. Grossman and Kaplan (1988) sort out what they term "commentaries" on gender within Freud's writing. They note many instances in which Freud produces a simplified trait theory of gender, but they also extract from Freud's work a commentary in which gender is preserved as a psychodynamic category. Mitchell (1988), on the other hand, draws out the biological tropisms in Freud and in drive theory. Freud's essay on the case of female homosexuality contains ample evidence for each of these readings, reminding us that the arduous task Freud set himself—to build an account of sexual object choice and identity that broke with previous biological models—was one he both succeeded at and failed.

In this essay, Freud both perpetuates and breaks with the conventional patriarchal thinking on homosexuality and femininity. Freud's contradictions are embodied in the very circumstances of agreeing to undertake the analysis. As with Dora, he has responded to a father's insistence that a daughter be brought to heel. This father, "an earnest, worthy man, at bottom very tenderhearted," actually reacts to his daughter's homosexual tendencies with "rage," "threats," and "bitterness." Should psychoanalysis fail, the father's fallback position is "a speedy marriage . . . to awaken the natural instincts of the girl and stifle her unnatural tendencies" (p. 149). Tracking the voice of patriarchy through this essay, we hear the outraged voice of the father of a disobedient, rebellious girl. Freud's alliance and, I would suggest, his identification with this father thus undermine his theoretical claims for the constructed and complex dynamics in all forms of sexuality and identity.

This essay exemplifies a historically new censorious attention to female friendship. The girl's relationship to her love-object, so disagreeable to her father, is characterized as an instance of the devotion of friendship taken to excess. Carroll Smith-Rosenberg (1985) identifies a shift late in the nineteenth century when female friendship, which had formerly enjoyed much social and moral approval, became problematic and pathological. Freud's essay shows the unmistakable signs of a cautionary tale on the forms and fate of female friendship, on the potentially dangerous connections between women. This narrative of danger is one theoretical move through which deviance can be constructed. Empowered scientific discourse simultaneously lights up female desire and problematizes it.

Yet Freud places so many cool and rigorously argued ideas before the reader. Following the radical insight of the *Three Essays,* Freud traces out the view that sexuality and identity can never be simply some hard-wired, constitutionally driven forms but, rather, that the formation of sex and identity operates like the rules of grammar. As Chomsky (1965) demonstrated formally in the case of language, any given sentence has no inherent linkages or simple linear connections. His theory of generative grammar demonstrates that all human language creatively combines elements according to a set of special combinatorial rules, which permit many optional selections and arrangements. If we extend this analogy to the sphere of sexuality, any human experience of sexuality and identity is built on a unique and particular sexual sentence in which the elements of subjectivity, action, and object are never inherent or inevitable. Unlinking aim from object and allowing the play of sexual forms and symbolic meanings for bodies, selves, and acts are the radical core of Freud's theory of desire and gender.

The theoretical revolution Freud (1920) proposes is set within an essay whose opening paragraph enigmatically invokes the law and whose closing paragraph evokes gender surgeons and a rather horrible prefiguring of fascist medicine: "the remarkable transformations that Steinach has effected in some cases by his operations" (p. 171).

We can track the contradictions in the tonal variations in Freud's voice and stance in regard to this patient. A Foucauldian twinning of science and power sets a doomy beginning to the essay. A hitherto hidden practice, homosexuality in women, ignored by the law and neglected by psychoanalysis, is to be excavated to make "a claim" on our attention. At the very beginning, the patient is brought into Freud's sight-lines. All the exits seem closed off. "It is possible to trace [the origin of this case] in complete certainty and almost without a gap" (p. 147). But later, Freud likens treatment to a train ride (though which of Freud's trains is not so clear). "An analysis falls into two clearly distinguishable phases" (p. 152), he writes. In the first the analyst does the explaining; and in the second "the patient himself gets hold of the material put before him" (p. 152). The analyst is then a powerless passenger, sitting passively with ticket in hand until the patient-engineer agrees to start the journey.

Ticket and seat offer up only the "right" and the "possibility" of voyage, never the necessity. But perhaps what is in sight here is "a journey to another country," the preoedipal home of femininity. Freud (1931) writes his own Baedeker to this country in his essay on femininity by sketching out the trip into that terrain of womanhood as a place of gaps and silences, a place without certainty, a "pre-Minoan-Mycenaen civilization" whose tourism Freud left finally to the women analysts. Late in the essay and late in the short-lived treatment, Freud must acknowledge that gaps yawn open in the "hypocritical dreams" in which revenge and the wish to please are reverberating transforms of each other, played out in respect to Freud and to the father.

> Warned through some slight impression or other, I told her one day that I did not believe these dreams, that I regarded them as false or hypocritical, and that she intended to deceive me just as she habitually deceived her father. I was right: after I had made this clear, this kind of dream ceased. (p. 165)

Freud's harshness and the sermonizing admonitions in his commentary to the patient about her wish to distort and deceive her analyst are stunning. Then the tone shifts, and in a more wondering, open register, so different from the imperious voice of his conclusions about this patient, Freud speculates on how little we know of whom and why we love. "It would seem that the information received by our consciousness about our erotic life is especially liable to be incomplete, full of gaps, or falsified" (pp. 166–167). These unsettled and unsettling moments in the essay are its golden possibilities.

The contradictions move not merely through the structure and style of the essay but in the alternation between the theory and the particularities of the treatment. We should take up what Freud says, not what he does. Views on the manifold causes of homosexual object-choice and homosexual identity and the subtlety of parallel dynamics in respect to a child's connection to mother and to father are lost to the rigid choice Freud makes as analyst in his insistence on the conventional Oedipal structure, the primacy of disappointment in losing the father's love.

"Her Facial Features Were Sharp"

Within the body of this essay, Freud (1920) establishes his commitment to the independence of physical constitution, mental traits, and love object-choice. The idea that sexual object-choice is necessarily fixed and immutable is undermined in various ways. In the discussion of situational homosexuality, the power of setting to shape drive and counter inhibition is considered. In the discussions of motives for accepting treatment, the person's youth, vulnerability, and commitment to family and object ties are all proposed as elements in the shaping of sexuality. Indeed, in the very term "choice," the role of consciousness, and the multiplicity of options, decisions, and reflections are all raised in regard to experiences that are often considered to be immutable. Paradoxically, Freud also describes the entrenched resistance of sexual object-choice.

Freud seems to speak here against two different literary and scientific traditions. In regard to one, medical psychiatry, with its commitment to taxonomies and the rigid alignment of constitution and sexuality, Freud marks his great revolutionary stance, the disjunction of body and culture. But in repudiating the idea of a "third sex," he also speaks against a politicizing polemic of the nineteenth century that sought to carve out a psychic and social space for homosexual persons (see Weeks, 1979, for an analysis of these historical developments). It is interesting that psychoanalysis is still poised against both these traditions, though they themselves are so implacably oppositional.

Political works in gay liberation have often refused any account of sexuality as a developmental achievement and have considered that a constitution-based sexual identity offered safer and securer ground for a politics and a lifestyle organized around sexual object-choice and homosexual identity. This politicized stance served another important function, namely to protect gay people from institutional practices that privilege one gender (male) and one object-choice (heterosexual) as unremarkable and thus unquestioned, while homosexuality becomes a developmental dilemma that needs to be understood. Gender identity and sexuality can perhaps be "freely" investigated only in a social, institutional, and therefore political situation in which everything may be put in question and nothing is fixed or "natural." This utopian possibility was sketched in Freud's theory of sexuality and was at the heart of his method in the technique of "free" association. This hope for a freedom to question and this radical skepticism are also psychoanalytic feminism's deepest utopian vision.

Conventional thinking in psychoanalysis, in academic psychology, and in psychiatry frequently opted for the apparent security of a biologically based treatment of sexuality. Freud defers from considering "the problem of homosexuality," yet this essay requires that we consider homosexuality not as a problem but as a solution, the solution any child might make to the dynamics of a family, the conflicted process of object-choice.

There is a magisterial flow to the final section of the essay. Sexual object choice is achieved, not given. Any individual contains and, in some forms, retains multiple sexual needs and objectives. Only a reflective, psychoanalytically based study of an individual's history yields some understanding of the relative potency of homosexual and heterosexual libido. Femininity is connected to maternal attachment. The Oedipal moment is a developmental hinge for boy

and girl in which each must give up the mother, though with differing symbolic meanings attached to each repudiation. But as Freud always insisted, nothing is ever fully given up, merely displaced.

Yet how curious the final paragraph. Freud makes a pitch for a hermeneutic
method for psychoanalysis as opposed to prescriptive and predictive scientism.
Then enigmatically he speaks of a masculinity that fades into activity and a femininity that fades into passivity. And, finally, he counterposes powerful surgery
against a puny, feminized, castrated psychology. As against the more phallic, surgical interventions of Steinach, Freud presents psychoanalysis in rather the same
way as he presents the female genital: "When one compares the extent to which
we can influence it with the remarkable transformations that Steinach has
effected in some cases by his operations, it does not make a very imposing
impression" (p. 170).

Even more curious is the final sentence: "A woman who has felt herself a
man and has loved in masculine fashion, will hardly let herself be forced into
playing the part of a woman, when she must pay for this transformation,
which is not in every way advantageous, by renouncing all hope of motherhood" (p. 172). If a woman homosexual were to give up her hermaphroditic
organs, she would be one sex but would be deprived of motherhood. She would
be doubly punished through a loss of masculinity and a loss of that phallic possibility offered to femininity, the birth of a child. From the high ground of theory, the writing drifts into enigma and defeated retreat. This movement has
continued to operate within psychoanalysis. Lacan (1977) initially seeks to recuperate Freud's notion of a complex and fragmentary sexuality but ends in a position that displaces women, conflates them with the place of the Other, and
mystifies social power by a reified treatment of language's relation to subjectivity. Chasseguet-Smirgel (1966, 1986) critiques phallic monism but puts in its
place biologically based feminine and masculine drives.

It is tempting to ask whether, within psychoanalysis, there are two genders
or one. As in comparable debates about a one-person or two-person psychology, we can inquire whether psychoanalysis makes a commitment to a one-
gender (male) or two-gender system. Could gender fluctuate like any system of
meaning? But if we insist on the symbolic meaning of the body, can we, in our
practice and our theories, tolerate the ambiguity and instability of these profoundly personal and ideologically charged categories of experience?

In Freud's treatment of this patient his own insights fail him. He tells us that
this sharp-featured, tall girl has a body that evokes that of her father and a mind
that echoes this body: sharp, imperious, tough. Constitution as an explanation
for homosexual identity and object-choice is rejected in theory but sneaks in at
the back door of practice and countertransference.

"She Changed into a Man"

As Freud sets out the case, he puts into a play a fascinating set of possibilities, a complexity of attachments and identifications. The girl faces a set of relational problematics to which sexual object-choice could offer a resolution. First, there is the girl's relation to her mother, an attractive young woman who Freud thinks may be content with a daughter who refuses to compete with her.

One strand of explanation woven throughout the case material is that the primary object-choice for the girl, the mother, is never fully given up but transferred to other mothers and finally to the lady love. In this way, the patient continues a "masculine protest" (which for Freud never quite attains the legitimacy of male identification).

We can take a moment to look at the Freudian position on the differences between male identification and masculine protest. The former is thought to rise wholesomely from libido and desire; the latter is thought to be a more unsavory outcome of aggression. This position only restates the valuative judgment and double standard in different terms. The problem still remains. Why would a girl's identification with her father arise solely from envy and aggression? Jessica Benjamin (1988) addresses this question by proposing a legitimate role for a girl's identificatory love for her father and examining the conflicts and inhibitions that arise for women when this process of loving identification is thwarted.

Alternatively, a feminine object-choice is the resentful consolation prize after an Oedipal defeat. In this case, mother gets father's boy baby (when the girl is 5 or 6 and again in adolescence), and the daughter spurned gives up men altogether and "changes into a man." The spoiling of her chances for a love-object lead, in extreme form, to an abandonment of gender identity. The changeling now enacts the conventions of male love.

This interpretation allows us to see the contradictions in the theory of normative male heterosexual choice that Freud brings to bear on the case of this young girl. He lays out the unconscious dynamic of masculine love, both in its Oedipal and its narcissistic components. Certain men choose an idealized yet degraded woman lover. Freud understands this choice as an aspect of masculine idealized love operating as a defensive distortion within the Oedipus complex. This scene goes as follows: An idealized pure love develops for a degraded creature who is really a stand-in for mother. In the boy's fantasy, mother stays with father only for protection and convenience; her sexual love for father is degraded and bad, and she saves her purity for the devoted son. The boy loves a pure mother and will save her from the degradation of heterosexuality.

There is also the narcissistic element in mature male object-choice. The man defers to the pleasure and the narcissistic preoccupations of the lover: "the humility and the sublime overvaluation of the sexual object . . . the renunciation of all narcissistic satisfaction and the preference for being the lover rather than the beloved" (p. 154). This position is somewhat of a theoretical double standard. A man's love of women is cast in the language of submission and deferral, of living through the narcissism and pleasure of the Other. A comparable construction in a woman would have been tagged with the epithet of masochism. This aspect of male love of women, perhaps the theoretical twin of penis envy in a woman, has none of that construct's negative play. The central point to extricate from this piece of theory that Freud produces is the feature of distortion and defense in normal heterosexual development that is nonetheless not introduced as a "problem."

Freud's interpretive solution to this patient's problem is a relational solution: Sexuality and desire are at the mercy of object relations. Choosing a woman or rechoosing a woman comes after a defeat and a disappointment in respect to her longing for her father. She seems then, to Freud, to have jumped tracks from a positive to a negative Oedipal complex, changed into a man, taken on a rebellious struggle with her father (surely a version of the Oedipal identificatory struggles of father and son), and fallen in love with a mother substitute, whom symbolically she will win back from the degraded sexualilty of heterosexual life.

For a contemporary reader of this case who operates with the insights of object relations theories, the intersubjective treatment of transference and countertransference, and the current appreciations of the potency of maternal attachment, the question is how to decide between the alterative models of identity and object-choice that Freud sets up.

I want to take up first the fate and form of Freud's patient's primary love object, her mother, who consistently deserts her for men, for father, and for flirtations and male attention. The most crucial abandonments occur when the girl is 5 or 6, (when the mother gives birth to a male baby) and at yet another crucial developmental juncture, adolescence. The trauma of these narcissistic injuries might well be measured in the girl's obliteration of any thought that these births have been psychically disruptive. But perhaps the trauma resurfaces, disguised, in an attempted solution when she begins to play with a 3-year-old boy. Freud connects this play to maternal and feminine identification. But it is also possible that the identification is with the rapprochement boy, an alter ego who represents her child self before the narcissistic (and obviously also Oedipal) disaster. If she is a little boy, she retains the exclusivity of her mother. There is not yet a new baby boy. Also if she retains "boyness," the discovery and despairing loss associated with femininity are warded off. Did she change into a man or simply always stay one, imagining within her family that to be loved by mother you have to be a boy? As a mother's boy, she looks for an adored love-object and seeks to love an ego ideal that Chasseguet–Smirgel (1985) has always connected to the longing for narcissistic healing and reunion with the preoedipal mother.

At the same time, many factors (father and culture) prevent her from occupying the privileged position of adult masculinity. Perhaps one compromise solution is to be a rebellious "boy" in a failed relation to a heterosexual woman. Loving the *cocotte* serves multiple functions. It symbolically plays out the Oedipal defeat and the preoedipal possibilities and hope, also finally defeated. The suicide attempt signals the futility, not merely the Oedipal enactment of the wish for father's baby. Rather, we are back at the railroad as the girl falls on the tracks, symbolically expresses having nowhere to go, and "finds herself" caught in a preoedipal and Oedipal no person's land. Her chastity then arises from confusion and a double inhibition. This enactment of futility could also preserve the elements Freud sees in the suicide attempt, its mixture of hate and excitement. Stasis and refusal remain the fundamental stance, hidden behind a mask of compliance and interest.

The suicide attempt, however, demands a closer look. It is introduced as an example of her mixture of openness and deceitful disobedience. "She paid for this undoubtedly serious attempt at suicide with a considerable time on her back in bed, though fortunately little permanent damage was done. After her recovery she found it easier to get her own way than before" (p. 148). We might note Freud's rather chilling refusal to privilege the girl's despair, to see the integrity and seriousness of her hopelessness and her confusion. Lauffer and Lauffer (1989), working on adolescent breakdown and suicide attempts, consider some adolescent suicidal crises as expressions of intolerable conflict over the integration of gender, body ego, and sexuality.

One poignant dilemma for this girl is the contradiction between the preoedipal and Oedipal mother, the mother of longed-for exclusivity and the mother who rivalrously reserves the ground of femininity for herself. We cannot know, in this woman's case, whether she chooses masculine identity as a solution to defeat at mother's hands, at father's, or at both. We know more, I suspect, of the creative resolution of her object-choice as it preserves the complexity of her sexuality.

Freud suggests that the patient's love-object is a complex solution, a fusion of male and female object-choice, the expression of homosexual and heterosexual libido. An object-choice ideally represents a world of multiple sexualities and the preserving of all prior forms of loving. The love-object technically must be one gender or another, that is, formally either female or male, but unconsciously and symbolically, this object-choice is a multilayered, multisexed creation. It is not, of course, that the gender identity of the lover is unimportant, but that it both expresses a powerful resolution of conflicting aims and preserves all elements of the conflict.

In formal identity terms, the patient makes a homosexual object-choice. But in the more subtle terms of identity and unconscious meaning, I read this patient's love relation as a heterosexual object-choice in which a fictive "boy" chooses a mother to idealize and save from an Oedipal father. Despite Freud's reading of the girl's disappointment in respect to her father, the transference-countertransference deadlock suggests this Oedipal battle has not been conceded. The mother's body and feelings are still contested zones.

"Russian Tactics" by the Patient, So the Analyst "Breaks It Off"

Like an Escher engraving, the question of who drives and who buys a train ticket and sits waiting on this treatment journey is constantly fluctuating. "In the case of our patient, it was not doubt but the affective factor of revenge against her father that made her cool reserve possible. . . . As soon as I recognized the girl's attitude to her father, I broke off treatment" (p. 164). Freud claims to see through the false self-analysis and the subterfuge, a repetition of tactics with the father. He sees that envy and defeat are the real project, refuses the charade, and stops the work.

There is now a tradition of thought in object relations theory, notably the work of Little (1981) and Bollas (1987) and others in which countertransference is viewed as an induced experience of the object history of the patient. Using that model in this case, we might ask how this clever girl of 18 maneuvers Freud to play out the father, to act out the rejecting and rejected patriarch, and to admit defeat by referral to a woman analyst.

In another enactment, Freud's response to the dream reports is to make a transference interpretation, not a dream interpretation. The reporting of dreams of marriage and heterosexual happiness is given transference meaning as an enactment of the wish to deceive the father by presenting him with "hypocritical" dreams. Although he uses the judgmental term, "hypocritical" in the footnoted section in *The Interpretation of Dreams* (1900), he simply presents the dual level, manifest and latent, in any dream and notes that dreams disguise just as they express. Worth remarking on is the dream example he uses—a dream in which his relation with Fliess is played out and hidden (p. 52). This hidden association can be connected to the poetic paragraphs earlier in the essay, in which Freud invokes the mystery of not knowing why or whom one loves. I am suggesting a buried countertext of rivalries involving Freud, Fliess, and Tausk in a complex scenario of love and contest.

The enactment of silenced, disowned countertransference in the treatment of the girl in "Psychogenesis" is the story of father-son rivalry. Freud plays out the struggle of father versus girl-who-is-really-a-boy and consistently relates to the patient both as a ridiculous rival for male terrain and as a girl refusing to give up the position of masculine protest and accept and internalize the analyst's interpretations. I would say it is less clear that she wants these interpretations (for Freud the symbolic equivalent of the father's babies) than that she wishes to be the boy to mother and thus comes into a situation of difficult rivalry with her father and then with Freud.

Freud interprets the patient's single quoted comment in the essay, "How very interesting," as an intellectualized defense. Yes, but also a masculinized one, as if the patient were saying: "We are two colleagues sitting here discussing a patient we have in common, who happens to be me. How very interesting." This patient practices, as Freud suggests, a Russian tactic: an entrenched, defensive resistance against which penetration must fail. Freud notes with some exasperation the mildly interested attention the girl gives to the analytic work. He sees resistance, certainly. But perhaps she is calm because he is so obviously off target. Freud presses on as if he were treating a young girl who is vengeful because she has been betrayed by her father. One thinks of Winnicott (1971) glimpsing one gender masked behind another. In the daring move Winnicott makes in making the acquaintance of the "girl" in his male patient, the treatment lights up and moves.

In this case there are evocations of Freud's (1905b) work with Dora. Both are cases of resistant, oppositional young women, and both are treatment struggles in which shame and defeat are the stakes. Dora votes with her feet and gives Freud notice as though he were a servant. This other patient, "the clever and beautiful girl of 18," from "a family of good standing, beautiful and well made, . . . a spirited girl, always ready for romping and fighting, . . ." (p. 169) is sent away. In Freud's language we can note that the Oedipal blow of castration has been struck: "I broke it off." This girl must not dare to inhabit male space, to represent phallic desire. He recommends that she be dispatched to a woman analyst. And here is the complexity of the defeat/victory, for perhaps he has sent the fox into the henhouse.

There are two moments in the clinical management of this treatment that are striking. The first arises when the girl's dreams are rejected as "hypocritical." The second is the censorious tone in which the analysis is ended. Both these moments may be seen as instances in which Freud, the stern, gate-keeping patriach, refuses the rivalry of this fictive boy, this woman who appears to make a claim for masculinity. This refusal raises a question in respect to masculine identification in women. When, for whom, and with whom is it permitted? In Helene Deutsch's analysis, which Freud conducted, her masculine identification, her father complex, was left deliberately unanalyzed. In the essay on femininity, female analysts as a group are given a kind of dispensation from the humiliating requirement to confess penis envy and repudiate phallic aims (Freud, 1931).

The date of his first publication of Freud's essay is 1920. Drawing on Jones's (1957) biographical treatment of this period and Roazen's (1969) book on Freud's young colleague, Victor Tausk, I propose a linkage between these biographical events and the themes of this case. Tausk's suicide occurred in July 1919. Freud's complex preoccupations with Tausk and his death are evident in a rather cold, dispassionate interpretation of the suicide as a loss to the "father ghost," an interpretation that he includes in a frank letter to their mutual friend, Frau Lou Salomé. Later that year, Freud produced a respectful obituary, as Roazen (1969) has noted, the longest obituary Freud wrote. Jones (1957) records that Freud wrote the essay on this case of homosexuality in the fall of 1919, thus in the immediate aftermath of Tausk's suicide and in the same period as the composition of the obituary. In the obituary, Tausk is described as "passionate," "sharp," and "brilliant," several terms also used to describe Freud's young suicidal patient.

These links between the events surrounding Tausk's death and the writing of the case are evocative, not causal. Nonetheless, I interpret the end of this young woman's treatment as both castration and reparation. It enacts the father's punishment of a contesting son, a guilty repetition of Freud's treatment of Tausk. Freud had earlier refused to take Tausk into analysis and had sent him instead, in a humiliating move, to work with Helene Deutsch, an analyst quite junior in experience and reputation to Tausk. Then, when Deutsch was overwhelmed by this analytic task and found herself using her sessions with Freud to talk over the work with Tausk, Freud forced a choice: Deutsch could give up her work with Tausk or her analysis with Freud. She abandoned Tausk, and several months later he killed himself. There is one other parallel between Tausk and the young patient discussed in Freud's case. Tausk died gruesomely, shooting himself in the head and simultaneously hanging himself. Roazen interprets this suicide as a double death, reflecting both the loss of Freud and the failure of a love relationship. Tausk had been poised against a double loss, as the young woman patient is at the moment on the railroad tracks when she is threatened with rageful abandonment by her father and the loss of her love for the *cocotte*. The resolution of the case acknowledges a potential healing power in the mother-analyst, for Freud recommends turning the errant "boy" over to a woman analyst. I read this referral as a symbolic reparation to Tausk and perhaps also to Deutsch.

Yet the danger in this way of thinking and in Freud's own language as he announces the resolution to this case is that mother and father analysts become a newly reified category. What if we could imagine the term "woman analyst" as a provisional title for a range of analytic responses or strategies? This construct would make a theoretical space for the "woman" analyst (which could, of course, be an aspect of any analyst) to hear rivalry, masculinity, competitiveness, and ambition without triangulating. Maternal identity in the analyst is usually invoked in issues of separation or preoedipal functioning. Here is a position not for an Oedipal mother who will be object, but for an Oedipal mother who could be subject as well, untempted to do same-sex battle with a child who is trying to assert self in adult psychic territory.

To summarize this reading of the case, I hope to suggest some advantages to reading gender identity as a complex, multiply figured, and fluid experience. This view is in contradiction to work on core gender identity, such as that of Fast (1984), but it does not preclude experiences of the sort Coates (1994) has written about in which young boys feel profoundly in opposition to their gender. In fact, Coates's interpretation of gender identity disorder in boys, in which a disruption in gender coincides with a disruption in separation experience and self-structure, rather supports this view that gender can become heavily freighted with meaning and can be put to the service of crucial psychic work.

The position I am suggesting is one in which gender is neither reified nor simply liminal and evanescent. Rather, in any one person's experience, gender may occupy both positions. Gender may in some contexts be as thick and reified, as plausibly real as anything in our character. At other moments, gender may seem porous and insubstantial. Furthermore, there may be multiple genders or embodied selves. For some individuals these gendered experiences may feel integrated, ego-syntonic. For others, the gender contradictions and alternatives seem dangerous and frightening and so are maintained as splits in the self, dissociated part-objects. Any view of sex, object-choice, or gender that grounds these phenomena as categories of biology or "the real" misses the heart of Freud's radical intervention in our understanding of personality. Biologically determined theories keep such experiences as gender and sexuality outside the system of meaning itself. To be meaningful, these experiences must be understood as symbolizable. Gender, then, and the relation of gender to love-object can be understood only by acts of interpretation. In that way the density of their unconscious and conscious elaborations are brought into the realm of language. Only with the reflective narratives on which psychoanalysis depends can we know the complex meaning of "masculine," "feminine," "boy," "girl," "same," "different."

In the remainder of this paper I want to begin to translate this perspective into clinical work and refuse any monolithic, single-determinant, and single dynamic theory of homosexuality or gender. This view is not a prescription for total relativism or for the idea that everyone is everything and all choices are equally plausible or equally privileged. Any experienced gender- or sexuality-based identity or sexual choice arises in a historical and culturally laden context that becomes part of the internal experience of gender.

In considering two contemporary clinical examples in the light of Freud's work, I will keep formal gender identity as a point of comparison. I consider the consciously experienced totality of being a male or female person a necessary fiction, as Lacan (1977) noted. I will therefore write about my work with two women who use love-objects as points of identification as well as desire. The symbolic meaning of these loves undermines the surface meanings of their choices. I have also chosen to highlight women's problem of masculine or father identification as well as the complexity of conscious and unconscious gender meanings. These two women are preoccupied with and conflicted over the meaning and symbols of masculinity as internal aspects of ego functioning and of self-structure. As gender identity and sexual choice become more complex, so the constructs of maternal and paternal images become more complexly figured as they appear, develop, and alter in the patients' internal worlds as aspects of gender identity and self. Each woman, in unique ways, struggles with the complexity of her gender identifications and the ways in which her body reflects and at the same time spoils identity.

"I Don't Like To Be Encumbered"

This statement is my patient Hannah's explanation of a routine of daily work-outs at the gym and her refusal to risk weight gain by giving up smoking. For Hannah, flesh itself symbolizes encumbrance, the entangling encumbrance of need and desire. A beautiful and delicate young woman, an aspiring performer, always freshly turned out, she seems the platonic form of the lovely, contemporary urban girl. As her mother wryly observed, in a town where girls cannot find a date, Hannah always has a line of suitors. At first glance, then, she does not present an obvious case of masculine identity.

Indeed, considering her relationships to her father and stepfather, I have found no simple stage of idealization, no obvious clear point of connection to an admired and enabling male parent. Her own father is positioned in the family as the degraded outsider. Her stepfather is quite an exciting, powerful figure but never offers Hannah entry into the charmed circle of his life in the artistic world.

Each life arena in which aggression, activity, and mobility may hold sway has been excruciatingly difficult for Hannah to occupy. She is torn and enraged with frustration over her career and her possibilities, she is furious in the knowledge that she must thwart herself from having the success and contentment she longs for, she is furious that she cannot seem to stop her mind from turning on itself and destroying any sense of ampleness or possibility. The prohibition on action touches many spheres of life, both fundamental and trivial.

Achieving sexual pleasure, learning to drive and securing a license, serving at tennis, succeeding at intellectual projects at a university, being hired by an employer—each of these experiences, which entail accepting one's own power and desire, has been powerfully forbidden, and only grudgingly have the rights and access been won.

The daughter of a seductive and intrusive father, she spent many early confusing years (her parents divorced when she was an infant) listening to her father bind her to him in complex identifications against the maternal family and against society. This father kept his daughter in a *folie à deux* of outsiders and oddballs. Later in her adolescence he treated her as his perfect feminine object. In a kind of seductive initiation into exhibitionism, she would be told in any public setting that all eyes were on her, that everyone wanted her. The unspoken implication was that she, the one wanted, was Daddy's. Yet this understanding has given way to a deeper and more unsettling possibility, for Hannah had always sensed her father's investment in attracting the interest of young men. One of her favorite dramatic monologues is the scene from *Suddenly Last Summer* in which a beautiful young girl discovers she has been bait for her male homosexual companion's interest in young men. This scene reappears in fantasy in many guises, a sort of disabling myth. Hannah's father's feminine identification and homosexual desires disrupt her own possibilities for display and power; that is, not only must she deal with her own fantasies of grandiose display and exhibitionism, the delight in being seen and admired, but she must also struggle with the complex projections of her father's exhibitionist and homosexual desires, which contaminate her fantasy life.

One of the *Suddenly Last Summer* subtexts is that the man is devoured, cannibalized by the objects of his desire. Desire can be fatally dangerous. Her guilty excitement in her complicity in this scene is also powerful and problematic. Desire and the desire for empowered visibility are contaminated from many points of view. One of Hannah's psychic solutions follows the line of masochistic fantasy in which she becomes wildly excited and out of control, is desired, and then is attacked. The behavioral outcome of these conflicts is the avoidance of any moment of success or visible empowerment.

Identification and attachment to her mother have become problematic in another way. In the marital dynamic, the mother ruled, and the father was defeated and castrated. So her mother, in the world of work and in her interactions with Hannah's father, embodies phallic power and hegemony. Her mother's understanding of her own life connects efficacy, ambition, and power to her liberation from men altogether. One of the tasks of Hannah's adolescence was to begin to integrate and manage the meaning her mother's lesbian identification and its correlation with greater happiness and power for her mother. There is one other feature of this confusing family dynamic—the pre-oedipal mother. For Hannah, this relation is split between her mother and grandmother. Her memories of the mother of her early childhood are terrifying. An angry, unhappy woman, furious at any evidence of need in a child, corrosively contemptuous of weakness or dependency, her mother discovered a capacity to parent and love a child only upon the birth of Hannah's younger brother, when Hannah was 6. This injury to narcissism has been excruciating for Hannah to acknowledge. It remains layered in feelings of shame and self-doubt. The grandmother is sweet, somewhat ineffectual, a comforting but distanced presence. As an internal object, this grandmother is no match for the murderous mother, so derisive of need or weakness, so contemptuous of Hannah's striving for competition.

Where is masculinity? Primarily in Hannah's relation to her body, which is experienced and maintained as a place of phallic triumph. She lifts weights, works out, monitors appetite, eats sensibly if somewhat obsessively, and contains in her own body the fusion of masculine and feminine ideals. To draw on Bertram Lewin's (1933) idea of the body concretizing as a phallic object, we can say that Hannah at the gym is pure phallus, pure object; she embodies the male desire, but as its object, and is thus usually rendered powerless to act in any personal way on her own authority.

Second, there is her relationship to men. She is never without a boyfriend for very long and always chooses handsome, aggressive men. What is powerfully clear in these relationships is that they are founded as much on processes of identification as on processes of desire. She wants to be with these men and to be like them. What she enjoys is a life on male turf, hanging out at clubs, playing late night poker games. She prides herself on being able to outdo, outtalk, outdrink, and outplay any boyfriend and his coterie of male buddies. Her relations with men are a mixture of object-choice and identification. In these heterosexual object relations, which she finds compelling and exciting, she is also working out masculine identification. A recent, intriguing analysis of this process is found in Mikkel Borch-Jacobsen's *The Freudian Subject* (1988). Drawing on Freud's work on dream interpretation, he notes the placement or displacement of some wish or desire into being the one who possesses the desired object: If I cannot have something for myself, I will be like one who can or does. Hannah then encounters, in her wish to be subject like these hypermasculine men, the paradox that they themselves insist on highly conventional feminine attitudes in women.

Finally, she plays out in her analysis her idea and ideal of masculine identification. I am experienced as a version of her well-meaning, ineffectual grandmother—distanced, unskilled, impotent in regard to the treatment. Any insight she will have to develop for herself. She attends her analysis politely, dutifully, but without hope of her change or of my efficacy. She monitors and maintains all systems of control. She cannot know or experience any need for me. She can need analysis in some abstract sense, but her sessions with me are lined up with duty visits to grandmother and other burdensome obligations. To feel need in her analysis would be to give in to terrifying possibilities, to be, in her derisive words, "a betty," apparently a code word she uses to signify any dependent, weak girl. It is also a term her mother reserves for her girlfriends. She is depressed but bewildered whenever a separation from the analysis presents itself. Sessions are canceled for headaches and stomachaches, but if I question the absences, there are angry outbursts at the banality of my suggestions, at the ordeal of having to come for analysis that cannot help because she is hopeless. There is, above all, the terrible, degrading idea that if she needs her analyst, she is hopelessly female and I will become the triumphant, contemptuous, masculinized figure to whom she must submit.

"Look Ma, No Cavities"

A greeting at the beginning of a session. B.K. continues: "The good news is that I went to the dentist. No cavities. The bad news is that I went to the gynecologist." B.K. tells more than a medical history. The good news is that she could be a boy, my boy, teeth without holes, body without messy insides. The bad news is that it is not the whole truth; she is a girl with a long-standing relationship to gynecology and its ministrations. Perhaps the analyst can cast the deciding vote.

I have chosen this "homosexual" patient to challenge the idea of "homosexuality" as a monolithic, simple, transhistorical category. An important guide in this work has been Eisenbud's (1982) paper on lesbian identity. B.K. has her own form of ironic linguistic markers, humorous commentaries that embrace and transform conventional descriptions of lesbian identity. She uses the term "little butch" as a self-description but lives this identity in a social and personal space that is marked by feminism and by urban culture. Freud's patient was struggling with conflicts in male identification while simultaneously living within the conventions of respectability and bourgeois culture. B.K. experiences and expresses symbolically through her body a more frankly male identification but one complexly set within a woman-based scene.

Male identification for B.K. works and does not work. In the urban world she inhabits—part subculture, part community—she has constructed a personal, social, and occupational world in which boyish style, feminist stance, and working-class identity all coexist. Her self structures mix and disrupt. Crew-cut, always in pants, shorts, or work suits, tattooed, she has fashioned a body ego and self-presentation that express her identification through the blurring of gender boundaries. Moreover, she has found a way to live in a social world in which this stance is unremarkable. She tailors her name to suit her particular notion of her gender and gives up a rather feminine name, first for androgynous nicknames and later for initials.

In work, she is socially permitted and has permitted herself to choose a working-class, skilled trade and to live out an occupational life akin to her father's. But she cannot permit herself fully to thrive and succeed in this world. She thwarts herself, doubts that she can bear the "responsibility" of the full title of tradesman. She stays defensively at the level of "helper," occasionally having to defeat the practitioners of equal opportunity programs by deliberately failing various exams. Her dream life is full of images of workmates driving cars while she is stuck in parking lots or is never quite in the driver's seat. Nothing can occur to disrupt the reign of the idealized father. Does fear of male retaliation play a role in her inhibition? Perhaps. But loyalty and love also play a role. And recently she has come upon the questionable idea that she cannot have what she wants at work and also live a gay lifestyle. That idea, though certainly plausible at a social level, given cultural homophobia, runs against some reality on her job. A gay woman, B.K's. age, obtained a senior administrative position. The practical possibilities of advancement seem to make the psychic taboos against such successes even fiercer. B.K. tells me she cannot come to know this woman, and she avoids any contact. Indeed she assures me that this whole problem of work and success is impossible to think about, unknowable. To underscore this point, she brings in a dream in which she was decapitated.

B.K. is the daughter of an adored and idealized father, who ran a store. As he appears in her material, the father is warm, funny, big, and hairy (there are many gorilla dreams both scary and fun). He is seen as responsible, hardworking. Curiously, he is the only parent about whom any memories of feeding and sensory care remain. His deli was the source of treats and food. There is an evocative memory of this father sitting in the kitchen and dozing by a stove on which eggs are boiling. This vision of the responsible, docile father-giant is a source of warmth and identity. There is also melancholy in this memory. The father's exhaustion signals his ordeal in caring for his wife, B.K.'s mother, who progressively declined to invalidism from multiple sclerosis, an ordeal that seems to have contributed to the father's early death.

Her mother, by contrast, was experienced as first absent, then horribly controlling, and later sick and frighteningly debilitated. When B.K. was 2, a sister was born, and her mother simultaneously began the slow, inexorable slide to debility. A double loss experienced by B.K. because of the mother's preoccupation both with the new baby and with her mysterious and terrifying illness. What seems relevant here is that B.K. enters all relationships with the conviction that she cannot be interesting, that the other will be bored and drift away, and that a rival may at any moment exclude her. In a dream early in treatment, she is at a café, and a waitress wants her to spoon cocaine over her Rice Krispies. She spies her former girlfriend buying coffee and rolls to go. B.K. reports a panicky feeling as she tries to see if the bag the lover is holding is "big enough to hold food for two." She is riven with jealously.

In a striking and powerful way, B.K. has used sexual excitement and later drugs to regulate tension and to cover separation anxiety and depressive loss. Constant masturbation, a lifelong habit of thumb sucking, and, in her childhood, the frantic excitement of sports and sex play with boys were placed against the constriction and anxiety of school and home. B.K. was a child who could play hard and wildly but who often felt speechless at school. Outside, she felt alive and sure. Inside, she felt ashamed, silent, bored, and boring. In the wildness of outdoor play, she remembers pulling down boys' pants "to have a look." As an adolescent this frantic quest for identity and soothing emerged in an intense sexual and love relation with a boy. Locked in combat with her mother over this relationship, she experienced in it a quality of absolute desperation, an obsessional and addictive tie later overlaid with drugs. The potency and power of this experience are a mix of desire and identity. B.K. seems most determined to inhabit and have pleasure in a homosexual space as one of the boys, freed from the maternal eye and control and looking for pleasure and freedom. I am terming "homosexual" her love of a young adolescent boy in that it is a choice of an object experienced as same-sexed, at least in unconscious fantasy.

This period coincided with the escalation of the mother's illness. In a dream that takes place in the street and back alley of her childhood, she is trying to escape on a bicycle as her mother comes toward her. But it is B.K. who is wearing the hospital gown, which is covered with shit. She is humiliated, carrying her mother's shame, the horror at physical collapse and loss of control. Associating to the dream, B.K. tearfully remembers the ordeal of caring for her mother during this preadolescent and adolescent period. The mother lost bladder control; an operation was performed that permitted catheterization, a duty both father and daughter had to perform. This memory allowed us to make sense of a series of dream images in which flaps of skin, sores on feet, and catheterized genitals could now be understood in terms of her desperation to repudiate a femininity that seemed ill and damaged and a female genital that was sordid and shameful.

Behind the memories of a shamed and damaged mother is a depressed and withholding mother, a silent mother who is longed for. A memory of this mother partially inspires the lovers chosen in adulthood. Romantic enactment is always orchestrated around bringing a woman to life. For B.K. as she says,

pleasure for herself is "at best second." Her relationships are primarily heterosexual in the sense that B.K. enacts symbolically the role of "boy/butch" court-
ing mother. She is, in symbolic terms, not exactly the same sex as her
love-object. In making this claim, I am preserving Freud's insight into the distinction between biology and culture and Lacan's insistence on the fictive nature
of sexuality and gender.

What is developing for this patient within the realm of object-choice is quite
interesting. There is a new willingness to have pleasure, not merely to give it.
This willingness seems to require greater comfort with an experience she is calling "being baby," a passivity that is frightening but fascinating. There is some
wonderment at the possibility that pleasure might occur for her and for another
person from acts of incorporation, being inside.

In these more ample relationships, she combines excitement with personal
connection, although at key moments they threaten to recapture or imitate or
outdo some fantasied primal scene, B.K. draws back to a mode of phallic play,
of deferral. Taking her lover away for a weekend was to be a time when, in her
words, she could "be daddy." Things went well until the moment for sex. It
was a Sunday afternoon, a time, B.K. later remembered, when her parents
would shoo the children away so they could make love. At that moment, B.K.
to her surprise, turned away from the bedroom and went out to play softball.

B.K. has a quality about her that has always puzzled me. For a person with such
a florid and elaborate sexual history, the term "latency" does not exactly hold. Yet,
stylistically, B.K. lives like a latency boy. Her apartment is full of toys, games, and
projects. She builds rockets, takes craft classes, does handiwork for friends. In this
way she is caught as boy, not able to inhabit adult masculinity, and this inhibition
is sharply problematic to her in her work. "It's natural for them. They always knew
how to do it." She is talking about her workmates, and if we hear penis envy here,
we can think of Marie Torok's (1966) account of that structure as a defensive move
against owning and inhabiting one's own life, body, and prospects. "In penis envy,
there is a projection into the Other of some desire, deemed natural to that other
and treated as fundamentally unavailable to the self" (p. 140).

Conclusion

Despite the shortcomings and contradictions in Freud's work with his patient,
there is still an astonishing richness in his ideas of sexuality and gender. This
complexity in the structure of anyone's gender and object-choice now meets
up with the analyses in feminism and in current deconstructionist and semiotic
theory. These perspectives argue for a multiply figured and multiply determined
model of gender, for the fluid and fragmentary nature of desire, and for the
potency of culture to shape and construct both identity and desire.

What might be helpful is to maintain a contradictory model of gender in which it is a serious, fully lived, conscious experience of self, often "core" to one's being, and at the same time it can dissolve or transmute under our very gaze. Ann Snitow (1989) has argued for this approach as one that keeps in play the currently unresolvable conflicts within and around this category.

We might try to hold to a paradox. What is persistent is that gender and sexuality are fluid and unsettled and labile. What can be consistently addressed is the disruptive and complex and multiply determined developments that end up in adult identity and adult love. Giving up commitments to a bifurcation of normality and abnormality where object-choice and identity are concerned means that other criteria can be watchfully considered.

The French psychoanalytic school proposes a definition of perversion as one in which difference is refused. Yet Chasseguet-Smirgel (1985) and others using this framework often secure "difference" as a solely biological term. But "nature" is no guarantee of difference. A more promising line of thought is in Winnicott's (1971) criteria for normal versus pathological play, which are echoed in McDougall's (1980) consideration of perversion as the enactment of a rigidly programmatic and fetishistic object relation, a refusal of fluidity and playfulness in respect to sex and identity.

Yet even with a revitalized vision of the complexity of gender structure and sexual choice, there is still the problem of politics, culture, and power. Freud's theory of the construction of the relation of sexual aim and object, of the free play of associations and symbolic meaning that arise for any child in regard to the body can sound remarkably idealistic. Our society marks some practices as wholesome and some as pathological, and these markings hold powerful meanings for all of us. Feminist and gay liberation texts have revalenced the degraded positions of homosexual practices and refused patriarchal culture hegemony. What is needed is a theory that recognizes the social power of categories like gender and sexuality in both conscious and unconscious experience but can also account for the way in which these categories, at certain moments, lose salience and become more porous. Benjamin's (1988) groundbreaking work holds that promise.

Hannah and B.K. each in her own way, express the rage and conflict they feel at the absence of social power. But whatever binds them as women struggling with the phallic position, the differences are equally profound. B.K. lives her life in a community of women and gay people. Her lovers are women, even as she wryly worries that not all lesbian women like to hear her talk about "dicks and being inside people." Hannah competes and lives in a rather relentlessly heterosexual world as a woman who hates the feminine in herself while operating fully within the conventions of femininity in dress, look, and style. She groans, "The only good thing about being a girl is the clothes."

In one of those coincidences about which psychoanalysis teaches us to be curious, during a week in which I was revising this paper, both Hannah and B.K. brought in stories about dancing. B.K. talked about the pleasure of dancing with her shirt off at a Gay Pride Day dance, and she contrasted this pleasure with the shame she felt looking at her body with her T-shirt on. Covered, she felt female and saw rolls of flesh. Uncovered, she felt full and pleased and safe. Hannah had gone to a benefit at which there were mostly gay men. She also talked of the pleasure in dancing freely. Why this freedom for Hannah in a crowd of gay men? She would say, graphically, "No one stares at your tits." I would theorize that at this moment she is freed from pure object status and can inhabit her own subjectivity. Yet the contradiction comes in her meticulous development of her body along ideals and stereotypes of feminine beauty. Hannah's ideally slim, feminine body concretizes phallic power, but as object. It is phallic power more in enactment than in conscious function. This conflict, lived at the level of the body, is a thwarting of a masculine identification that could infuse her subjectivity. In both these women's experiences, masculine life and possibility are highly idealized. Maleness seems to equate with freedom itself. Torok's (1966) analysis of penis envy notes this defensive stance in women as the idealizing into masculinity desires and possibilities too dangerous to own as aspects of self.

At this point historically, we need to understand the psychic costs of contesting for entry as a subject in the Symbolic order, a privileged psychic space from which women are barred, both in unconscious fantasy as well as in social reality. We need a theory to encompass the complexity of rebellion in masculine and feminine character, its liberating potential and its painful costs. We need a theory of gender with room for both reified categories and fluid new forms of social and personal life. Psychoanalysis and Freud's radical model of sexuality, as he theorized it in the essay on homosexuality in a woman, can be one crucial resource in such a project.

References

Benjamin, J. (1988). *The bonds of love*. New York: Pantheon Press.

Bollas, C. (1987). *The shadow of the object*. New York: Columbia University Press.

Borch-Jacobsen, M. (1988). *The Freudian subject*. Stanford, CA: Stanford University Press.

Chasseguet-Smirgel, J. (1966). *Feminine sexuality*. Ann Arbor, MI: University of Michigan Press.

Chasseguet-Smirgel, J. (1986). *Sexuality and mind*. New York: Basic Books.

Chasseguet-Smirgel, S. (1985). *The ego ideal*. New York: Norton.

Chodorow, N. (1976). *The reproduction of mothering*. Berkeley, CA: University of California Press.

Chomsky, N. (1965). *Aspects of a theory of syntax*. Cambridge, MA: M.I.T. Press.

Coates, S. (1994). The ontogenesis of gender identity disorder in boys. *J. Amer. Acad. Psychoanal.*

Dinnerstein, D. (1976). *The mermaid and the minotaur.* New York: Harper & Row.

Eisenbud, R. (1982). Early and later determinants of lesbian identity. *Psychoanalytic Review, 69,* 85–109.

Fast, I. (1984). *Gender identity: A differentiation model.* Hillsdale, NJ: The Analytic Press.

Freud, S. (1953–1974). Female sexuality. In J. Strachey (Ed. and Trans.), *The standard edition of the complete psychological works of Sigmund Freud.* (Vol. 21, pp. 223–242). London: Hogarth. (Original work published 1931)

Freud, S. (1953–1974). Fragment of an analysis of a case of hysteria. In J. Strachey (Ed. and Trans.), *The standard edition of the complete psychological works of Sigmund Freud.* (Vol. 7, pp. 7–122). London: Hogarth. (Original work published 1905)

Freud, S. (1953–1974). The interpretation of dreams. In J. Strachey (Ed. and Trans.), *The standard edition of the complete psychological works of Sigmund Freud.* (Vols. 4 & 5). London: Hogarth. (Original work published 1900)

Freud, S. (1953–1974). The psychogenesis of a case of homosexuality in a woman. In J. Strachey (Ed. and Trans.), *The standard edition of the complete psychological works of Sigmund Freud.* (Vol. 18, pp. 145–172). London: Hogarth. (Original work published 1920)

Freud, S. (1953–1974). Three essays on the theory of sexuality. In J. Strachey (Ed. and Trans.), *The standard edition of the complete psychological works of Sigmund Freud.* (Vol. 7, pp. 123–243). London: Hogarth. (Original work published 1905)

Grossman, W. & Kaplan, D. (1988). Three commentaries on gender in Freud's thought: A prologue to the psychoanalytic theory of sexuality. In *Fantasy, myth and reality.* New York: International Universities Press.

Jones, E. (1957). *The life and work of Sigmund Freud.* (Vol. 3). New York: Basic Books.

Lacan, J. (1977). *Écrits.* New York: Norton.

Lauffer, M. & Lauffer, M. (1989). *Developmental breakdown and adolescent psychopathology.* New Haven, CT: Yale University Press.

Lewin, B. (1973). The body as phallus. In *The selected writings of Bertram D. Lewin.* New York: Psychoanalytic Quarterly Press. (Original work published 1933)

Little, M. (1981). *Transference neurosis and transference psychosis.* New York: Aronson.

McDougall, J. (1980). *Plea for a measure of abnormality.* New York: International Universities Press.

Mitchell, J. (1975). *Psychoanalysis and feminism.* New York: Basic Books.

Mitchell, S. (1988). *Relational concepts in psychoanalysis: An integration.* Cambridge, MA: Harvard University Press.

Roazen, P. (1969). *Brother animal: The story of Freud and Tausk.* New York: Knopf.

Rosenberg, C. (1985). *Disorderly conduct.* New York: Knopf.

Snitow, A. (1989). A gender diary. In A. Harris & Y. King (Ed.), *Rocking the ship of state: Towards a feminist peace politics.* Boulder, CO: Westview Press.

Torok, M. (1966). The significance of penis envy for a woman. In J. Chasseguet-Smirgel (Ed.), *Feminine Sexuality.* (pp. 135–169). Ann Arbor, MI: University of Michigan Press,

Weeks, J. (1979). *Coming out: A history of homosexuality from the nineteenth century to the present.* New York: Quartet Books.

Winnicott, D. W. (1971). *Playing and reality.* London: Tavistock.

11

FREUD, THE REVIVAL

~

Linda I. Meyers

Prologue

I am a dramaturge hired by Lesser and Schoenberg to solicit backing for a revival of a little-known play by Sigmund Freud. Following is the proposal I presented to a select group of analytically minded Broadway Angels in early 1998. It was a successful presentation and won the backing of the group. I offer it as encouragement to those of you who would consider a similar enterprise.

Presentation

The name of the play, as you know, is "The Psychogenesis of a Case of Homosexuality in a Woman." Written in 1919 by Sigmund Freud, it was first presented to the psychoanalytic community in the *International Z. Psychoanalysis* in 1920. Starring in the original production were the highly controversial psychoanalyst, Dr. Sigmund Freud, and his newly devised theory of female homosexuality. The theory and the analyst were developed and played by Freud himself. The young patient, aptly conceived by her father and Freud for the supporting role, was an intriguing ingenue. Other members of the original cast included the father, the mother, and the *"cocotte."* There were also several walk-on parts.

To our knowledge, there were only six legitimate productions between the play's debut in 1920 and the *Gesammette Werke* in 1947. There were two English translations: the 1920 *International Journal of Psychoanalysis* and the 1924 *Collected Papers* (p. 146). We have been unable to locate any reviews but conclude, by virtue of the fact that there have been few if any revivals, that this work was not particularly well-regarded, a mistake we intend to turn to our advantage.

I do not know if the early audiences appreciated the risk Freud took when he presented this piece. Since the late 1800s, he had stayed away from any direct consideration of female sexuality. He preferred to infer women's psychology from the safe, familiar perspective of male sexuality. He knew there was far more to women's sexuality than he had investigated in *Studies on Hysteria* (1895). However, by his own acknowledgment, women confused him, and for 20 years he skirted the issue. (This may actually be a double entendre as Anna [b. 1895] was the Freuds' last child and "the method of contraception her parents resorted to was abstinence" [Young-Bruehl, 1988, p. 35]. Freud's active sexual life with Martha ended with Anna's birth.) With the presentation of this case in 1920, he intellectually reentered the dark realm of female sexuality.

Why did Freud use this patient for his comeback? She purportedly was a "non-neurotic" (pp. 150–151) woman, an invert clearly resistant to his interventions. As such, she hardly provided supportive material for his nascent efforts in an arena he already deemed difficult. Surely he had seen other women patients in the interim, yet he opted to present this rather unwieldy vehicle. Why? And why did he choose to produce this case at that time? The rationale behind this revival can be found in the answers to these questions. These are the questions that are pertinent to a contemporary audience as they speak directly to Freud's subjectivity.

Resistances

In preparation for this presentation, in an effort to win your support, I, like any good analyst, have attempted to anticipate your resistances toward this project. No doubt, there will be some I've missed. There will be plenty of time at the conclusion of the presentation to raise questions. For those of you who prefer confidentiality, I am also available for private consultation and will be happy to set up individual sessions at the end of the meeting.

Isn't Psychoanalysis Dead?

While I know this audience is generally supportive of psychoanalysis, you still may find it difficult to invest your money in a discipline you've been repeatedly told is dead. Let me say categorically that this simply is not true. What you are hearing are false rumors widely circulated by the American health insurance cartel. Lesser and Schoenberg, clinicians on the front lines, are fully aware of the current climate and are undaunted. They have complete trust in the efficacy and vibrancy of contemporary psychoanalysis and understand that it has become far more than the metapsychology of its founder.

They also appreciate that for many in our audience psychoanalysis and Freud are the same; to say Freud is dead is to bury the discipline. It is not our intent, nor would it be possible, to separate Freud and psychoanalysis. Our goal is to integrate him into the whole. Freud and psychoanalysis are very much alive. The lay public continues to esteem Freud (*LIFE* magazine's "millennium issue" currently lists Freud as the thirteenth most influential man of the century). The professional community still uses him as the standard against which all psycho-analytic process and progress is measured, and, within the subfield of human sexuality, his thinking is rarely, if ever, ignored. We do not ask you to take any risks that we ourselves are not taking. We solicit your backing with the complete confidence that all will profit from the investment.

If you doubt that there is contemporary interest in the field, may I remind you that *The New York Review of Books* does not miss an opportunity to review psychoanalysis. Although their coverage is generally negative, their consistent attention is indicative of psychoanalysis' vitality. Our public relations department assures me that we can count on them to review our production.

Why Revive an Obscure Play by Freud?

If we want to illustrate the vitality of psychoanalysis, why revive an obscure play by Freud? Although *Mrs. Klein,* a play about Melanie Klein, recently completed a very successful off-Broadway run, perhaps that's enough of the old world psychoanalysts. Shouldn't we update the audience and produce a contemporary theorist, maybe a relationist or at the least an interpersonalist? What's to be gained by reviving an unknown play by Freud?

Paradoxically, the play's intrigue lies in its anonymity. Unlike "Dora" and "Anna O.," cases that are annually presented in institute classrooms worldwide, this drama remains obscure to all but Freud's most ardent aficionados. The general psychoanalytic audience has never heard of the case, or they've rejected it out of hand. It's old Freud, but it's new to the public.

Having read the piece, I know that many of you have decided that it's been ignored for good reason. I'm here to tell you that you're assessing it from the wrong perspective. The lack of interest in this play is not as high-minded as to be rooted in what we might call the play's "intellectual" deficiencies; other of Freud's productions have elicited similar if not more strident criticism without being relegated to obscurity. The reasons this case has been ignored or rejected in the past are the very reasons it has value in the present. I'm referring to the base human propensity toward prejudice, specifically the anti-homosexual sentiment within psychoanalysis, and to an unusual conjunction of transferences, explicitly the confluence between Freud's countertransference toward this patient and the audience's continued idealization of Freud. It is our contention that it was the interaction of these variables that resulted in the play's either being overlooked or perhaps actively suppressed by the psychoanalytic cognoscenti. In the current production, we will turn these impediments to our advantage.

Prejudice

Prejudice against homosexuals in psychoanalysis is being altered through an ongoing cultural and professional evolution. A successful revival would be further evidence of the change. What I'm saying here is that until recently it would have been impossible for a revival of "The Psychogenesis Case of Homosexuality in a Woman" to get an audience. Two possible audiences had existed for this production: One believed and supported cases that portrayed homosexuality as pathology; the other consisted of homosexuals themselves. The first audience was dissolved and the second was disallowed.

Homosexual analysts were unable to fill a house or guarantee a draw. This was not a reflection of disinterest but of the unwritten Institute codes that had kept all homosexual analysts and candidates closeted. Unwelcomed or disguised, they could not carry the box office. The other audience that perceived homosexuality as pathology was, in essence, negated. Homosexuality had lost its cache as perversion. Kicked out of the DSM-II in 1987, gays and lesbians were in effect "blacklisted."[1] There was no longer an impetus to produce plays with a homosexual theme. Prejudice could now be underwritten as "legitimate" disregard; if "they" are simply a variation of "normal," they're outside the rubric of pathology, so why feature them at all? (I should like to note that small, clandestine groups of "classical" analysts on the Upper West Side of New York City and in certain sectors of Paris have refused to accept this nonclassification. To a closed and biased audience, cases depicting homosexuals as "perverts" are presented to this day. Although our revival will disappoint those classical analysts, they will still encourage each other to come if only to shake their heads in disapproval.)

Evidence that the climate is changing can be found in the reception Lesser and Domenici received for their 1995 production, *Disorienting Sexuality*. Lesser and Schoenberg intend to build on the audience base generated by that success. They believe, and I agree, that with proper marketing the preferred audience for this play is in place and ready to support the production—the revival, that is, not the original play. Freud's script had serious problems. Which brings me to the second, and most significant, impediment to the original work—the countertransferences.

Countertransference

As you are probably aware by now, our enthusiasm for this project is not commensurate with Freud's theoretical perspective on female homosexuality or with his clinical interventions with this patient. Our umbrage with his conceptualization and treatment of this patient is definitive. This revival is an endorsement of our continued respect for Freud's import and the efficacy of contemporary psychoanalysis, not for the specific content of the original piece. Although I've stated that we have an audience for this production, it is not for the play as Freud wrote it.

Did you notice when you read the play that none of the characters is likable? The theory, a featured player in the original production, is convoluted and difficult to understand. The patient is portrayed as either brash or affectively absent. Freud writes her as more recalcitrant than troubled. Freud, the other star of the play, comes across as unempathic. His contempt for his patient, the "*grande damme*" (p. 163) elicits the audience's contempt for him. Our goal is to show that his manner in this case was not indicative of a general attitude but specific to his countertransference.

Ironically, "The Psychogenesis of a Case of Homosexuality in a Woman," by today's standards, would hardly be considered a psychological play. It is cultural exposé, but it is not analysis. If reproduced as written, this play would be justifiably dismissed as an outdated, generic presentation of Victorian patriarchy and sexual small-mindedness. It would not hold the interest of a psychoanalytically sophisticated assemblage. (I am referring to an educated audience well versed in issues of overdetermination, multiple causality, and subjectivity.) The so-called "neutral analyst" featured in the original play is out. While Freud concentrated on the patient's transferences, our script must emphasize and deconstruct his countertransference. It is there that we will find the key that opens up this drama. It is our contention that with this patient, perhaps even more than with his other analysands, Freud was conflicted and constrained by a powerful and unacknowledged countertransference.

Countertransference issues are at the heart of this proposal. The substance of this work is within the audience and the author himself. The complex visionary who's perspicacity propelled the concept of infant sexuality into the twentieth century is barely recognizable in this case, nor is the man who welcomed women to his profession. We meet instead the conventional Viennese patriarch. The modernization of this production does not lie in the revision of theory or technique but rather in the exposition of Freud's unconscious and the audiences' transference to Freud. Unless we can connect the humanity of Freud and the contemporary audience, there is no drama.

In anticipation of criticism that the investigation and assumption of a deceased's countertransference are by definition invalid and, by process, unethical, I ask you to consider the following: While all case documentation is subjective rendering, this case is more so than usual. In fact, we come away from the reading feeling more certain in our inferences about Freud than we are in his inferences about the patient. Furthermore, Freud would encourage us to speculate. He was far less reticent to self-disclose than the "Freudians" he spawned.

His subjectivity, unsheathed in jargon, is as seductive an invitation to enter his unconscious as the lure of the rabbit hole was to Alice. His analysis of Leonardo da Vinci (1910) is further precedence for this type of adventure. Leonardo's presence was unnecessary for Freud's purposes. He obviously believed that there was a validity in conjecture beyond that of his own projections.

As dramaturge, it is not my intention to rewrite the case but to edit it, develop relevant themes, and suggest the inclusion of pertinent scenes. Consistent with our approach to the revival, these scenes are meant to illustrate Freud's countertransference. They will be the fantasized elucidations of his unconscious. A conflation of fact and innuendo, based upon material from the original case and from other writings by and about Freud, will be crafted into each scene to give the audience entry into Freud's psyche. The off-Broadway play *Gross Indecency: The Three Trials of Oscar Wilde* uses this technique. It has proven to be very successful.

Woven throughout the countertransferences are the dangling threads of an unfinished idealization process. Issues of idealization are what connect Freud and the patient, as well as the audience and Freud. If our interpretation is on the money, this theme will resonate with the audiences and the play will be felt to contain an inherent truth. It need not be Freud's truth. I repeat, it need not be Freud's truth. We have no way of knowing Freud's truth any more than he had of knowing Leonardo's or we have of knowing the childhood "truths" of our patients. It need only be a narrative so believable that it speaks directly to the audience's subjectivity. Issues of idealization provide such a narrative.

For those of you who are still uncomfortable with the tack we're taking and think that I protest too much, I ask you to hold onto your thoughts and feelings. They may be at the core of the audience's countertransference issues. I will get back to them shortly. Hopefully, for the moment I've assuaged enough resistance that we can move on to several specific ideas I have for the revival.

The Revival

If you turn your attention to the overhead monitors, you will see sketches for the set: Freud's consultation room with its familiar artifacts and paintings. The cluttered shelves and leather-bound books exude a strange blend of the personal and the erudite. The couch covered, as you know, with Victorian rugs and pillows invites as it intimidates. The warm sepia tones we associate with the turn of the century will be exquisitely reproduced in the furnishings and lighting. Our emphasis will be on authenticity in the replication of Freud's study, costumes, and props. This is very important, as inattention to detail will distract the unconscious of the audience. If they are unable to enter Freud's context, the play will be farce rather than drama. Without the social construction there is no context for meaning.

The drama will be explicated in the subtleties that elucidate Freud's conflicts with the patient. Therefore, the audience must see her as Freud sees her. His descriptions reflect his personal, theoretical, and cultural conflicts with her sexuality. Remember, he describes her as "a beautiful and clever girl of eighteen" (p. 147). He states that she was "well-made" (p. 154), a propitious and decidedly female adjective that evokes his awareness of her sexuality yet cloaks it in an air of propriety. He also defeminizes her by stating that she has "her father's tall figure," "sharp features," and the "acuteness of comprehension" and "lucid objectivity" of a man (p. 154). Remember, too, that he never names her. Unlike most of her female predecessors (Dora and Anna O, for example), she is never formally introduced. Lacking even a pseudonym, we have no choice but to refer to her throughout the play as "the patient." I was tempted to infer a respect by naming her but decided that was counter to our aims. Her anonymity, intellectual cogency, and affective absence make her an extremely useful object for Freud's projections. The audience should take no less privilege and will be encouraged to use her similarly.

In the original 1920s production, there were several important characters that went largely unnoted. If you look closely at the overhead monitors, you can just about make out three shadowy figures standing behind Freud. In this blow-up you can see that they are Freud's daughter Anna, his father Jacob, and his friend Fliess. These characters stood, unmoving, through the original play. They are the amorphous embodiment of Freud's subjectivity. They potentially illuminate his countertransference. Without them, viewing this play is like watching a foreign film without subtitles. In the revival they will become the featured players.

Freud and His Antigone

The first figure to emerge from behind Freud is his daughter Anna. At approximately the same time that he is treating the patient, or shortly thereafter, Anna has also become her father's analysand.[2] The patient has no way of knowing that she is being affected by Freud's clandestine treatment of his youngest daughter. It is doubtful that Freud is consciously aware of the impact. The audience will come to see that there are provocative similarities between the patient and Anna, and they will note that the characteristics Freud appreciates in his daughter, he disdains in the patient.

Both Anna and the patient have what Freud termed a "masculine intellect" (p. 154). Although he uses it to infer a masculine sexuality in the patient, he does not offer a similar interpretation to Anna. Freud writes to Fliess in 1897, "Annerl is turning into a charming child; she is of the same type as Martin, physically and mentally" (Young-Bruehl, 1988, p. 46). He is proud and supportive of Anna's intellect, particularly her interest in psychoanalysis. Freud nurtures

Anna, telling her: "You have turned out a little differently from Math[ilde] and Sophie" and "have more intellectual interests and will not be quite so satisfied with some purely feminine activity" (Gay, 1988, p. 430). It is Anna who will be the recipient of Freud's legacy. He does not leave it to his sons, for they show no particular "acuteness of comprehension," he gives psychoanalysis to Anna: Anna was "the mother of psychoanalysis; the one to whom primary responsibility for its spirit, its future, was passed. Sigmund Freud . . . called his daughter 'Anna Antigone' " (Young-Bruehl, p. 15). Antigone, as you may recall, was Oedipus' devoted daughter, who cared for and supported him throughout his exile until his death.[3]

Anna, like the patient, has little interest in men. They both prefer the company of older, independent women. While Freud disparages the patient's desire for the *cocotte,* he clearly supports these proclivities in Anna. He not only accepts Anna's preference for older women, but he also actively solicits their companionship on her behalf. After Freud invites Lou Andreas-Salomé to spend time with them, Freud writes to Eitingon: "Enough is left over of her [Andreas-Salomé] to occupy Anna, for whom I mainly invited her" (Young-Bruehl, 1988, p. 110). The visit initiates a long-term attachment between the two women, of which Freud gratefully approves (Gay, 1988, p. 439). Freud would probably argue that there is no comparison between the *cocotte* and Lou. The *cocotte* would be unsuitable company for any "proper" young lady. Henri Ellenberger (1970) refers to Lou as a "femme inspiratrice" who "was to play an important role in the lives of a succession of great men" (Ellenberger, p. 294). It leaves us to wonder how she was perceived by conventional bourgeois women of the day.

The audience is not to assume that Freud's identification with the patient's father and Freud's attitude toward the patient reflect his feelings toward Anna—at least not his conscious feelings. There's no doubt that Freud cares a great deal about Anna. We will make sure that his love is evident, as the audience's empathy toward Freud is dependent upon their awareness of his caring. Our contention is that it is his concern for Anna and his inability to directly deal with that concern that results in his mistreatment of the patient. The patient is the unfortunate recipient of Freud's defensive maneuvers with his daughter. In his theory and in his clinical work, Freud may portend to objectivity, but as a father, he knows that neutrality is impossible. He splits off his hostile feelings toward his daughter and projects them onto the patient. Without Anna's presence in the play, without an understanding of Freud's subjectivity, the audience would be able to use similar defenses. They would be rescued from the natural anxiety one experiences when attempting to hold the good and bad object together by splitting Freud and the patient. The complexity of the play would be lost. We want them to feel these conflicts, to experience the discomfort Freud defends against. This is a fault in the original script. We do not intend to make the same mistake.

Freud worries about Anna's sexuality, as he writes to Lou in 1924: "I am afraid that her suppressed genitality may someday play her a mean trick. I cannot free her from me and nobody is helping me with it" (Gay, 1988, p. 441). He attributes her "suppressed genitality" to her undue attachment to him. This worry is more palatable than fears that Anna is a lesbian. Freud is too astute an observer not to entertain the question that his concerns automatically induce in others, and the patient interferes with his ability to suppress that seminal worry. He believes himself culpable in Anna's persistent idealization of him. If this were the sole constraint on her libidinal development, analysis might help. But how invested is Freud in actually freeing Anna, particularly if freedom from him means indulgence in homosexuality? Even if Anna is heterosexual, he is conflicted between his desire for her to marry and the fear that she will leave him. He colludes with Anna in discouraging male suitors.[4]

For any of you that may be trying to maintain a fantasy about Freud's sexual liberalism and wish to believe that his collusion is a covert endorsement of a lesbian sexuality, forget it. We want to show Freud's caring for Anna, but we do not want to feed a false idealization of Freud. His "open-mindedness" toward homosexuality is theoretical at best. Aside from his attitude toward this patient, I will remind you of his treatment of Wortis. Wortis, Freud's analysand in 1933, asks Freud why one needs to choose: Couldn't both sides of sexuality be engaged and enjoyed? Freud's response is

> Normal people have a certain homosexual component. The homosexual component should be sublimated as it now is in society; it is one of the most valuable human assets, and should be put to social uses. One cannot give one's impulses free rein. Your attitude reminds me of a child who just discovered everybody defecates and who then demands that everybody ought to defecate in public; that cannot be. (Drescher, 1996, p. 99–100)

Even though Freud writes to a mother encouraging her to accept the naturalness of her son's homosexuality in 1935, his theoretical acceptance of homosexuality certainly does not extend to his daughter; however, it is the patient, not Anna, who bears the brunt of his disapproval.

In case you are wondering if this play takes a definitive position on Anna's sexual orientation, it does not. Her sexual orientation will be ambiguous. In true postmodern application, the script will not permit the audience to escape into the protection of socially constructed categories. We want to raise the audience's eyebrows, not their defenses. We want them to experience Freud's ambivalence and confusion, to experience all of the ambiguity. It is much more pertinent for them to be asking who is treating the patient, Freud the father or Freud the analyst, than to be asking if Anna is gay.

This raises the important issue of deceit. Freud, as you remember, bases his major interpretations of the patient on his belief that she is deceitful. He tells us that even her dreams are manipulations unconsciously fashioned to delude (p. 165). Why is he so mistrustful? If she is manipulative, why does he label it deceit instead of defense? He is able to enjoy similar qualities in Anna. Doesn't he call her his "black devil" (Gay, 1988, p. 431), an endearing term intimating his fondness for Anna's defiant nature? Anna strives throughout her childhood to secure him for herself. Anna pursues Freud with a tenacity he admires and to which he eventually succumbs. Her aspirations, particularly her interest in psychoanalysis, are all taken up with him in mind. Any father would have been flattered; any analyst would have been suspicious. The audience will question Freud's "deceit" when he labels the patient's pursuit of the *cocotte* as obsession and Anna's pursuit of him as devotion.

Our intent is to develop the complexity that was missed in the original production. Every character in this play is honest and every character is deceitful. The audience will identify with Freud because they will recognize their own desires to seduce and be seduced by their children. Freud's treatment of Anna seems impossible and perhaps ill-advised. But it wasn't that simple and here again, the social context becomes paramount. It was not unusual for analysts at the time to treat family members and friends, although Freud himself advised against it. (Gay, 1988, p. 114). All of you are Institute graduates. Most of you had choices when applying for analytic training, nevertheless, you complained that treatment and training were incestuous. Such problems are endemic to psychoanalysis. But let us take ourselves back to Vienna in the early twentieth century. The only analysts Freud can consider for Anna live in Budapest and Berlin, and Anna is teaching in Vienna (Gay, p. 115). Freud is understandably conflicted between his desire to help his daughter and his wish to protect himself. He continually struggles with the paranoia induced by his insecurities and the envy of his colleagues induced by his accomplishments. Given Anna's loyalty to Freud, with whom can she explore her unconscious hostility toward her father or confess family secrets? Certainly not with any of his colleagues, certainly not with any of his sibling analysands, and, unfortunately, probably not with her father.

The patient obviously suffers the consequences of Freud and Anna's dilemma; Freud is frustrated and angry during his treatment of the patient. Whatever hostility he feels toward Anna for his impossible situation, for her manipulation of his needs and affections, he projects onto the patient. Whatever guilt he carries for accepting the position as Anna's analyst becomes resentment turned on the patient. Now we begin to understand his overidentification with the patient's father. To Freud's credit, in the end he is able to do for the patient what he cannot do for his daughter: rescue her from his countertransference by referring her to a female analyst.

There is no doubt that Freud wants to succeed with the patient. He appreciates her father's desperation in considering a treatment that is almost as disreputable as his daughter's behavior (p. 149), yet he declares the treatment impossible. It is hard to know where he suffers the greater narcissistic injury: in relinquishing the patient or in treating her. She never develops an idealizing transference toward him. He experiences this as a negative therapeutic reaction. He also experiences it as her disrespect. His daughter never de-idealizes her analyst, and it's not clear if Freud questions Anna's "transference" at all. Even if he does, it would be impossible to analyze. You can't analyze idealization when the real object and the transference object are the same, nor can you analyze countertransference when the patient is the real object. Freud's ability to work with the idealization process, whether for the patient or for Anna, is impeded by his own unresolved idealization issues.

Freud, the Idealized Object and the Patient

In the second act, Jacob Freud moves out from behind Freud and takes center stage. Freud tells us he has been extremely moved by his father's death. He claims it is the most significant event of his life (Gay, 1988, p. 89). Yet, there is little in Jacob Freud's life or Sigmund Freud's biographies to indicate that the "real" Jacob is truly a loss to Freud. Much older than his son, raised in a very different social environment, Jacob provides little for Sigmund to emulate. The often-told story of Freud's shame when his father recounts the tale of his harassment at the hands of the Gentiles stands as a seminal story (Gay, pp. 11–12). Equivalent to a screen memory, we read it as symbolic of Freud's overall disappointment in his father. This is not to deny that Freud is sincerely moved by his father's loss but to raise the question: Who, or what, is he actually mourning?

Once again we pick up the thread of idealization. The audience, watching Freud's reaction to Jacob, will identify with their own disappointments in their same-sex parent. They will recognize Freud's depression after the death of his father as disappointment turned inward. Freud is faced with the untenable task of separating and establishing himself as a male presence in a patriarchal culture but without the help of a patriarch. His controlling mother's adulation, the presence of four older sisters, and then the unfortunate fulfillment of his death wish toward his baby brother compounds Freud's difficulty. Remember, too, that

Freud's mother is considerably younger than her husband, and closer to the ages of her stepsons. We can only assume the effect these facts have on the sexual dynamics in the Freud household and the effect of these dynamics on Sigmund's Oedipal development.

As is typical of an arrest in the idealization process, Freud is confused as to the limits of his power. Without the secure boundary provided by an idealizable father, Freud can only be frightened by the strength of his sadistic and Oedipal wishes. It is through Jacob's presence that the audience begins to identify with Freud's handicap. It will be implied that Freud's unconscious need for a strong father delays his emergence into his profession and extends his engagement to Martha. Until he can idealize and incorporate a same-sex object, he cannot separate from his mother and take his place in the adult world.

The patient's childhood position, in the context of the idealization process, is not dissimilar to Freud's. She too has a mother unworthy of idealization. Freud describes the patient's mother as vain and childlike, narcissistically invested in her youthful appearance, and unwilling to give ground to her adolescent daughter (p. 149). As is typical of innovative and relatively well-functioning egos, Freud and his patient each seek and find the necessary substitute objects. Freud, uncomfortable with his hostility and disappointment toward his father, does not want to identify with the patient's feelings toward her mother. The audience sees Freud's denial when Fliess moves from the shadows into the spotlight.

Freud loves Fliess in the same way the patient loves the *cocotte*. Fliess is Freud's hero and, like the *cocotte*, is an unorthodox character. He supports Freud's desire to move beyond the conventional. Freud says of his friend in 1893, "Fliess is a most unusual person, good nature personified: and I believe, if it came to it, he would for all his genius be goodness itself. Therefore his sunlike clarity, his pluck" (Masson, cited in Young-Bruehl, 1988, p. 464). Fliess, unlike Jacob, stands up to his, and Freud's critics. He understands and supports Freud's passions. He bolsters Freud's creativity with the flight of his own ideas. Freud does not see Fliess' limitations. Just as Freud seriously questions the patient's adoration of the *cocotte,* Freud's colleagues must puzzle over his adoration of Fliess. Freud's intellect is far superior to his friend's, yet Freud for many years acts more than deferential to Fliess (Gay, 1988, pp. 56–57).

The need to idealize overrides the confines of reality. It is only when the idealized object has served its purpose and been incorporated into the ego that we can emerge from the fusion. Until that psychological work is accomplished, we strongly resist any outside attempt to differentiate the real person from the idealized object; any direct interference is likely to increase our resistance. The *cocotte* is to the patient what Fliess is to Freud: She holds out the promise of a progressive, independent, sexual existence in a culture where females are only girls, wives, or mothers. There were extensions of men and rarely sexual beings in their own right. Perhaps unresolved grief at the premature loss of the idealized object and shame at the depth of his needs thwart Freud's ability to use his own experiences with his father and Fliess to empathically connect with the patient.

Freud, aware of the permeable membrane between idealization and homosexual desire, defends against his identification with the patient. He admits to homosexual feelings toward Fliess. In fact, in 1906, 1908, and then again in 1909, after the friendship ends he, like his patient, takes a "fall." Freud has several fainting spells that he attributes to the remnants of "some piece of unruly sexual feelings towards Fliess" (Gay, 1988, p. 275). He contends that these spells are activated by the revival of death wishes toward his brother that cover over his homoerotic desire for his friend. Similarly the patient jumps onto the railroad trestle after she and the *cocotte* are sighted by her father. It is Freud's unconscious identification with the patient that leads him to assume that her "fall," as his, is fueled by death wishes toward her own baby brother (p. 162). This is convoluted theory invented to support Freud's defenses. He still has not resolved his sexual desire for his friend or his need to idealize him. To do so, Freud would have to experience his anger and disappointment with his father. If he were able to accomplish this important psychological task, he would be empathetic toward his own need to idealize, and he would not have to sublimate his longing into theory at the expense of his connection to the patient.

The audience will be more tolerant of Freud than he is of himself or than he is of the patient. The scenes with Freud and Fliess will show his worship and their homoerotic desire. It will become clear why Freud needs to dissociate from his feelings and disidentify with the patient: The patient's endeavor with the *cocotte* is too reminiscent of Freud's shame with Fliess. Once again, he is unable to use his subjectivity to empathize with the patient. Our intent, however, is to engage the audience's subjectivity so that they may empathize with Freud.

We will recruit Henri Ellenberger (*The Discovery of the Unconscious: The History and Education of Dynamic Psychiatry,* 1970) to help us tie together issues of idealization and connect Freud with the patient and the audience with Freud. Using Ellenberger's concept of a "creative illness," we will draw the parallel between Freud's strange illness after the death of his father and during his friendship with Fliess (Ellenberger, 1970, p. 447) to the patient's adoration of the *cocotte.* Symptoms include a characteristic sense of isolation and a feeling of being ill-treated. There is an intense preoccupation with an idea or a search for a certain imminent truth. The person has a sense of blazing a new trail and needs a guide to help him or her. The idealized object serves as the needed guide. In the original script Freud fails to recognize the patient's creativity. He negates her independence of thought by labeling it resistance. In fact, she, like Freud, is attempting to forge a unique path. Unlike Fliess, the *cocotte* is a deficient guide. She is inaccessible and unreceptive to the patient's love. Through the natural bisexual properties inherent in transference love, Freud could eventually replace the *cocotte* and become this much-needed object for the patient. Unfortunately, Freud is too constrained by his countertransference to play this role.

While Freud does not provide the patient with a replacement for the *cocotte,* he finds an excellent replacement for Fliess: Leonardo da Vinci. He continues to work through the idealization process by exploiting his identification with Leonardo. He writes his analysis of Leonardo in 1910. Leonardo's undisputed genius provides Freud with the safety of a posthumous object. Leonardo, unlike Fliess, cannot be impugned by the vicissitudes of actual human failings. Freud contends that Leonardo's homosexuality results from his fatherlessness and intense erotic attachment to the mother. These similarities facilitate Freud's identification with Leonardo while ameliorating whatever shame Freud may feel regarding his longing for Fliess. The patient, in the throes of her idealiza-tion with the *cocotte,* has no Leonardo in the wings. The *cocotte* has not yet accomplished for her what Fliess, and then Leonardo, accomplishes for Freud. Her suicide attempt is an expression of her despair and her continued need for the help of an idealizable same-sex object. To dismiss it as simply the expres-sion of jealousy toward her mother is to sacrifice the patient to the theory.

By the end of Act Two, the audience will begin to identify Freud's subjec-tivity with their own. They won't like it, but they will understand it; after all, it talks directly to their unresolved idealization of him.

The Audience's Idealized Transference to Freud

If you recall, earlier I asked those of you who were still uncomfortable with our analysis of Freud's countertransference to hold on to your thoughts and feel-ings. I did so because I suspect that they relate to my own. I have a confession to make; there was far more tentativeness behind my convictions in taking this tack than I let on. In fact, I embarked on this exploration of Freud's subjectiv-ity with definite trepidation and voyeuristic shame. Earlier, when discussing the reasons this case was ignored, I referred to the confluence between Freud's countertransference with this patient and the audience's idealization of Freud. As I began to work with the script, I had a memory that elucidates this conver-gence and that helped me to understand my reticence.

I was reminded of an old mansion in the woods near where I lived as a child. The proprietor had once owned all the surrounding land. For reasons we couldn't know, the property was sold off in large parcels and then odd lots. All around the mansion, builders constructed little monopoly-style houses for the dreams and ready money that had accumulated during the war. In an excited rush, returning G.I.s with FHA mortgages bought the American dream. They sat upon their sectional couches, looked out on their newly planted azaleas, and prided themselves on having purchased the "good life." The prototype, the real thing, was less than a half a mile away. It stood, without artifice, alone in the woods. Although its large frame appeared to spill over the small piece of land it retained, it did not lack dignity. The owners of the new "estates" preferred to ignore the old house, as if acknowledgment diminished the integrity of its offspring. Rumor had it that the mansion was still occupied by the original owner. She, entrenched in the past, refused to leave her home. It was believed she lived alone in the big house with only one servant to help her. No one had ever claimed to see her.

My friend and I developed a fascination with this old house and its occupant. We wanted to confirm her existence and perhaps seek her forgiveness for deforming her legacy. Banking on the necessities of daily life, we assumed she must emerge sometime to go to a doctor's appointment or to the hairdresser. All that was required was our patience and vigilance. Each unrainy day, we brought Mallomars and Good 'n Plenty for sustenance, hid ourselves at a safe distance, and waited. We passed the time conjuring intriguing tales of "her" former life. We imagined a genteel existence—mornings spent letter writing in the library and afternoon teas on the verandah. We were sure she was bereft and that she resented the disbursement of her mannered estate to an unrefined bourgeois. How could she not resent seeing the magnificence of that home distilled into unimaginative plastic representations? Glory reduced to allegory. In the parlance of the day, she'd become a knock-off. We decided that she was unable to tolerate the bastardization of her creation and chose, instead, a reclusive existence. We imagined she hated us.

Believing ourselves to be the only ones who "cared," our grandiosity bolstered an errant sense of responsibility and kept us at our post long after most other kids would have given up. As Indian summer turned into autumn, the leaves dropped. Daily, we lost our cover, and we felt increasingly exposed. Certain to be discovered, we decided to take the risk, extend our trespass, and actually peer through the windows. We were sure we saw her: a small bowed figure, moving slowly through the unlit parlor. As if we'd actually rung the bell, the clock inside the hall chimed, and she looked up and saw us. She was not intimidated. She unlocked the big oak door and invited us in. Stunned and embarrassed by the unexpected welcome, we ran like hell and never went back.

If we and our audience have sufficiently progressed in the idealization process, we will experience our differentiation from Freud not as abandonment but as individuation. Then, we will be free to accept his invitation to enter.

Conclusion

The need to idealize can easily elicit shame. Self-esteem is a delicate commodity easily wounded if the adult is insensitively confronted by his or her childlike impotence and gratitude. While it is the child's helplessness that constructs the hero, it is the hero who affords the illusion of security and thereby eventually empowers his or her own destruction. If we shame Freud, we will also shame the audience. By interpreting Freud's need to enhance his self-esteem through an identification with greatness and the incorporation of an idealizable same-sex object, we locate ourselves. Freud's struggle is our own. Through an understanding of Freud's countertransference, "The Psychogenesis of a Case of Homosexuality In a Woman," a play, which at first appears theoretically and clinically obsolete, becomes timely and ripe for revival.

Ladies and gentlemen, I thank you for your time and attention.

Epilogue

The revival of "The Psychogenesis of A Case of Homosexuality In a Woman" opened in the spring of 2000. *The New York Review of Books* heralded its appearance with yet another article on Freud's demise and the obsolescence of psychoanalysis. The play is sold out and expected to run at least through the first two years of the century.

Notes

1. It wasn't until 1973 that attempts were made to remove *homosexuality* from the DSM-II manual. When it was removed, psychoanalytic organizations and psychoanalysts protested vociferously (Bayer, as cited in Drescher, 1995). In 1980, an attempt was made to retain the perception of homosexuality as pathology, but the burden was transferred from the psychoanalytic establishment to the pathology of the patient; hence, the category of ego-dystonic homosexuality was created. I suspect that as a reaction to its untreatability, rather than to any true change in beliefs, it was finally removed in 1987.

2. Anna began analysis with her father in 1918, continuing for 3 years until 1921. In 1924 her analysis was resumed for an additional year (Gay, 1988, p. 439).

3. "Antigone was preeminent among Oedipus's children. She was his gallant and loyal companion, just as Anna became her father's chosen comrade over the years. It was Antigone who, in *Oedipus at Colonnus,* leads her blind father by the hand, and by 1923, it was Anna Freud who was firmly installed as her wounded father's secretary, confidante, representative, colleague, and nurse" (Gay, 1988, p. 442).

4. In 1914, Freud actively discourages Ernest Jones' interest in Anna by writing to him: "She [Anna] does not claim to be treated as a woman, being still far away from sexual longings and rather refusing man" (Gay, 1988, p. 434). Again in 1920, Freud and Anna collude in discouraging the advances of Hans Lampl. Anna writes to her father in 1921, "I am often together with Lampl in a friendly relationship, but I also have daily opportunities to confirm our judgment of him from last year and rejoice that we judged correctly" (Young-Bruehl, 1988, pp. 95–96).

References

Domenici, T. & Lesser, R. (1995). *Disorienting sexuality: Psychoanalytic reappraisals of sexual identities*. New York: Routledge.

Drescher, J. (1996). Reflections of a gay male analyst. *Gender & Psychoanalysis, 1,* 223–237.

Ellenberger, H. (1970). *The discovery of the unconscious: The history and evolution of dynamic psychiatry*. New York: Basic Books.

Freud, S. (1953–1974). Leonardo da Vinci and a memory of his childhood. In J. Strachey (Ed. and Trans.), *The standard edition of the complete psychological works of Sigmund Freud*. (Vol. 2). London: Hogarth. (Original work published 1910)

Freud, S. (1953–1974). The psychogenesis of a case of homosexuality in a woman. In J. Strachey (Ed. and Trans.), *The standard edition of the complete psycholocal works of Sigmund Freud*. (Vol. 18). London: Hogarth. (Original work published 1920)

Freud, S. & Breuer, J. (1895). Studies on hysteria. *The standard edition of the complete psychological works of Sigmund Freud*. (Vol. 2). London: Hogarth.

Gay, P. (1988) *Freud, a life for our time*. New York: W. W. Norton & Company.

Young-Bruehl, E. (1988). *Anna Freud, a biography*. New York: W. W. Norton & Company.

12

THE FEMALE HOMOSEXUAL
C'est Nous

~

Donald Moss & Lynne Zeavin

This paper is an extended improvisation provoked by a reading of a classical Freudian text: "The Psychogenesis of a Case of Homosexuality in a Woman."

By "classical" we mean two things: first, that the text has achieved canonical status and second, that it contains and gives voice to ideological tensions that characterize Freud's entire oeuvre and that continue to enrich and bedevil psychoanalytic theory and practice today.

Our improvisation means to illuminate and utilize those tensions.

Contemporary texts establish their legitimacy by explicit or implicit reference to predecessors. "Classical" texts form the foundation on which all pertinent predecessors rest. They are an enduring presence. Whether sensed as resource, debt, or hindrance, the classical—no matter how thickly mediated or disguised—provides form and structure to the new. One speaks into, against, or around the classical but never independently of it. The classical exerts force.

In Freud's (1920) text on the female homosexual, one manifestation of this force is the text's pedestrian employment of misogynist and homophobic sentiments. Planted elsewhere in history, we have no trouble spotting these sentiments, and our ability to see through homophobic and misogynist rhetoric tempts us to think ourselves free of the forces that engendered those offensive sentiments.

But this presumption ironically exemplifies the force of the classical in action. As modern as we are, we have become habitually alert to the deforming power of the classical—its misogynist and/or homophobic premises, say. We defend

197

ourselves against that power, and in the process we grow less alert to our
defenses than to the ostensible threats that they so effectively ward off. Thus
protected from our "classical" past, we grow confident in our contemporary
habits of thought.

We want to attend not so much to the loud and openly deforming influences
of the classical but rather to its more quiet and often less noticeable legacy of
confidence. This legacy of confidence underwrites a belief in our own texts'
freedom from deformation. It is only by a mixture of direct and indirect appeals
to our classical predecessors that we distinguish texts produced by thought and
experience from those produced by fantasy and prejudice. Validity depends
upon continuity. The classical, thus, grants legitimacy to the contemporary.

Freud's text is an occasion for this project. As psychoanalysts, we are in continuous relation to our discipline's ongoing output and distant history. That history originates with Freud. No psychoanalytic output can avert the original
Freudian theme. And through that theme we remain tethered, no matter how
loosely, to the classical traditions from which it was produced.

In what follows, we purposely avoid referencing potential intersections with
contemporary arguments and discussions. We suppress intervening contexts in
order to intensify our sense of contact with Freud's text. The potential costs of
this tactic include a possible narrowing or pinching of perspective; the potential gain is a heightening of focus.

Besides the obvious debt to Freud, we sense an explicit theoretical obligation
only to Laplanche and Pontalis' improvisational text, "Fantasy and the Origins
of Sexuality."

In "The Psychogenesis of a Case of Homosexuality in a Woman," Freud
interprets a clinical situation whose main feature is the emergence of homosexual feeling and action in a young woman. At the crux of his interpretation is the
notion of disappointment. Freud posits the woman of his study as doubly disappointed: no phallus and no heterosexual object. He then interprets her homosexual object-choice as an embittering and vengeful compensation for these
disappointments. Her revenge is prompted by a sense of unjust deprivation,
while her bitterness derives from the fundamental ineffectiveness of her fantasied
solution. Freud then argues, in effect, that this ineffectiveness is categorical, that
fantasied solutions like hers do not, and can never, compensate for real disappointments.

Freud's "double disappointment" interpretation of this paradigm case of
homosexuality in a woman does not originate solely from a consideration of the
case's sexual particulars. It necessarily emerges instead from the application of a
preexisting and more general theory of sexuality. By *necessarily,* we mean simply that, explicitly or implicitly, a general theory supports and determines any

particular clinical interpretation. Therefore, although we will take Freud to task for his use of the "double disappointment" interpretation in this case, the object of our argument will be that aspect of his general sexual theory on which this particular interpretation seems to lean.

The aspect of the theory we will look at most critically is Freud's classical notion that phallic disappointment is fundamentally a female problem. We will argue that this interpretation represents a constricted use of Freud's own theory of sexuality and that a consistent reading of that theory posits phallic disappointment as an intrinsic element of genital sexuality regardless of gender and regardless of heterosexual or homosexual object-choice. After explicitly addressing the pertinent theoretical issues, we will offer two exemplary clinical vignettes.

Since we aim to counter Freud's sexual theorizing with Freudian sexual theorizing, we will begin with a consideration of the status of sexual theory itself, particularly of the conditions that make sexual theorizing a continuing necessity for psychoanalysis.

The necessity of sexual theory in psychoanalysis derives from our conviction—our knowledge even—that regarding the origins, raw ingredients, and meanings of its own sexuality, the first-person singular voice labors under severe epistemological constraints. Whether via introspection or interview, the yield from first-person direct inquiry is radically fragmentary—inevitably, and on its face, insufficient. At its most comprehensive, regarding sexual origins, the first-person voice chronicles an apparently coherent sequence of influences. But the starting point for these narratives of influence is either overtly inaccessible or is obscured by the clarity provided by interpretable myths of origin.

We think of the sexual narrative directly available to the reflective first-person voice as referring to manifest sexuality, a sexuality whose relation to its own underlying generative sexual thoughts resembles the relation between the manifest dream and its underlying generative dream thoughts. Just as the dream's formative thoughts are opaque to the dreamer, so sexuality's formative impulses remain opaque to the sexualized person. And with sexuality, as with dreams, where the first-person voice does not know, it constructs. The story it tells itself, or tells us, about its own sexual origins is a product of secondary elaboration.

Therefore, although the first-person voice may speak with precision about the clusters of sexual sensations and erotized persons it currently pursues and avoids, that voice, no matter how meticulous, is structurally unreliable when it comes to the infantile history and original precursors of those sensations and persons.

The most convincing feature of the honest and straightforward first-person voice is its sincerity. Sincerity is epistemologically self-enclosed; it functions as its own validation. It appeals to an experience of direct access and is therefore radically antitheoretical. There is a kind of hallucinatory conviction to sincerity's claims. What it knows, the first-person sincere voice knows via experiences that have been mediated so as to feel immediate and vivid.

The resultant sense of perceptual contact generates the idea that one has encountered the real thing. Knowledge so gained is particularly hard to forswear. Even when conscious of both the cost and the insufficiency of relying on this kind of knowledge—as in the presence of symptoms—the sincere first-person voice will aim to preserve its confidence in its own privileged position; it will believe that to it alone do sexuality's mysteries become clear. Insufficiency and cost—pain, in the Freudian sense—are not enough to displace the first-person voice from its own sincere ground. It seems a constituent element of "I" that it must "know" more about its own sexuality than might any "You" or "He" or "She."

Regarding sexual origins, it is only because we reject both the validity and reliability of truth claims grounded in sincerity that sexual theorizing becomes a necessity. Via sexual theorizing, we place ourselves in direct argument with the foundational premises of first-person erotic sincerity.

Sincerity is sexuality's voice of urgency—"I *really* want this," or "I *really* am this." To theorize thoroughly the formation, and therefore the meaning, of sexuality is, then, to theorize simultaneously the formation, and meaning, of the sincere first-person voice. An adequate psychoanalytic theory of sexuality would have three intertwined objects: (1) sexuality itself: the fantasies and deeds through which the erotized body seeks satisfaction; (2) the voice through which that seeking is given expression; (3) the relation between the voice and the erotized body.

None of the three objects can be read directly; none is transparent. When the object appears transparent and directly legible to its interpreter, we can assume that in that moment of transparency the interpreter has abandoned theory in favor of sincerity.

Regarding both infantile and female sexuality, Freud writes as a theoretician. That is, his ideas are derived. The theorized objects of his inquiry are posited as out of the reach of direct observation. From the wide array of adult sexual manifestations, Freud infers the particulars of both infantile and female sexuality. At the heart of his inference, for both infant and female, is a body inadequate to the task of wish-fulfillment. Lacking the phallus, infant and woman must make do with renunciations (i.e, clitoral masturbation for the girl) and fantasy.

Freud's voice turns sincere and nontheoretical, though, when he writes about male sexuality. For Freud, the male body—in contrast to both the female's and the infant's—is transparent. He reads penis = phallus directly, as though here reality is suddenly transparent, shorn of mediations. And it is this reading that reads the realized male subject as one freed from the specter of phallic disappointment. For Freud here, the male genital is beyond the reach of meaning; it simply *is:* propping up all sexuality, male and female, and sufficient unto itself. For its bearer, the main danger becomes castration—a reduction to the insufficiency of woman or child. For Freud, man has what infant and female want.

This picture of male sufficiency is constructed sincerely—with the confidence of someone who already knows. Here lurks the influence of classical thought, not only in this particular confidence surrounding the essentially metaphysical status of the male genital but also in the more general confidence in metaphysics itself. Freud does not ask what seems an obvious, though nonetheless theoretical, question: "What is it that *men* lack, such that, lacking this, they so urgently want?"

For Freud, male sexuality is disappointed only once, in relation to attaining its object, while female sexuality is disappointed twice, in relation to both its body and to its object. The clinically pertinent disappointments associated with "female sexuality"are arrived at indirectly, via theory, while the contrasting, clinically employed notion of the adequacy of male sexuality is arrived at directly, via sincerity.

The sexualized body, as such, does not speak. Rather, it provokes speech. What speaks in its stead is a thickly mediated, and thickly mediating, "I." A theory of sexuality is, therefore, also a theory of voice. In clinical psychoanalysis, we understand voice by its theorized relation to body; we understand sexuality by its theorized relation to voice. At the heart of our clinical practice, we aim to interpret the ways in which voice and body simultaneously construct and destabilize each other.

The dynamics binding voice and body are not fixed. They are under perpetual negotiation. The priority of the body is immediacy of discharge, while the priority of voice is organization. Infancy is the original and quintessential site for these negotiations. In principle, given bodily pain, the infant's cry (like the adult's) is an argument by direct appeal. It is an alloy of the voice and the body. It therefore aims for both the immediate and organized repetition of a satisfaction already known. And also in principle, given pain, caretakers' responses blend a capitulation to immediacy with an argument for a new organization. The caretaker aspires to oversee a more or less precipitous, more or less gradual, series of renunciations and replacements. To the infant, the caretaker "says" change your aim from the direct repetition of that earlier mode of pleasurable organization to this newer one, which is, after all, bound to the first either by similarity or by metaphoric and associational propinquity.

In the negotiations of infancy, voice encounters voice. The theme of this encounter is repetition versus renunciation. And of course, the ground of this ongoing argument (the "civilizing" argument) is fundamentally unsteady because it is fundamentally determined via dialogical dynamics of power and persuasion. The stakes of the dialogue are high, and neither of the participants—infant or caregiver—is in full control of himself or herself.

Both "speak" sincerely. For both parties, unconsciously originating desires are felt as conscious necessities. The civilizing process entails sustained, forced contact between often incompatible necessities. The process takes place as demand encounters demand; flesh alternately presses against and withdraws from flesh. In these contacts of the flesh, bodies are being put to rhetorical use; rhetoric is being put to the bodily use. For the infant, the cry and its vicissitudes are in the service of a body becoming sexual, while on the caregiver's side the vicissitudes of touch and word are in the service of a body already saturated with sexual habit, a voice accustomed to having its say.

The infant's impulse to immediacy directly collides with the caregiver's impulse to pause and consider. The caretaker aims at negotiation, finding the right way to proceed, the proper response. What is right for the caretaker is never entirely self-determined. The voice of the caregiver is not singular; it includes the voice of tradition, the influence of the classical.

Infant and caregiver both mesh and collide. The caretaker looks for traditional solutions to traditional problems. For the infant, each of these proposed solutions results in a mix of satisfaction and disappointment. These mixed experiences both stock memory and seed anticipation. As such, they serve to put the formal, temporally organized structures of subjectivity into place.

In these encounters, caregiver and infant both undergo enormous strain. For the infant, the strain is obvious—needs and desires are overwhelming and satisfaction is far from guaranteed. For the caregiver, the strain resides most pointedly in the reopening of a discourse long ago thought closed—contending with a body-in-formation, giving structure to that body's cries and silences. Each voice in the encounter is vying to define optimally a field of mutually engendered pains and pleasures. *Optimal* here means keeping pleasure inside and pain outside. "Inside" and "outside" are themselves objects of negotiation, since the emerging subjective borders are blurred by unstable identifications—projective and introjective.

The caregiver's ministrations necessarily include an erotic dimension. Voice encounters voice in an immediate asymmetry—the infant needs; the caregiver wants. The organizational imperatives of need are different from those of want. Want allows for substitution while need demands the thing itself.

It is this rhetorical asymmetry that gives child care its necessarily "seductive" dimension. The caregiver gives what is wanted to someone else. This giving necessarily resonates with significance. To give or to refuse what is wanted, to satisfy or not to satisfy—such activities cannot take place without an erotic dimension. A theory of sexuality will have to account for the infant's interiorization of this erotic dimension—the moment when the infant meets the caregiver's long-standing sexualized voice with a newly sexualized voice of his or her own. This is the moment when both parties seem intently engaged in putting the infant's mouth, say, to uses that suddenly have taken on only a coincidental relation to purposes of nourishment.

At that moment, we can say that two erotized voices are "speaking." Both speak sincerely, and the meanings of each must be found via theory.

For each voice, suddenly, there is a surface and a depth. By *surface,* we mean, for example, the skin and mucosa of the mouth, sites on which there is a mutual enactment of wishes. For each voice, these wishes originated earlier and are now mediated by memory. For both voices, the satisfaction of these wishes will depend not only upon the empirical actions taken but also, and more importantly, on the dynamics of representation and resemblance through which those actions are linked to earlier ones. Action will satisfy if and only if it can be represented as a repetition of a previous satisfaction.

Each voice aims at repeating a remembered pleasure. Each voice, then, can now be said to have the capacity to argue its own cause, to work the surface so as to have both the surface and the means by which the surface is represented optimally coincide with the representation of what it wants. A sexual argument is taking place, a play of accommodation and opposition between a newly emerging voice (one with a meager repertoire from which to draw resemblances) and a traditional one (one with a vast repertoire).

Infant and caregiver bracket the infant's mouth and together create the possibility of it becoming sexualized. Both participate in sexuality's origin, but neither witnesses it. Suddenly, it is upon them. Regarding sexuality's origin, both are left with only inference, only "theory." With its earliest words, its earliest reports on what it wants and therefore wants to do again, the first-person voice reports a knowledge it has gained only after the fact.

To theorize sexuality is to give it a history, a context, to insert it "within the chain of the person's psychic experiences" (Freud, 1900). This act of insertion is problematic. It is often met with resistance, and when it is, the interpretation of sexuality will necessarily expand to include an interpretation of that resistance. Every element of sexuality is open to interpretation and is therefore resistable—from the terms by which its explicit acts are described to the concepts by which its beclouded origins are imagined.

In general, the contest is most fierce when the interpretation claims manifest sexual expression as an anxious version of disavowed sexual origin. This is the interpretation that most directly offends sincerity's sensibilities. A sexual theory, then, will receive its most severe test when it interprets ardent desire as covert defense.

And indeed, this is the cardinal orienting interpretation of the psychoanalytic theory of sexuality. When we place sexuality's origin within the field set up by the bodily mediated rhetoric surrounding sensual sucking, we are necessarily driven to think of the entire subsequent range of sexual expression as an elaboration of, and a series of transformations performed on, this original oral theme.

The original aim and object of sucking is not easily, nor ever fully, abandoned. Instead of abandonment, then, our sexual theory postulates a series of transformations. Each of these transformations takes place via new versions of the conflict-laden civilizing rhetoric, a rhetoric produced by incompatible necessities placed in irreversible sustained contact. These new versions, like the original one, pit impulses toward repetition against impulses toward modification, though with each party now coming to be differentially invested in what ought to be preserved and what ought to be changed. The infant no longer can be identified as solely on the side of repetition, the caretaker no longer solely on the side of modification. The terms of the new sexual argument, though, remain intact: It is a contest, via sexuality, over what is necessary, what is good, and what is real.

At the interface of this argument are two competing sincere voices. Both infant and caregiver give voice to what is necessary, what is good, and what is real. Each knows itself as wishing; neither knows itself as in flight. Thus, both voices are unreliable. The absence of directly articulated anxiety at the civilizing/sexualizing interface engenders the later necessity for sexual theorizing. Since sincerity and sexuality, on both sides of the interface, are each in part a product of anxiety, each side is necessarily disqualified as a reliable historian.

There is nothing contingent about the psychoanalytic reluctance to take at face value the sincere, affirmative claims of first-person sexual histories. That reluctance is axiomatic. Where the first-person voice necessarily speaks only of a series of affirmations in this narrative, we grant an essential place to anxiety. We assume that danger mingles with pleasure in spurring the renunciation of x and y on the way to z.

For the first-person voice, though, to the extent that its sexual expression is sincere, this theorized dimension of anxious aversion cannot be known. Invested in establishing its own sexuality as positive, the first-person voice is therefore also invested in effacing any sign of anxiety from what it can deduce of the determinants of its sexual preferences.

In defense of its own sincerity, the first-person voice might therefore argue for a theory of sexuality in which only first-person testimony would be admissable. Such theory would be grounded in a methodology of introspection. Its power would be measured by its capacity to produce affect sensed as authentic. Its yield would be a report on *my* sexuality or perhaps, in the presence of a sympathetic witness, on *ours*. This is often the epistemological position of voices explicitly aiming to transfigure the scars left by a history of oppression. For such voices, any theorization of "reality" risks ceding authority to the outside. But to locate epistemological authority outside is to recreate the original oppressive condition. Theory itself takes on an oppressive valence and is therefore pushed aside in favor of liberatory "directness"—sincerity.

Contesting the presumed link between liberation and sincerity is a voice that links privileged sincerity not to liberation but to tyranny. This voice would have a direct interest in preserving the contemporary from undue assault. It would counter the epistemological appeals of sincerity with an appeal to epistemological disinterest.

This is the premise of the traditional clinical voice. It refuses the claims of raw introspection, no matter how meticulous, and insists on the balancing presence of a disinterested second-person voice. This second voice is a theorized one. It is constructed out of controlled processes of identification and disidentification and will, in principle, be able to resist the blunt appeal of affect as a measure of truth. Therefore, via the insertion of theory, it will be capable of speaking, with authority, not of its own sexuality and not necessarily of sexuality in general but of *your* sexuality.

Yet another position, the traditionally scientific one—even more cautious— would refuse to grant epistemological authority to either monads or dyads, no matter their methods, and would demand a disengaged third-person voice, one obliged to a mathematically constructed plurality. This voice would then be licensed to speak of a sexuality neither its own nor yours but rather, via the controlled and disinterested observation of many, of *human* sexuality.

Freud's sincerity casts its shadow on his theorizing. We intend to relook at Freud's theorization via a consideration more of the voice in which it was written than of the findings it announces. What it finds, first and foremost, is the determining role of disappointments in the construction of femininity and indeed of female homosexuality. Our grounding assumption will be that the disappointments Freud finds as constitutive of the female homosexual—no phallus, no Oedipal object—hardly mark her as a unique subject. Rather than theorizing these disappointments as the determinants of femaleness and/or female homosexuality, we will regard them as the preconditions of sexuality itself. We will look at the female homosexual not as a special case but as a general one. Freud's theorization, then, will come into focus not as inaccurate on its face but as inaccurate in its context. What he saw in the female homosexual can be seen in any "sexual." The corrective we offer is to universalize the disappointments that Freud here symptomatically saw as the single hallmarks of both the "female" and the "homosexual."

What Freud's female homosexual seeks in her erotic life is to restore a state whose very existence is entirely fantastic—the state of erotic sufficiency. This is the promise she hopes to realize via her two-pronged strategy of renunciation and embrace. Freud focuses on this strategy as particular to her and to the category of female homosexuality. We mean to argue that belief in the promise of erotic sufficiency inevitably depends upon just such a two-pronged tactic.

Disappointment presumes expectation, and to expect is to expect *again,* to anticipate the repetition of a satisfaction once had. To be disappointed, then, is to have now lost what one once had.

Sexuality, wanting via one's body, necessarily confesses both to a want in one's body and to the fantasy of that want assuaged. For psychoanalysis, disappointment remains a mundanely ordinary feature of quotidian life as long as the object both lost and wanted can again, literally, be found. The paradigm here is food: the bread once had, now gone, soon to reappear. Though fantasy may accrue to this sequence, it need not accrue for there to be both disappointment and satisfaction. For Freud, those wants that could be satisfied without the mediation of fantasy were called needs. At the same time, disappointment is always layered with fantasy and as such is psychoanalytically meaningful.

Sexuality is sexual, for Freud, to the extent that all three elements in the sequence—the object once had, the object lost, the object again to be found—are fantastic. In contrast to need, sexual desire, for Freud, cannot be satisfied. Whatever is found can only resemble the object represented as lost. Hunger might be temporarily fooled by, but never permanently satisfied by, something like food. This "something like" is the condition of sexuality's object, for Freud.

For Freud, all of sexuality is grounded in double disappointment. Our original genitals are inadequate to their original aims, and our original objects prove finally to be unavailable. But the foundational status of double disappointment is only made explicit in his theorization of female development. For the girl, Freud posits a unique moment of genital disappointment. He writes of her "realizing" its inadequacy "in a flash." This "realization" then incites a turning away from the whole of her previously satisfactory masturbatory activity. It also incites a turning toward the male genital, whose adequacy is "realized" in the self-same "flash." She is certain that what she has lost can only be found again through the self-punishing renunciation of her own active pleasure, which she achieves through turning toward the man who is deemed capable of fulfilling her.

Freud treats the girl's "flash" as inspired. That is, he completely identifies with the girl he is theorizing. Each believes in the *material* reality of her disappointed condition. A theorized psychic reality has been transfigured into an untheorized material reality. With this, Freud and the little girl both see passivity as her only solution.

Freud also identifies with the theorized girl's counterpart, the adequate boy. But unlike the girl, this boy is at no point theorized. His adequacy is simply asserted. Male concern about genital inadequacy is then, by simple inference, construed as concern about feminization.

Here, an untheorized psychic reality—the adequate genital—is now transfigured into an untheorized material reality. Freud confidently uses this figure. It functions like a fetish might. It fills an absence that sincerity reads as material with an object that theory reads as imaginary.

Both theoretically and clinically, the interpretation of defensively driven identifications has long been a Freudian motif. Via Freud, we have been empowered to see and interpret the fiction that these identifications sustain. At the heart of that fiction are the notions that the lost predecessor is present and adequate and that via identification both that presence and that adequacy can be claimed for oneself.

Theory grounded in similar identifications—*sincere theory*—sustains and yields a similar fiction. Such is the case with Freud's representation of male sexuality as grounded in genital adequacy. Via a consideration of the following two cases, we mean to expose some features of the theoretically mediated fictions that follow from such a representation.

Case #1: Ms. A. entered analysis 5 years ago, a 35-year-old woman troubled by a sense that she was "not as happy as she might be." At that time she was single and having a series of unsatisfactory and transient sexual relationships with men. She characterized her desire in terms of her need to have these men want her. Her focus would be on getting them to want to have sex with her, which seemed to quiet her own wanting for a time. Frequently, these liaisons would cease after one encounter, and Ms. A. would be bewildered and alarmed, feeling "as though I am nothing."

Only after a lengthy period of psychotherapeutic work did Ms. A. achieve any stable sense of self-regard. Up until then her conscious desire was entirely organized around getting men; she wanted their total attention. Once her self-esteem was somewhat stabilized, she realized that the men chosen were inevitably "beneath" her—never her intellectual, social, or economic equals. Often they were men she "didn't even like."

She was preoccupied with hope organized around the idea of having the man's penis inside of her. Most encounters, however brief, would have an initial effect of making her feel "better," "fuller," just after sex. Afterward, she experienced terrible defeat if the man did not call; if the man called, it meant that she had something worth wanting. She felt that the man's desire was based on what she did or did not have.

If a man suggested disinterest in her, she experienced "crushing disappoint-ment." She sensed everything meaningful about her was lost. Instantaneously, she could lose her sense of desirability, well-being, and efficacy. She would feel "back to being on my own, alone" and "lacking," "less." These states of defi-ciency were particularly acute when she would calculate her assets as compared to women who seemed successfully coupled with a man. Via such calculations, she always "came up short."

Our theorized sketch of Ms. A.'s initial presentation: For Ms. A., sexual coupling assumes a quantitative dimension. Coupling makes her "more," "bigger," and "extends" her sense of self. Working against the idea that "on her own" she is painfully deficient, she targets a man as the remedy to a persistent sense of insuf-ficiency. On the surface she resembles Freud's classic girl. She imagines herself having once been something she can no longer be unless added onto by a man. The fantasy of sexual having goes only so far. She must concretely have the penis in order to feel completed by it. She then, in fantasy, is restored, her sense of disappointment quieted temporarily as she feels whole again.

Despite great strides and economic success in work (also viewed as making her feel "bigger"), not yet having a relationship with a man continues to be evi-dence of her inferiority to other women who *have*. With her analyst, Ms. A. senses herself particularly lacking. The analyst *has*—men, babies, a kind of vital internal substance. She feels herself "full of shit" by comparison.

As Ms. A. contends with oscillations in her picture of herself, she simultane-ously imagines women thinking about her, evaluating her, basing their thoughts and assessments on what she has acquired. If she is with a man, she seeks affir-mation in the eyes of a woman—any woman. Such affirmation makes her feel "glorified." Especially if the man in question is unequivocally beautiful, she is reassured of her own sense of goodness through knowing that it is she, not other women, who inspires the man's wanting. Beauty and goodness are linked and reassure her of her special ability to be desired.

A more imperfect man is a mirror onto her own failings. "I realize the prob-lem with P. is he is small, dark, he is average. There is no problem with that except it is like me—and I do not want to be seen that way, small, dark. It is not the image I wish to have of myself." Emotional vulnerability in a man is another mark of imperfection. A man who is "too open" seems weak to her, distinctly not in possession of "the hard penis I was hoping to have from him." This hard penis has become a central element in the structure of her own desire.

If many women do not want what he has, how important can what he has be? Getting a man wanted by few women only confirms her sense of herself as "damaged goods."

Shadowing Ms. A.'s conscious preoccupying fantasy of getting and having a man is her wish to be at the center of a woman's attention and from there to receive her approbation. Her orienting heterosexual fantasy of getting a man, therefore, is linked to a homosexual fantasy in which she establishes an erotic tie with a woman against whom she can prove herself superior. She must outdo all others, and she must succeed in this outdoing for all time; otherwise she, feels herself to be nothing.

As the youngest of three children, Ms. A. assumed herself to be an afterthought. The parents' relationship was a source of constant anguish for her. She would peer from the window waiting for their return from evenings together. The mere fact of her parents being together was an ongoing sign of their rejection of her. She still says with conviction that she does not understand why or how they could want to have excluded her.

Her feeling of wanting to be chosen, of needing to outdo all others as a prerequisite for a sense of self-regard, originated in relation to her siblings. She felt that they had already had her mother, and that her mother, "the busiest of women," was too distracted to attend to her. She felt especially jealous of a brother 10 years her senior. He had a long period of drug abuse, with extended hospitalizations. Though debilitated, he was also idealized, especially by his younger sister. He fostered this idealization and exploited it, getting her to sell drugs for him. In adolescence, Ms. A. herself had a history of lying and shoplifting and was once expelled from school for cheating.

But unlike for her older brother, for her these unruly behaviors did not elicit affirmation. Rather, she repeatedly had the sense that even her problems "did not add up," "were not big enough," in comparison to her brother's. When she was expelled from school, her mother slapped her and said, "I cannot have another M.!" In other words, there was only room for one.

The analysis has revealed the painful wish to be first: first with her mother and then—that repressed wish's derivative expression—first with a man. Longing for a woman has been replaced in consciousness with longing for a man. And the longing is to be wanted, to be all important, to be so valuable and so superior that no one will ever be able to outdo her.

What Ms. A. visits and revisits in her recurrent disappointment is the hope that she possesses what it takes to win. What she ultimately wants is her mother's love. She wants to fill the mind of the mother, as her brother once had. Her despair is grounded in the sense that in this instance, once is for all time.

To possess the mother's mind she must be bigger, larger, and more solid. The brother has the mother; she doesn't. The problem of difference is approached via a fantasy of difference. He has what she both wants and needs—needs in order to attract and keep the mother.

The brother's "big" problems and "big" penis are means to enter and fill the mother's mind and body. Having neither her mother's love nor the mind and body to secure it constitutes a brutal attack on her own narcissistic equilibrium. She therefore constantly appraises herself—always in relation to other women. Is she as smart as they? Is she as beautiful? If a woman who is fantastically beautiful sits at a table beside her, she is suddenly stricken with the awful sense of being less. She maintains two representations of herself that work to elide each other. In one she is identified with the brother and capable of being "the be all and end all" to those around her. In another she is nothing—if she cannot be the most beautiful, the most intelligent, the most charming, her self-esteem plummets.

At times, she speaks of being the woman wanted above all others. But the slightest evidence that she is not all-important leads to crushing disappointment. She generally characterizes it as a disappointment fundamental to being feminine—a genital disappointment. But this attribution of the disappointment to her anatomical difference obscures a preanatomical and more central disappointment—the failure to have ever attained sufficient proof of her mother's love.

Ms. A. has tried to account for this formative absence via sexual and narcissistic fantasies. She imagines herself an imperfect person and then lives imperfectly both to prove this and to disprove it by finally winning her mother's attentions.

Ms. A. envies the brother his capacity to fill their mother's mind and body. Her own inability is construed as the result of being the third child: last in line, a girl, and filled with envy/shit. The interworkings of envy, longing, and narcissistic fragility in this woman might well, to a naive eye, appear to be the consequence of intractable penis envy. Such an interpretation might be equivalent in this case to Freud's attribution of disappointment in his case of the female homosexual. Disappointment figures largely in Ms. A., as it does for Freud's young woman. Both women might be understood to want something from their mothers that is unforthcoming. While each has developed a different manifest solution, the underlying fantasy content seems to be a hybrid of heterosexual desire and homoerotic longing. Each is disappointed—the narcissistic self-accusation of genital deficiency comes as a belated mode of accounting for perceived failures in the mother, the expression of which might further drive the mother away. Without the mother's secure presence, each of these women finds entry into more mutually gratifying sexual relations intensely problematic. The persistence of disappointment is like the persistence of hope. The "female homosexual" and our patient, the female heterosexual, employ the same tactic. Each retreats from both her own body and some of her own objects so as to maintain a fantasy that the mother is still accessible: that *her* love and *her* body will be renunciation's reward.

Case #2: J. is a 40-year-old man who initially sought analysis because of inhibitions regarding his career as a singer. Immediately after the analysis began, however, it became clear that he would use the analysis much differently than he had originally proposed. It was to be a prop by which he could completely withdraw from singing, from social life, from commitments in general, so as to descend into full-time clerical work, a life organized around staying occupied and therefore distracted from ever having to think about what he might "want."

The analyst was no longer there to help but rather to construct a setting that affirmed the patient's sense of self-sufficiency. Self-sufficiency meant an emotional coolness that was grounded in "wanting nothing." Explaining this, J. said, "We have an understanding. What we know is that everything is in its proper place. All is well. Everyone is happy."

J. is a male heterosexual. But the mere fact of his sexuality challenges his notion of self-sufficiency. Like Freud's patient, and like Ms. A., J.'s entire sexual life is oriented around defending against the awareness of irreversible disappointment and the attendant loss of hope.

His sexual behavior seems to offer him neither satisfaction nor disappointment. He has sex with the woman he lives with, but as he puts it, "not really." "I could never really have sex with her. Not because of her, though. It's anyone. How could I ever have sex with anyone? Then I'd have to explain why I'm not having sex with all the other possible women. My sex has to take place with no possibility of ever having to account for it, for why I wanted it, and for why I did it with the person I did it with. What I have isn't sex, it's the idea of sex. That idea will come true later. For now, I'm still getting ready."

For J., wanting is intolerable. Wanting is pathetic, weak, horrifying. To want is to admit that the world contains what you are missing.

Fundamentally, J. lives in a quasi-dream state: a state of continuous, near-hallucinatory wish-fulfillment. Primary process rules. There are no substantive contradictions, there is no operative "no," and time is reversible. By conflating idea and perception, he averts what Freud calls "bitter experience" and thus averts the necessity of calling secondary process into play. As J. says "I have what I want because I want it."

This omnipotent concatenation—"I have what I want because I want it"— undoes the unbearable idea that "I want what I want because I don't have it." Each element—the manic sense of omnipotence and the depressive sense of insufficiency—are necessary ingredients of all wishing and thus of all sexuality. J. protects against any awareness of insufficiency either in himself or in his object. By psychic definition, disappointment has no place. Conscious life is designed to approximate a state of uninterrupted wish-fulfillment. Instead of "real" sexuality, J. experiences what he calls "the idea of sexuality." His conscious sexual life is structured as the obverse of Freud's patient's. She, falling prey to double disappointment, turns depressively away from both her own body and her own original object. J., on the other hand, fends off both disappointments but nonetheless must turn away from both his own body and his object's in order to sustain this victory. "Bitter experience" has been too much for Freud's patient, while for J., "bitter experience" is located in an ever-receding future. Each of them, like Ms. A., has been unable to reconcile the depressive impact of double disappointment with the omnipotent promises of sexual coupling.

On the way to his early morning analytic appointments, J. regularly sees a group of schoolgirls on the street. He imagines that they, like he, are excited by the passing encounter. "That's enough for me," he says. The idea of actually doing something to become a schoolteacher and therefore, perhaps, a school-girl's heartthrob is a horrible one. "Perhaps" is the problem. J. lives in a state of perpetual certainty. There are no contingencies. Of pursuing a teaching career, he says, "I would be despicable and pathetic, some man who wanted something from some girls." If J. has a favorite sweater, he never wears it. If he has a good idea, he keeps it to himself. Anything he likes, he hides, he keeps pristine. His aspiration for himself is to become an admired "pristine object on the shelf." Fantasy is not only equivalent to deed, it is superior. Deed "dirties" the thing done; fantasy keeps it pure. Deed takes place in the world of bodies and objects. Fantasy takes place anterior to them both. Deed is contiguous with disappoint-ment while fantasy trumps it.

To become the "pristine object on the shelf" is, for J., to restore himself to a state of fullness and plenitude, a status once his and then lost catastrophically at the time of what he calls his "breakdown." This breakdown took place as he realized that singing had been, for him, a means to "get it all," "to have it all fall in my lap without ever having to want something," and that this was not going to happen.

What is meant by pristine is virginal—never having been had, never having wanted. J.'s Bartleby-like descent into the lowest levels of office work offers relief from any moment of wanting. While at work he actively "thinks"that his firm's highest-ranking executives secretly admire him, see his genius, wish they had the courage to have given it all up like he did, and realize that it is they who have made the big mistake and fallen for all the tricks: the wish for family, pur-suit of love, and so forth.

A recent session:

J.: I had a dream. Nothing important. Not really useful to talk about.

Analyst: You are not sure I will be able to see its relevance to what we're doing.

J.: I was at a party with Mick Jagger. It was very cool. The important thing was to make sure that Mick Jagger did not know how cool I thought it was. If he found out, then he would no longer want to be with me.

Analyst: You were unsure if you deserved to be with him.

J.: I don't know if I ever told you about the rock and roll band I was in in high school. I played guitar. Ever since I stopped and took up singing, not a day has gone by when I don't regret it. By now, I could have been a rock star.

I got my girlfriend to listen to Sheryl Crow. She's a fan now. We were listening last night. I liked how excited my girlfriend got. I was listening to the backup guitar. I could play like that. I could be her backup. Be on tour with her. Have a relation with her. I would be the guy she'd always been waiting for but never really believed was possible. She would have fucked so many other guys, but the moment it was me she would know that I was the one. We would be onstage, even fuck onstage. Nothing would be greater, her and me, everyone knowing. The sexiest woman alive, the sexiest man alive, together. It's that or nothing. It's that. It's like it's true. Nothing else is as true as that.

Discussion: The backdrop for J.'s heterosexual activities is the fantasy that, in effect, they are not taking place. The necessary fiction is that what he is doing is entertaining an idea and not performing an action. J. can be sexual as long as he never has a sexual experience. Experience is the problem. And the problematic element integral to experience is the possibility of disappointment.

Freud's patient, like our two, comes to know her own body as a site of insufficiency, a site from which she has to turn away if she is to find any compensatory relief. This initial turning away is, of course, the precondition for any turning toward. Erotic object-seeking is premised on the possibility of finding elsewhere what one has somehow lost, and cannot find, on one's own body. In this sense, one's own necessarily disappoints. Object-choice, the organized turning away from one's own body and toward another's, will depend on the set of fantasies by which one accounts for that disappointment. Those fantasies organize one's wanting, making possible a narrative that tells what one has lost, why one has lost it, where it can be found, the conditions by which it can be obtained, and so forth.

One's body and one's objects are both held to account for one's "bitter experience." Each is turned away from because each is sensed, alternatively, as the primary cause of pain.

In sexuality, the body of one's own that one seeks, like the object that one seeks, is necessarily fantastic. Body and object—if not one, then the other—

will protect against loss. This is sexuality's orienting wish, the wish to eradicate loss.

Sincerity drives the search; theory, beholden to "bitter experience," accounts for both the endurance and the failure of sincerity's search.

References

Laplanche, J. & Portalis, J. B. (1968). Fantasy and the orgins of sexuality. *International Journal of Psychoanalysis, 49,* part I, 1–18.

13

WRITING SEX, ERASING RACE
Rereading Freud's Lesbian Dream

~

Erica Schoenberg

What would it mean if, instead of viewing sexual differentiation as more fundamental than other forms . . ., we considered the disjunctive ordering of masculine/feminine as taking place not only through a heterosexualizing symbolic, with its taboo on homosexuality, but through a complex set of racial injunctions which operate in part through a taboo on miscegenation? Does reproduction of a racialized version of the species require and reproduce a normative heterosexuality in its service? (Butler, 1993, p. 167)

The abject has only one quality of the object—that of being opposed to I . . . Thus, braided, woven, ambivalent, a heterogeneous flux that marks out a territory that I can call my own because the Other, having dwelt in me as alter ego, points it out to me through loathing. (Kristeva, 1982, pp. 9, 10)

You can be in my dream if I can be in yours. (Bob Dylan)

This paper is a meditation on voice: voices heard and silenced, voices objective and subjective, voices confident and authoritative and those hesitant and fragmentary. Its concern is the multiplicity of voices, both within and outside us, which may roar or whisper to be heard. It is a consideration of the problems I encountered trying to orchestrate the cacophany of these voices that blared forth when I attempted to listen to the characters in "Psychogenesis" and to address both their concerns and my own. And it is an exploration of the clash between Freud's modern voice and my postmodern one and of the difficulties communicating across the divide. Accordingly, it reflects my recognition that since disparate metaphors and attitudes structure our respective narrative voices, I will not at the end uncover the Truth, either about Freud's account or about his patient's life, but rather may simply find a view of matters that I can live with.

This essay is also concerned with the voices of the two participants in the case, Freud's own and that of his patient, and with Freud's commitment to distinguishing absolutely between them. For committed he is, claiming for himself the high road, the unmarked story whose "origin and development" are traceable "in the mind with certainty and almost without a gap" (1920, p. 133), while relegating to his patient the manipulative, deceitful path of "lying dreams." I contest this claim by using a dream I had while composing this piece. By using it, I attempt to rectify Freud's determined silencing of one female homosexual, his patient, by giving full voice to another, myself. My dream is also a vehicle to explore questions of voice that Freud foreclosed, since I maintain that my dream voice—by definition personal, subjective, associative and contextual—is in important ways no different from Freud's putatively objective voice in this narrative, which resonates with scientific authority and confidence. I suggest that since the price of Freud's certainty is the total excision of his patient from his account, all traces of her voice omitted and even pseudonymous recognition denied her, then his report, like my dream, exists in a fantastical space outside sociality. This suggests that the boundaries between science and dreams are substantially more permeable than Freud would have it, not because his narrative also lies—although in its own way it does—but because I believe it is his dream (Wineapple, this volume).

Thus, I intend with my dream to reconfigure the boundary Freud drew between fact and fiction, science and dreams. My use of it as a window onto Freud's case/dream reflects my conviction that while in certain respects my nocturnal dream and his psychoanalytic dream share a detachment from reality, they simultaneously and paradoxically share being thoroughly imbricated by reality. This is so because, while our narratives speak of it in quite different voices, both are shaped by the concerns and attitudes that characterize our social worlds. Thus, Freud straddles the perspectival fence, foreshadowing postmodernism by theorizing the preeminently fragmented, multivocal unconscious on the one hand (Freud, 1905) while on the other assuming the thoroughly modernist position of disinterested, univocal narrator (whose patient is likewise rendered univocal) in "Psychogenesis." My repudiation of the latter position reflects the postmodern stamp that causes me to identify Freud's lie as his claim of objectivity and detachment where none is possible.

From my vantage point, "Psychogenesis" is not a dispassionate scientific account of the etiology of his lesbian patient's private unconscious but rather a chronicle of Freud's systematic and determined effort to make sense of his world given the dominant metaphors and concerns of his time and place. Consequently, in lieu of a story of homosexuality in a female, I read an "elaborate ethnography of the white Western male, middle class psyche" (Doan, cited in Tate, 1996).

While feminist discourse has critiqued this ethnography in terms of the formative influence of patriarchy on Freud's thought, I believe that the prominent role of other social factors remains inadequately theorized. Specifically, I suggest that the undeniably powerful influence of anti-Semitism, conceived at the time as a racial issue, has been largely underestimated. Jews in Freud's Vienna were perceived as diseased and degenerate and consequently were widely degraded and abhorred (see Lesser, this volume). This was true not only in the whispered undercurrents of private prejudice. The science of the day legitimized the hatred by theorizing Jews as negatively as Jensen and others of that ilk have theorized African Americans. To be Jewish was to figure Otherness profoundly, for not only were Jewish men considered emasculated and therefore feminized by circumcision, but they were also "quite literally seen as black. . . . By mid-century, being black, being Jewish, being diseased and being 'ugly' came to be inexorably linked" (Tate, 1996, p. 56).

The effects of this on Freud were manifold and warrant much greater discussion (Gilman, 1993; Lesser, this volume; Tate, 1996). However, one vignette that illustrates anti-Semitism's impact will have to suffice for my purposes. According to Jones (1957, p. 105), Freud had a favorite joke that he told numerous times over several years and in which he reportedly found great amusement. He called this his "Negro joke," and in it he disparagingly referred to his patients as "Negroes." Tate suggests that since racial bias was pervasive in Freud's society, it is perhaps not entirely surprising to find racism in his humor. More noteworthy for my purposes is Freud's need to redraw racial boundaries and displace his own degraded status onto the even more vulnerable "Negro" in order to claim for himself a legitimate place in white, male, bourgeois society (Tate, 1996). His need to stabilize and legitimize his own position permeates his theory as well. Freud's metaphor of the Dark Continent to represent the Otherness of women's sexuality, which conflates racial and sexual difference, speaks to the prominence and pressure of both concerns (Gates, 1986a). By employing these rhetorical strategies, Freud becomes the white master while both the "Negro" patient and "woman" become colonial property. Such transformation "goes double for the female homosexual, who not only must turn into a man, but who (also) has no name"(Tate, 1996, p. 59).

Since I insist on locating Freud's comments in his social world, it seems only fitting that I require the same of myself. I believe that the most salient consideration in that regard is my having come of age in the 1960s, a time marked by concern with many muted voices, but particularly with the silencing and oppression of people of color. Part of my dream then, both the nocturnal dream I will report and the waking dream I have maintained as an adult, is to link the discredited voice of Freud's lesbian with other voices of abjection, for all such groups share the considerable burden of carrying the despised aspects of themselves that the powerful in Western society project onto the less powerful in order to maintain their own sense of goodness. Specifically, I mean to link the derogating rhetorical strategies of this case with the marginalizing strategies of psychoanalytic discourse, which continue to erase racial voices. For certainly, in addition to being male, our standard bearer of mental health is undeniably also white. Mindful of Wole Soyinka's (cited in Gates, 1986b) caution to "[b]eware the neocolonial wolf dressed in the sheep's clothing of 'universality,'" I intend in my discussion to vex both the psychoanalytic voice of uniformity that requires us to call difference pathology and its damagingly privatized, individualistic voice, a function of our astonishing preoccupation with sex and personal pleasure (Cushman, 1995; Flax, 1996). For not only have these voices served to sever the collective bonds of our sociality, but they have also stated most clearly to those excluded from our narrative that psychoanalysis "all(ies) itself as much or more with the forces of white privilege than those of racial equality" (Tate, 1996, p. 53). If we can learn to introduce the plural voices of diversity into our discourse, making use of what Gates (cited in Gilbert-Moore, 1997) terms the "multiplication of margins," we can augment our vectors of analysis, opening our ears to those whose concerns we have ignored. By so doing, we seek not simply to rectify past bias but to create the conditions necessary if psychoanalysis is to survive. For I believe that unless we dramatically broaden the range and variety of voices whose legitimacy we recognize and appreciate, we will find ourselves speaking loudly and authoritatively to no one. Perhaps we already are.

Interestingly, several papers in this volume have as their focus problems related to voice, which they have dealt with in quite inventive and productive ways, (e.g., Grey, Meyers, Moss & Zeavin, Pérez Foster, and Wineapple). Despite their success, I have had great difficulty writing this essay. Despite, or perhaps because of, being immersed in issues of voice, I have found it nearly impossible to find my own. Over the several weeks of working on this piece, I have felt confused, detached, and stuck, banging repeatedly into walls, unable to find my way out. What's more, the "I" authoring my comments and the voice used to express them seems to keep shifting and changing. I'm never sure who will be at the keyboard on any given day. On some days I have sounded like a postmodern heavy or an academic pedant, on others as though Allen

Ginsberg were using me as a channel for his prose. I am finding this most perplexing, as I usually find writing a very engrossing and pleasurable process. I enjoy creating a shape for the text, going over and over the words to craft a combination that pleases me and that expresses my meaning as elegantly as possible. So why, I wonder, has finding, refining, and using my voice been so painfully aborted in this essay, leaving me mute on the one hand and multivocal to the point of obliteration on the other? Clearly, I have become so enmired in the very problem of my essay that my own voice is thoroughly implicated.

My decision to base my comments on my dream came from having had it during a period of frustration and despair about ever successfully completing this essay. Feeling immediately upon waking that its triptych of images vividly embodied and refracted my thoughts about Freud's case, I marvelled at how three dream snapshots, drawn from both my personal life and my work with a patient, managed in a few brief instants to express all I had been struggling to say. I realized, however, that what the dream allowed and what a linear presentation prohibited was a simultaneity of voices and perspectives. Feeling substantially more grounded once I had my dream, I concluded that perhaps I might find my way through my dislocation in this essay if I used my dream voice as my vehicle and tried to weave my dream images into my discussion of the case. However, locating myself in my dream seemed to present as many new problems as it solved. My dream seemed so personally revealing, so naked and exposed, so solipsistic and exhibitionistic a mode of commentary. I feared that once it became my focus, the line between a scholarly presentation and an episode on *Oprah* might become too fine.

My sense that there was no firm ground for me in this essay, that even an apparently viable solution evaporated in a moment, caused me to consider more carefully what the problems might be that caused me to feel so thoroughly silenced. As I began to look more closely at my relationship with the case, I realized that it raised a multitude of issues for me, including the tensions of identification and counteridentification, both with Freud and with his patient. For example, my position in this piece reflects my clear identification with the girl. However, this caused me to worry that in using my own lesbian dream to rectify the disparagement of hers, it is now my own voice that silences her yet again. Further, as I tried to give voice to the voiceless, the abject, I had a sense that many other erased voices were screaming to be heard, including those within Freud himself that he silenced with his assumption of disinterest (see Meyers, this volume). Further, I fear that by using this case to further my own agenda by introducing the silenced voices of color and promoting the possibility for a more collective, social vision that the use of such voices provides, I mirror the obliterating, opportunistic use of the "girl" for which I criticize Freud.

In addition, perhaps it is too difficult to venture beyond the "master's narrative." As de Lauretis (this volume) notes, a case study is much more the expression of its author's subjectivity than it is of its patient's. If I try to make this case my own through my dream of it, is this theft? Do I fear being too competitive with Freud, trying to one-up him in the dream game? Or is it too important, when a female homosexual confronts Freud in her own voice, that she do it right? Is too much at stake? Or does confronting Freud the all-knowing analyst mirror too closely the very issue upon which my own analysis foundered after years of remarkable intimacy and productivity?

The foregrounding of these issues of voice so deafens and fragments that wholeness and coherence seem increasingly artifactual. Binaries that usually rest quietly in their places now bounce around wildly like tiny, motorized balls of silly putty. The primary-secondary divide, for example, which usually seems to rest fairly neatly in place, now violently resists reconfiguration. I want to discuss the ways in which my dream plays not only as three snapshots of intensely private concerns but also as the hub of my musings on the case, scripted and cast according to my personal aesthetics and requirements. It is both my fantasy life and my treatise on Freud, as much a primary-process package for secondary-process activity as a secondary-process retelling of my primary-process images. Yet once disorganized, these categories refuse containment, and despite my frantic conducting, I seem unable to create a piece with any discernible form.

Furthermore, I need to play the dream stereophonically, adjusting the volume and balance so that the social harmonics that resonate through the more obviously personal voice become audible. Because in addition to hearing the dream as my unique, "authentic" voice, I hear ventriloquism, the voices of my time and place as they have scripted me and speak through me. So there are multiple tracks that require balancing, multiple voices that must be separated yet integrated if the whole is to work: my dream voice with Freud's scientific voice; my dream with its personal concerns as they resonate with Freud's concerns; both our dreams as they express our work with our patients; both his and my dreams as they resonate with the social concerns that structure them; resonances between him and me, between his patient and me, between my patient and his. . . . No wonder I feel fractured and deafened!

I see now that while the indissociability of primary and secondary, private and social, viewer and viewed, subject and Other, dreamer and dreamed, with its repeated reversals of figure and ground and its relentless rearranging of elements is at the very core of my discussion, it is dizzying. I am reminded of the way I felt some 20 years ago standing in Shinjuku Station in Tokyo, an enormous railway intersection with platforms everywhere, trains going every place, and me, thoroughly disoriented, unable to read the signs in an unrecognizable alphabet or make contact with any of the people hurrying by because they did not speak my language. Perhaps trying to author this essay as dreamer, lesbian, psychoanalyst, Jew, social progressive, premillenial American, and whoever else claims a piece of the action has left me feeling too unanchored and adrift, too multifaceted, too reconfigured. Have I lost any one recognizable voice because the postmodern promise of many partial voices renders each too faint and partial to be heard against Freud's modern, scientific voice, inflected as it is with absolute patriarchal authority?

I don't know. Perhaps many of these concerns, as well as others I have not even considered, are at play. What I do know is that while my dream is certainly about my own dance of life, alternatingly joyous and annihilating, it is choreographed to the music of my times, music composed in a not insignificant way by Freud. And I know that we three—Freud, his girl, and I—are united by this, for each of us can do nothing more—nor less, for that matter—than try to author our words and orchestrate our voices and our lives as honestly as we can, despite we ourselves being authored by our situations and sung by the melodies of our times. I cannot know the truth, not about the intent or accuracy of any of our dreams, nor about all our motives or conclusions. I didn't live in the world Freud and his patient inhabited, amidst the values and beliefs that characterized their milieu, nor could I have had a privileged view of the case even if I had lived then. What I can have is a perspective that orients me and that gives power and resonance to my voice(s). Fortunately, this is rather a lot, since recognizing that all facts exist only within a particular worldview saves me from drowning in a sea of relativism. We must always evaluate the information at hand from our own perspective (Tompkins, 1986). This is what both participants in the case did as well. From my perspective we have no choice.

My Dream

Scene 1

I discover, while picking a little black girl up in my arms, that she and I can almost fly. I think we are dancing, but it is a dance I don't recognize, in which we seem to glide through the air. As I hold her, we are propelled by my wriggling my body back and forth as I do when seeking the surface of the water after diving in. My ability to fly is clearly and inextricably connected with our being partnered: that is, I cannot do this alone. In the dream, I think of having seen Nureyev dance when I was in high school. His leaps were so graceful and extended that he seemed to defy the laws of gravity and I remember wondering how he'd learned to freeze time and motion at the very apex of his arc.

Scene 2

My former husband R. is being very sweet to me, kind and attentive. I am filled with pleasure from his caring look. I feel myself become that person I used to become when I gained value and significance through that gaze.

Scene 3

As used so often to happen, I am sick with disappointment. R. is no longer paying attention to me. I am an afterthought, and I feel nauseated and deflated, as this seemingly endlessly repeated sequence occurs yet again. Through the hurt and rage I feel puzzled most of all. What did I do? Why did this happen? I feel shapeless, without identity.

Comments and Associations

I was surprised by this dream, immediately struck by its imagistic portrayal of the very ideas I've been mulling around about the case. I will try to get to this by taking the dream scene by scene, allowing my personal associations to form the basis for the commentary and weaving back and forth between them, their relevance to my ideas about the case and their relationship to Freud and his patient. This may at times be difficult to follow, like a maze that turns in, out, and back upon itself. However, as Freud puts it in the case, "[c]onsecutive presentation is not a very adequate means of describing complicated mental processes going on in different layers of the mind" (p. 147). Given this dream format, I can conceive no other way to proceed (Rosica, 1997).

Scene 1

My first association is to a session I had two days ago with D. a 33-year-old African-American woman I work with. During the session D. observed that in her family, if you are confronted by an obstacle, you never go for it and attempt to surmount it but rather turn around and give up. I am immediately struck by how closely this statement seems to me to summarize Freud's reaction to his "girl." She resisted him, stymied his efforts, looked down on him, and he turned around and abandoned any effort to actually relate to her or even to work with her. Instead, he sent her away and withdrew into his own dream of her. So am I, by presenting my dream, acting toward Freud as he did toward his patient? Is he as lost to me, as I attempt to locate him in my dream, as his patient was to him when he sought her in his dream/theory? Have I unwittingly assumed a dismissive, default position? Have we each dreamed our dream because we felt shut out? Has each of us, by dreaming in terms to which our subjects would never have agreed, erased and distorted them beyond recognition? Has it been my identification with Freud from the outset that perplexed my narrative, contradicting as it does my conscious intent?

Returning to my patient: As she and I discussed her family's habit of giving up when confronted by an obstacle, I heard myself commenting on how enslaved by their circumstances her family must have felt. Struck by my choice of words, I realized that I had no idea what her family's relationshp to slavery had been. I know that her roots are in the South, so I assume that her ancestors had been slaves. Is this an accurate assumption? If so, were there family stories about slavery? How did D. think this legacy had affected her family? I was startled to note that although we've worked together on a weekly basis for several years, we've never talked about this. I have asked D. on a couple of occasions whether she had any feelings about my being white, but she always responded to my question with denial and puzzlement, explaining that she had not been raised to consider race a significant or motivating factor in life. Her parents believed that people of color cried racism to mask their own failure and that with hard work she could accomplish whatever she chose. Her lack of interest in our racial differences led me to wonder whether bringing up the topic again was related more to my needs than to hers. However, is it possible that race is entirely irrelevent to our relationship? It's hard for me to believe. And I do know that D. felt racism was the cause when she was unable to complete her B.A. from the first college she attended because one of her professors failed her without advance notice the week before graduation. Furthermore, I first met D. when she was a student of mine at the local college she subsequently attended, where she is now in her last semester. Is it possible that she never associates me or her other white professors with the one who so disappointed and humiliated her?

Whatever D.'s relationship to race, however, I could not help but notice how acute my own feelings of discomfort were the moment I raised the issue of slavery. I felt as though I were shining a light on a topic that has been vigilantly remanded to the dark. D.'s family style is not to talk about any problems at all, so silence on racial matters may suit her. But what about me? Did I want to push it aside, avoid the subject? If so, why? Was I afraid of the guilt and self-recrimination I might feel if racism and slavery were discussed in detail? Deep in my heart, do I feel that by not being more politically active I've abdicated my progressive 1960s voice and turned into a complacent bourgeoise? Do I gain power and privilege by being white to D.'s blackness, as I was the professor to her student and now the analyst to her patient? Is she the little girl who enables my dance? Is D.'s powerlessness in relation to me the opportunity for, even the requirement of, my flight? Is it her smallness/blackness/less-than-ness that powers my larger-than-life dance? If so, how?

Do my concerns about self-augmentation by diminishing D. resonate with Freud's relationship to his patient? How large, powerful, and omniscient he must have felt when he so confidently concluded that he could see through his patient's dream to the lie on which it was founded. Pausing momentarily from his dismissive certainty, Freud acknowledged that "beside the intention to mislead me, the dreams partly expressed the wish to win my favour" (p. 152). Yet in the end he abandoned the possibility of a complex voice composed of disparate and conflicted partial voices in favor of simple unity. The patient's dream of "cure through the treatment, . . . joy over the prospects of life then opened up to her [and] longing for a man's love and for children" was simply a ruse, a trick. Despite having championed multiplicity in *Three Essays,* here Freud foreclosed it; the "girl" was either for him or against him, homosexual or heterosexual. Arrogantly justifying his conclusion of deceit on "some slight impression or other" (p. 152), Freud never recognized that his patient may have stopped dreaming these sorts of dreams not because they lied, but because he refused them.

The issue of silenced and refused dreams is prominent in my work with D. as well; in fact, it is probably the central issue around which the therapy has revolved. D. learned early to mute her desires, her fears, her passions. Not infrequently I've felt that I too silence her. I have caught myself arguing with her, acting like her mother—as well as like white superiors with their black inferiors—as though I know the right answer and she would do well to defer to me. Here too, as with direct questions about race, when I've tried to raise the topic of my bossiness, D. denies that it troubles her. She states that she always feels that I'm willing to listen to her and that, unlike her mother, I am interested and open-minded. Okay. But I'm also at times insistent and somewhat authoritarian with her. Did I dream about D. because my interaction with her reminds me of Freud's with his patient more than I like to admit? Do I want to portray myself as different from him—open-minded and nonauthoritarian—when my relationship with D. says otherwise? And do not D. and I each silence the other in our interactions, she by refusing to acknowledge the bossy me? Did Freud's patient silence him with her snottiness, rendering mute the part of him that was genuinely interested in understanding her?

Part of what has been silenced and condemned in D. is her wildness, her "badness." One of the few times she has felt free to "let her hair down" has been at the annual AIDS Dance-A-Thon, which she always attends. She goes alone and dances far into the night, until she's danced out. Although I too would enjoy dancing away the night at the Dance-A-Thon, I am aware that our exhilaration takes different forms. In my dream the dance is classical ballet. And in this paper I dance conservatively by interrogating Freud, a positioning that grants him authority, fatherhood.

Also, like D., I felt obliged in my early life to be a very "good" girl. In addition to identifying with her desire to be wild, do I identify with her struggle to loosen her inhibitions and allow the abandon that would energize her dance and her actions? Do I envy the possibility that she will free herself of them more than I was able to? Is this very essay, with its somewhat unusual format, my attempt to loosen the strictures of the father's word in my professional voice? Freud states that the "bad reputation of her 'Lady' . . . was positively a 'condition of love' for her" (p. 148). While he explains this on the basis of intrapsychic conditions for object-choice, might it not be that the patient admired her loved one's courage to live as she pleased (see D'Ercole, this volume)? Might Freud in some similar way have envied his patient her spunk? Both were fighting for acknowledgment of their right to their own point of view. Did he quit because she seemed the stronger in that struggle? Did he, and do I, envy her refusal to subjugate her wishes, despite the pressures exerted upon her by society, her family, and by the treatment?

Scene 2

Dance, Nureyev dancing, takes me to the second scene. I suppose it was in the mid 1960s, when I was in high school, that I first saw Nureyev and Fonteyn dance. I went with R., who was then my boyfriend and later my husband. I had met him through Youth for Human Rights, a civil rights group I joined as my first political act. He was a communist, party member and all, and I greatly admired his courage and his commitment, his voice. It was my utter dependence on that voice, so powerful in those years, that my dream captures.

I married R. knowing he was gay, or at least knowing he had been. He was open about this with me from the beginning, but when he proposed marriage I hoped he had put it aside. This, I think, was my projection, since it was probably I who had decided to put the issue of his sexuality aside. His therapist in the late 1960s —a very nice, well-intentioned, politically progressive man— supported his marrying me, hoping this would change his sexuality. It seems hard in the current gay-tolerant climate to remember how different American attitudes toward "homosexuality" were during those years. I know R.'s terror pushed him to grab the "respectability" of marriage. For my part, I married him in spite of our problems largely because I felt lost, with no voice of my own, silenced in ways similar to D. I hoped that if I powered R.'s dance from behind the scenes, he'd lift me in flight as Nureyev lifted Fonteyn. Of course, if I was the behind-the-scenes motor, it was actually I who would lift him, I who had the power. Our changing sexualities—he's now married to a woman and they have a child, I now live with the woman I love—echo D.'s changing, evolving sexuality.

Despite being in her mid–30s and desperately wanting to marry and have children, D. has until recently had only one sexual partner, her female roommate with whom she has been very close for many years. Recently, after much therapeutic work, she had her first sexual encounter with a man. At present she is planning to get her own aparment for the first time. Much of her excitement over this prospect comes from her plans to pursue the hot heterosexual sex life she has fantasized about for years. While Freud hoped to change his patient's sexuality, open it to its bisexual potential, I don't conceive of D. (or of myself, for that matter) as "being" either gay or straight. Rather, in my work with her, I have approached the issue as one of voice. She loves her roommate but yearns for a man. Prohibited from pursuing this by her mother's and her girlfriend's injunctions, D. has felt enslaved and muted by her loyalty to them and by her fear and guilt at the prospect of displeasing them. Thus, rather than seeing her sexuality as "changed," I believe that as D. has felt more entitled to a voice of her own, she has been increasingly able to pursue choices heretofore foreclosed.

I believe that D. also feels constrained by her loyalty to her father, whose sudden, unexpected death and the terrifying dreams she had following it were the precipitants for her entering therapy. D.'s father stopped spending time with her shortly before she entered puberty, perhaps because he was fearful of her incipient womanhood. Meyers (this volume) suggests that Freud's relationship with his own daughter resonated through his treatment of his patient. To what extent did his feelings about Anna's sexuality inform his hostility to his "girl"? Although Freud looked with suspicion on his patient's being "a feminist [who] felt it to be unjust that girls should not enjoy the same freedom as boys, and [who] rebelled against the lot of women in general," he also actively supported Anna's right to a central position in psychoanalysis and the right of other women to become analysts, a far from universal attitude in the community. How did Freud's ambivalence about Anna and the other women in his circle get played out with the patient? To what extent did Freud demand loyalty of Anna as his patient's father did of her?

In "Psychogenesis," the father figures as the love-object whose unavailability pushed his daughter to abandon men. Freud concludes that "furiously resentful and embittered, she turned away from her father, and from men altogether . . . [and thus] changed into a man, and took her mother in place of her father as her love-object" (pp. 144–145). In this narrative Freud dichotomizes identifications, loves, and roles into male and female choices and possibilities. He does not envision the multiplicity of combinations possible, in fact inevitable from a postmodern vantage point. Something in our world has so significantly changed from his that his description seems as anachronistic as if it had been written centuries ago.

My point in this essay is to suggest that dependence on an intrapsychic or intrafamilial perspective to the exclusion of a social one in this case is similarly anachronistic. That is, our readings will be profoundly skewed unless we consider the ways in which racism and anti-Semitism affected my patient's father and Freud respectively and how these degradations influenced their treatment of their "girls." Might their own personal degradation require that they separate themselves from the degradations of their girls' femaleness? Is it not likely that Freud's devaluing view of women and of same-sex choice of sexual partners reflected in part his projective response to the hatred and diminishment he regularly endured, hatred that resulted at the end in the murder of four of his own sisters by the Nazis?

Scene 3

This scene is about deflation and Othering, central themes of my thesis here, of Freud's patient's life and of his treatment of her. Certainly the scene can be understood on a psychological level to illustrate the enhancing and diminishing power of the self-object. In that sense my feeling of evaporation in the dream echoes a dynamic that reverberates through Freud's account. Diminishment and rage permeate the text: the patient's father's rage at his felt diminishment by his daughter's behavior; the patient's rage at her father's interference in her relationship with the *cocotte*; and the rage felt by both Freud and his patient at their mutual need for the recognition and respect of the other. The narrative reads almost as a boxing match in which each seeks to knock out the opponent, a series of preemptive and defensive punches, all aimed to destroy the other and minimize narcissistic injury to the self. The girl diminishes Freud by looking dismissively down her lorgnon at him (p. 150). He responds in kind by utterly discrediting her contribution to the work.

The psychological process of putting down the Other, either before or in response to being put down oneself, is certainly not news. In the case, it occasions some dramatic instances of projection, as in Freud's comment that he cannot

> miss the opportunity of expressing for once my astonishment that human beings can go through such great and momentous phases of their love-life without heeding . . . [unconscious intentions] much, sometimes even, indeed, without having the faintest suspicion of them; or else that, when they do become aware of these phases, they deceive themselves so thoroughly in their judgment of them. This happens not only with neurotics, . . . but seems also to be common enough in ordinary life. (p. 153)

Cannot Freud's treatment of his patient be described, at least in part, as his desire that she love and value him, or at least love and value his ideas? When she

thwarts his efforts to gain her acceptance, he accuses her of blindness and venge-
fulness, two attributes that equally characterize his attitude toward her. I do not
believe, as has been claimed elsewhere (Young–Bruehl, 1990), that Freud's
appreciation of his own countertransference has increased markedly in this case
compared to Dora. Rather, I read this narrative as a blaming, self-serving
account, essentially devoid of significant self-examination or self-awareness.
Freud sees only the unrecognized workings of his patient's unconscious, of her
inability to appreciate the complexity of her own mind. He is oblivious to the
truth of this for him as well.

I believe that most analysts would automatically attend to this psychological
level of the action, both in "Psychogenesis" and in their own work, and could
comment usefully on it. That's what we are trained to do. I mean here to suggest, however, that it is inadequate to restrict ourselves to this perspective to the
exclusion of the social level of our functioning and its larger ramifications.
Demonizing and Othering are not merely psychological reactions to intrapsychic
conflict or injury. They are also social processes that serve to consolidate the
power of certain groups to the detriment and destruction of others. Freud's narrative, with its silencing of his patient's voice in response to her difference, figures microcosmically the macrocosmic silencing of gay and lesbian voices
throughout psychoanalytic theorizing. Projecting lack onto his patient is not simply Freud's intrapsychic act of self-equilibration. It is also a social act of power.

Among the many strategies that exist for ordering and consolidating social
power is the cultural production of "scientific" taxonomies of sexuality and
race, justified as biologically natural (Laqueur, 1990). Freud's theorizing (as does
ours) took place amidst a variety of overlapping intellectual and social contexts
and discourses that created and legitimized power, including late nineteenth-
century intellectual discourses that justified the existence and expansion of
European empires. This body of thought included the modern tradition in
which universal attributes, dependent on the exclusions that defined them, created the ideological conditions for colonization. These discourses functioned
much as "with liberty and justice for all" did, defining "all" to exclude slaves
and women. Race and racism, no less than sex and gender, are deeply embedded in such universalizing modern discourses. They are formative features of
bourgeois liberalism, not aberrations from it.

> The most basic universalistic notions of "human nature" and "individ-
> ual liberty," elaborated by Locke and Mill, rested on combined notions
> of breeding and the learning of "naturalized" habits that set off those
> who exhibited such a "nature" and could exercise such liberty from the
> racially inferior. . . . [T]he very concept of universalism was [not only]
> gendered, . . . [it was also] racially inflected. (Stoler, 1997, p. 131)

That Freud figured his patient as Other was a function of the overlapping, mutually reverberating contexts in which he lived and thought. The personal context of his relationship with his daughter, the social context of being a hated Jew, and the intellectual context of modern universalism all contributed to his efforts to consolidate his power by projecting onto her his feared attributes of himself. Both sexual and racial concerns permeate the text, "inseparable axes" of social regulation and power distribution (Butler, 1993, p. 182).

In her discussion of black women writers, Mae Gwendolyn Henderson (1994) suggests that we engage a "simultaneity of discourse," an approach to their texts that includes perspectives of both race and gender and of the inter-action between the two. She posits that it is the subjective plurality (rather than a cohesive or a fractured subjectivity) of these authors, born of their inhabiting these socially differentiated spaces and of their multiply embodying the "other in ourselves" (p. 259), that enables them to speak in multiple languages of experience. Glossing Bakhtin and Gadamer, Henderson proposes that we recognize both the contestation of the Other and consensus and identification with the Other as aspects of black women writers' work. These intersecting lines, which articulate the Other within as well as the same within, provide the opportunity for an I/Thou experience based on the "fellowship born of not overlooking difference" (p. 264).

In this essay I have attempted to draw similar lines. Race and sex intersect the text and my dream, Freud's case and my own. If psychoanalysis can address the unacknowledged presence of race in our theorizing and engage a simultaneity of discourse, we may determine strategies to redress the Othering of difference as a means to power and to promote instead a recognition of difference as a means to true fellowship.

References

Butler, J. (1993). *Bodies that matter*. New York: Routledge.

Cushman, P. (1995). *Constructing the self, constructing America: A cultural history of psychotherapy*. Reading, MA: Addison-Wesley.

Flax, J. (1996). Review essay. *Psychoanalytic Dialogues*, 847–857.

Freud, S. (1963). The psychogenesis of a case of homosexuality in a female. In *Sexuality and the psychology of love*. New York: MacMillan. (Original work published 1920)

Freud, S. (1975). *Three essays on the theory of sexuality*. New York: Basic Books. (Original work published 1905)

Gates, H. L. (1986a). Introduction: Writing "race" and the difference it makes. In H. L. Gates (Ed.), *"Race," writing, and difference*. (pp. 1–20). Chicago: University of Chicago Press.

Gates, H. L. (1986b). Talkin' that talk. In H. L. Gates (Ed.), *"Race," writing and difference*. (pp. 402–409). Chicago: University of Chicago Press.

Gilbert-Moore, J. (1997). *Postcolonical theory: Contexts, practices, policies.* (p. 11). New York: Verso.

Gilman, S. (1993). *Freud, race and gender.* Princeton, NJ: Princeton University Press.

Henderson, M. G. (1994). Speaking in tongues. In P. Williams & L. Chrisman (Eds.), *Colonial discourse and post-colonial theory.* (pp. 257–267). New York: Columbia University Press.

Jones, E. (1957). *The life of Sigmund Freud.* (Vol. 3). New York: Basic Books.

Kristeva, J. (1982). *Powers of horror: An essay on abjection.* New York: Columbia University Press.

Laqueur, T. (1990). *Making sex: Body and gender from the Greeks to Freud.* Cambridge, MA: Harvard University Press.

Rosica, K. (1997). The evolution of a failed interpretation. *Psychoanalytic Dialogues,* 583–601.

Stoler, A. L. (1997). *Race and the education of desire: Foucault's history of sexuality and the colonial order of things.* Durham: Duke University Press.

Tate, C. (1996). Freud and his "Negro": Psychoanalysis as ally and enemy of African Americans. *Journal for the Psychoanalysis of Culture and Society.* Vol. 1, 1, 53–62.

Tompkins, J. (1986). "Indians": Textualism, morality and the problem of history. In H. L. Gates (Ed.), *"Race," writing and difference.* Chicago: University of Chicago Press.

Young-Bruehl, E. (1990). *Freud on women.* New York: W. W. Norton.

Part IV

~

DISCUSSION

14

UNFINISHED BUSINESS

~

Muriel Dimen

. . . our patient, who was in no way neurotic . . .
(Freud, 1920, p. 158, n. 1)

Introduction: Three Themes

What a mouthful! "The Psychogenesis of a Case of Homosexuality in a Woman" a title whose clunky concreteness suits the language of medical report, clashes with the pithy elegance of, say, *Civilization and Its Discontents*, to select just one of Freud's more gracefully titled cultural works. Hard to metabolize, it is altered with startling frequency. Sometimes it is abbreviated for literary convenience, much as *Three Essays* stands for Freud's *Three Essays on the Theory of Sexuality*. Sometimes an author will find syntax a compelling reason for emendation; in an essay published elsewhere, Jacobus (1995) cites but also abridges the full title depending on context. The most common truncation is "Case of Homosexuality in a Woman" (e.g., in Jacobus' own title; Schwartz, 1998), sometimes preceded by "A." But you also come across mistranscriptions like "Psychogenesis of Homosexuality in a Woman" (J. Rose, 1986), or, here and there, mysteriously degendered versions like "Psychogenesis of a Case of Homosexuality" or even, simply, "Case of Homosexuality." Indeed having finished this discussion, I was surprised to find, while proofing the galleys of another essay (1998), my own unconscious variation on this theme: "On the Psychogenesis of a Case of Homosexuality in a Woman." Without the benefit of others' mistakes, there's no doubt I would have missed my own and let the title as I had it go into print.

233

There's a message in this medium, and I am going to heed it. One might think of those apocryphal scribes copying out manuscripts by hand and making errors as they went. The instability of the title is, however, too pronounced to be attributable merely to carelessness of either the typographical or the authorial variety. In my discussion of this anthology about the many loose ends in Freud's account of his work with a very unhappy woman, I will go with, not resist, the tendency to rewrite his title. Like psychoanalysts listening to what their patients say in order to hear the repressed or dissociated unsaid, and like literary critics deconstructing their Freud to find out what has slipped through the cracks of silence, I want to read this community of error as a slip of many tongues that allows a plethora of silenced truths to speak out. In solidarity with the contributors to this volume, I seek both the coherence obscured by silence and the multiplicity hiding inside any uniform or totalizing account.

Within and among the essays in this interdisciplinary book, a conversation is taking place. Two worlds are engaged with psychoanalysis: the clinical and the academic. In this colloquy across a diversity of knowledge and practice, three themes emerge as a subtextual chain of thought that is imbricated with questions of sexuality and gender alive in clinic and culture. We are dealing here with an inconclusive text as well as a polyphony of sometimes discordant responses to it. Still, three centrifugal features hold the conversation together, keeping in play a variety of tropes and concepts inhabiting the intellectual space of this novel anthology.

1. *Dualism,* or the problem of binaries, will be familiar to the literary readers of this volume, as well as to clinicians who have availed themselves of the postmodernist and deconstructionist theories recently adumbrated in the academy. It appears variously in the essays: in deconstructing gender and desire; in interpreting the relationship of analyst and patient; in speculating about the structure and dynamics of the psyche; in decoding the interface of psyche and society, mind and body, nature and culture. The writers try mightily to contend with dualism's magnetic pull, and they invent diverse ways to inhabit the space between polarities.

2. *Intersubjectivity,* or the problem of other minds, is currently preoccupying many clinical practitioners of psychoanalysis who struggle with the post-Freudian after-shock introduced in Europe by Melanie Klein and in the United States by Harry Stack Sullivan and Heinz Kohut. Of chief interest to the writers here are the effect of the analyst's person on the process of treatment and the role of the analyst's countertransference in the patient's transference. Clinicians now ask how internal the psyche is; they wonder whether it exists in the space between selves. If there is no infant without the caretaker, to paraphrase D.W. Winnicott's insight, then there is no analyst without a patient, no patient without an analyst, no self

without an other. How we theorize psychological development and how we theorize clinical practice are just two of the dynamite matters at stake here.

3. *Authority,* or the problem of hierarchy and domination, registers a generation's worth of political contest now vividly ensconced and ongoing in academic life but only recently prominent on psychoanalytic turf. Not only Freud's authority over his patient and her defiance draw the essayists' attention; also extremely important are cultural and theoretical resistances to authority forged in the crucible of the political 1960s. The authority of personal experience, associated with the counterculture, feminism, and gay liberation, underlies the citation of both personal and clinical experience in the literary strategies of some of our authors. The critique of power embedded in Michel Foucault's theory of disciplinary authority finds its way into many discussions of psychoanalytic theory and practice in general and of Freud and his patient in particular.

With this community of thought and argument in mind, let us now return to that problematic title for a quasi-medical account that unsuccessfully tries to fit an unfinished treatment into a smooth narrative skin. There are, says the most common mis-citation, too many terms, the whole thing is too complicated. We don't want "Psychogenesis" and "Case" and "Homosexuality" and "Woman"; let's just simplify matters, let's just forget at least one of them, let's just call it "Case of Homosexuality in a Woman."

Case of Homosexuality . . .

Here, all our authors agree: There is no case. The academics and analysts in this volume, sharing an intellectual genealogy in the gender, sexual, and multicultural politics of the last 30 years, come together on this point. There is no case of homosexuality, nor is homosexuality a case. Unlike influenza, sexual preference is not an illness. When you have a case of flu, you need a physician. When you have homosexuality, you need a lover, not a doctor. The time when homosexuality was something to be "treated" by qualified medical personnel is just about over; Charles Socarides (1968) and John Nicolosi (1991) are, perhaps, the principal psychiatric holdouts for this version of a disciplinary psychoanalytic authority that overtly monitors desire. Since 1973, when homosexuality as a disease category was removed from the *Diagnostic and Statistical Manual of the American Psychiatric Association,* the official psychotherapy position has cohered: Homosexuality is an orientation, a legitimate type of object-choice.

Sexual preference, or object-choice, no longer fits into medical grammar. Once upon a time essays referred to "the treatment of homosexuality." You can't say things like that anymore. So goes the now commonplace rereading of classical nosology: To deem homosexuality an illness is heterosexist practice.

The authority of personal experience has made the case and, at least on paper, largely won the day: Homosexual desire is as normal, natural, healthy, and wholesome as any other form of sexual preference, orientation, or practice.

Case closed? Not exactly. That this book is necessary suggests unfinished business in psychoanalysis as well as in culture. Even after 1973, psychoanalysis continued to pathologize gays and lesbians (Drescher, 1997). Until about 5 minutes ago, "out" homosexuals were virtually prohibited from studying at analytic training institutes; this prohibition explains the still small number of self-identified lesbian and gay analysts. Predictably, this discrimination has inhibited the development of nonpathologizing theory. Historically, psychoanalytic thinkers who did not conform to the anti-homosexual hegemony risked being stigmatized and thereby discredited, prejudicially indicted as sympathetic or implicated as lesbian or gay, hence illegitimate. Homosexuality's increasing social acceptability, however, requires as well as permits advances that include but also exceed a critique of existing ideas. The new sexual tolerance stimulates a theoretical and clinical rethinking of sexual orientation altogether. Hence this book.

It is old news that Freud thought homosexual desire normal. He would have applauded when the official case was laid to rest in the books as they were written in the midst of the "sexual revolution" of the 1970s. His tolerance shows up repeatedly in text and footnote alike (see the quote that opens this essay, as well as 1910, p. 99, n. 2, added 1919). Yet throughout his surviving writings, he continues to speak in tongues. While he regards all human desire as fundamentally polymorphous, he also feels that heterosexuality is better. Biology and society constitute the good, sound "practical" reasons (1920, p.151) why, he says, we never attempt with heterosexual people what we dare with homosexual persons: to change their psychic signature—their desire. His *Three Essays on the Theory of Sexuality* begins as a red-hot manifesto for sexual liberation but concludes as a fiat for heterosexual, nuclear-family, monogamous order. Polymorphous perversity, primal but utopian, must narrow into heterosexual object-choice to fit the requirements of the human world and the demands of the species. Do not sorrow that your son is gay, he consoles the American mother of a homosexual man in a celebrated letter (1935) that points out how much homosexual people have contributed to our civilization. Unfortunately, he must admit, it is better to be straight than gay, if only because that is how society is set up. The dilemma endures. Not surprisingly, I know at least one lesbian single mother, a child of the feminist and sexual revolutions, who agrees: she prefers her daughter be straight because, as her own life has taugh her, being homosexual is just too hard.

. . . Homosexuality in a Woman . . .

One gets the feeling, however, that the practicalities are only part of the matter for Freud. His reason tells him one thing, his heart, another. Yes, he treats famous

lesbians like H.D. Still, he is bigoted. His "pedestrian . . . misogynist and homophobic sentiments," as Moss & Zeavin (p. 197, in this volume) label his prejudice, exist in parallel with his liberal sentiments, two clashing colors striping his
conscience. Why otherwise does he ally with the girl's father and accept the job
of forcing her to change?

You could almost say he hates her. Ken Corbett (1993) has proposed we
think of homophobia not as fear but as hatred. She "resists," she is "defiant,"
she condescends—indeed, she defeats him, as several of our authors (de
Lauretis, Gagnon, Wineapple, Woolwine) contend. Retaliating, he puts her
down: "In fact," he jibes, "she was a feminist." He erases her subjectivity by
rendering her nameless. Is he disgusted by her? If Freud champions homosexuality in general, maybe he does not really cotton to female homosexuality in
particular. Moss & Zeavin make perhaps too quick work of Freud's woman-
hating commitment to male domination, but other authors are quite disturbed,
though of course unsurprised that misogyny and patriarchy are as hard at work
as homophobia in both the clinical and theoretical spaces represented in this
account. Freud e-feminates his patient with a stroke of the pen, changing her
gender mid-paragraph, a subtlety first noted by Harris (in this volume). Pen
then morphs into sword: Can one not find revulsion in his concluding evoca-
tion of Steinach's sex-change operations, those "phallic, surgical interventions," as Harris (p. 162, in this volume) terms them?

He forces the girl, he forces the theory. Politics and knowledge converge in
Freud's massive effort to cobble fact and theory together. His language, Gagnon
(in this volume) shows us, repeatedly asserts his mastery over "the mystery of
homosexuality" even as the girl and her truths patently elude him, even as he
says that explaining homosexuality is not the job of psychoanalysis. In this text,
Woolwine contends, patriarchy thumps its chest in victory at the very moment
of failure: The "Freud of this text is . . . the Freud of power, the man who is
always willing to subordinate any 'liberal' inclinations he might have to a desire
for professional power and who, in order to do so, must in the last analysis be
the handmaiden of the 'normal', (i.e., of the heterosexual regime). He is the
failed liberal and takes revenge for his failure" (p. 103, in this volume).

Passions, we should note, run high in the responses to this case. Observe the
Schadenfreude enjoyed by Woolwine and Gagnon (both in this volume) upon
comtemplating Freud's failure: "The only thing," says Gagnon, "that makes this
particular text pleasurable to read is that ultimately, Freud is shown to be unsuccessful in his assertion of power (via his claims to knowledge and professional
standing) over an unruly object (lesbianism) and an unruly subject (a young
woman)" (in this volume). Lesser, interestingly, finds herself in this volume
departing from the customary feminist anger at Freud's dismissive handling of his
patient. Instead, the anti-Semitism of his history and milieu moves her to an unex-

pected sympathy. None of the essays here is without affect. Between the lines of even the most neutrally voiced essay in this volume, that of Moss & Zeavin, courses a river of deep feeling, if not for the patient, then for the position it defends: the validity of the voice of psychoanalytic tradition as against the "sincere" voice of first-person narrative, or what I am calling the authority of personal experience.

The psychoanalytical is political. Freud may efface his patient, as we have seen, but she likely obscures herself as well, resisting his mastery by refusing to let herself be known. "The 'Russian tactics' of my title are Freud's code name for the strategies employed by resistance in the face of psychoanalytic enlightenment," writes Jacobus (1995, p. 85). The girl has pulled back behind a line that Freud says he cannot conquer, just as lesbians in ordinary life have had to hide to protect their desire, a strategy that has reinforced the complementary ostracism on the part of the conventional society that made this defensive maneuver advisable in the first place. The text's silences speak loud and clear, too. The social invisibility of lesbians is a commonplace of feminist theory and activism, and this book may be said to be a theater in the battle against this effacement.

Is the girl, however, really homosexual? What is homosexuality anyway? Why homosexuality? Heterosexuality? What makes any given sexual preference cohere as an entity? Inquiring minds, like Freud, as well as the academics and analysts in this book, want to know. How far you can get with your theory of sex before having to take up your understanding of gender is a matter for some debate among our contributors. The two extremes represented in this collection in fact express a venerable tension in psychoanalytic thought and practice: On the one hand, one's sexual fate depends crucially on one's masculinity or femininity, on the other, sexuality is an impersonal and independently arising force shaping male and female, gay and straight alike.

This tension holds a debate about binaries between "either/or" and "both/and." At one extreme, D'Ercole (in this volume) argues that clinical psychoanalysis requires the fluidity and multiplicity postmodernism locates in gender to understand the sexual richness of this patient, whose psyche, needs, history, and desire have been distorted by Freud's conventionally narrow and rigid conception of women. Moss & Zeavin (in this volume), at the other, are clinical minimalists, preferring to theorize all sexuality down to its bare roots in primal loss, a time-honored and probably correct interpretation. Regarding lesbian desire as not a special case but a particular instance of a universal truth, they find differences of gender and object-choice to be irrelevant to the fundamental constitution of desire. As is so often the case, the extremes meet. At the end, D'Ercole seems led by gender's instability away from any certainty about its existence or effects at all, for she concludes by suggesting that sex needs to be theorized outside of gender. At the same time, gender seems a sufficiently puissant organizing concept that Moss & Zeavin's clinical examples follow its lines, albeit in untheorized fashion: a male analyst with a male patient, a female analyst with a female patient.

At stake in the debate in this volume between D'Ercole and Moss & Zeavin are vital questions of clinical and political theory and practice: on the one hand, the question of universality versus particularity, on the other, the validity of identity politics. Henry Mayer (1998, p. 13) asks of Ralph Ellison's *Invisible Man:* "Is it a great ethnic novel or a universal statement? Can it be both?" So we may ask about sexuality. Is it particular to individuals, types of object choice, or sorts of gender identification? Is it universal in origin, history, and manifestation? Can it be both? De Lauretis (this volume), who would seem to be in the "both/and" camp, combines the two extreme theoretical strategies. For her, too, loss universally begets desire. Equally important, however, the loss securing female homosexual desire is quite gender-specific: What gets dissociated for women is their finding of pleasure in their bodies through their relationships with other female bodies. The "'lost object of female perverse desire is . . . the subject's own lost body, which can be recovered in fantasy, in sexual practice, *in and with* another woman. This perverse desire . . . is based on the post-Oedipal disavowal of the loss . . . of one's body-ego, the loss of being" (p. 50, in this volume). The negative of this perverse female sexuality would, one might add, be the normal neurosis of female heterosexuality.

An Update on Intersubjectivity in Psychoanalysis

Note the profound matters raised here. Not only sex and gender, but one's very being are at stake—as was the patient's, for the case begins with her attempt at suicide. How does one become a being, a self? These questions are alive in the psychoanalytic world. How is the psyche structured? How does it come to be? Once again the problem of "both/and" versus "either/or": is psychic life *sui generis* or does it reduce to something else—to, say, relationship or culture or biology, to name three commonly invoked possibilities? How about all of the above?

If psychoanalysis once raised these questions in regard to the single psyche, it now considers that individual psychology may also equally entail plural minds. Intersubjectivity is much on the psychoanalytic agenda these days. The extraordinarily intricate world of individual subjectivity has at the end of the century been complicated by the complexities of multiple subjectivities. Several psychoanalytic stances on this matter are extant, and I will name three. Two branch from the original Freudian tree toward what is now called in some quarters relational psychoanalysis. One, the object-relations school of thought, imagines internal, unconscious representations of others: The psyche is formed of the rela-

tions among "objects." The other, the interpersonal school, thinks more literally about the lived relations among actual individuals, parent and child, analysts
and patients. Branching off from a quite different part of the trunk, Lacanian
theory takes up more globally the problem of alterity; it acknowledges that
dyadic relationship is psychically central but deems it illusory, valorizing instead
the Other of language, law, and culture.

The heritage of relational psychoanalysis, whose evolution I will sketch, is
polyglot. I privilege it here in part because it is less familiar to the literary readers
and writers of this volume, whose psychoanalytic home is more Freudian and
Lacanian, and in part because it is most germane to our next update, which will
be about the mother in psychoanalytic thought and practice.[1] Its point of origin,
classical psychoanalysis, answers the primal questions about the self's structure,
dynamism, and origins in terms of drives—forces that, lying on the border of mental and physical, motivate psychic structure and process in both health and illness.
Insofar as the psyche is deemed internal to the individual, the analyst's job is to
focus on the intrapsychic. The cause of illness being the repression of conflictual
desire, cure and health depend on the analyst helping the patient to make conscious the painful, conflicted wishes once rendered unconscious. The principal
tool at the analyst's disposal is interpretation, especially of the transference and,
within that, of the sexual transference. Sexuality in classical psychoanalysis is at the
heart of development and mind. A good example of the intrapsychic mode of theorizing and working is found in the essay in this volume by Moss & Zeavin.
There, sexuality emerges within body and psyche of the individual; although the
import of the parent–child connection for sexuality is mentioned, it is not theorized as such either developmentally or clinically.

Interpersonal psychoanalysis, a second source of relational thought, developed
as a direct response to orthodox Freudian psychoanalysis. As formulated by Harry
Stack Sullivan and Clara Thompson, among others, human psychology is matter
of human relationship; psychological difficulties are the result not of repression—
in which what is conscious becomes unconscious—but of problems in living,
especially patterns of relating that render suffering inevitable. Sexuality is not the
fons, origo, or telos of psychic process, but one of many motivations, modes of
being, and strategies of relating in the human spectrum. What goes on in the here-
and-now between people is at least as influential as what happened in the past.
Given the power of interpersonal relatedness to shape and repair the individual,
analysts should focus on what goes on between them and their patients; in this
practice, the internal workings of the psyche are imagined through the manifest
engagement between thr two parties to encounter. Think here of D'Erole's
account in this volume of her patient, in which growth is defined as the making
of human connection.

Relational psychoanalysis is also highly indebted to the object–relations school of thought (as well as to the self-psychology of Heinz Kohut, which my schematic formulation does not allow me to describe here). Object–relations is associated in the first place with Melanie Klein, who herself parted ways with Freud, and later with D. W. Winnicott, who parted ways with her, as well as with Ronald Fairbairn, who himself broke independently with classical concepts. Object–relations holds that the internal psychic world is made of representations or unconscious symbolic transformations of the early relations between self and other, that is, between "objects." Clinically, relational psychoanalysis may be said to operate in the tension of "one-person"—classical—and "two-person"—interpersonal—psychologies. In this intersubjective space, explicit parallels are drawn between treatment and development—that is, between parent–child and analyst–patient relations. The critique of binary thinking is an important relational project. Like consciousness and unconsciousness, neither the intrapsychic one-person psychology nor the interpersonal two-person psychology "holds a privileged position in relation to the other; rather, they stand in a relation of relative difference, each constituting the other through negation" (Ogden, 1994, p. 60). Here suffering is always both internal and external, interpretable by reference to the multiple dynamics of the early object world as well as to the way the analyst–patient relationship relives and revises ancient wounds. Not only the patient's subjectivity but the analyst's comes into technical and theoretical play. Interpreting countertransference as well as transference is held to be critical to successful and ethical treatment. Harris' essay in this volume, in which not only Freud's work with this patient but also two cases of her own unspool, is exemplary of the theoretical and clinical practices of relational psychoanalysis.

An Update on Mother

Emerging out of this internecine psychoanalytic fray is a figure lost not only to lesbian desire but also, until recently, to psychoanalytic desire: mother, who is central to these essays and to the intense questions of sex and selfhood they engage. The psychoanalytic discovery of intersubjectivity and the recovery of the mother in both the clinical and the academic worlds belong to one interdisciplinary evolution. It is one of the perhaps ironic curiosities of intellectual history that, in recognizing intersubjectivity, psychoanalysis and feminism, so often portrayed and self-represented as enemies (Dimen, 1997), have converged (Benjamin, 1984). In the footsteps of Melanie Klein, on the one hand, and Dorothy Dinnerstein and Nancy Chodorow, on the other, much is now made of the parallels and disjunctures between analyst and patient, mother and child. Some of the essays in this volume advance this long overdue recognition of the mother's force in mental process, psychological development, and transference/countertransference.

Consider the origins of the girl's love for her lady in Freud's essay. It entails, both academics and analysts agree, a primal relation to her mother, a relation that she and her analyst both occlude. There has been, you might say, a double dissociation or disavowal: Mother and lesbian desire together disappear at once from text, clinic, and experience, for the lost body of desire is wed to the body of the mother. An unvoiced prohibition, to put it differently, operates on sexual feelings between mother and daughter. A taboo so taboo it cannot be spoken, mother–daughter desire is the one form of incest that receives no mention whatsoever in Freud's (1913) foundational *Totem and Taboo*. Psychic and regulatory processes fuse here: The prohibition is simultaneously unconscious and institutional. "How deeply lesbian love threatens the patriarchal order," writes Pérez Foster (p. 130, in this volume) from the perspective of her Caribbean childhood, echoing Adrienne Rich's (1980) theory of how "compulsory heterosexuality" buries female homosexuality. And before that, at about the same time as homosexuality was being officially depathologized, Gayle Rubin (1975) was locating the cultural silencing of lesbian desire in patriarchal regulatory practice.

The silence is stentorian: Everyone, male or female, must be sexually oriented toward and by the phallus. Why, Fuss asks in her essay in this volume, does Freud read homosexuality as a turning back? Why is it not "a move *toward* the mother rather than 'a retreat *from* the father" (p. 60)? Freud presumes an original heterosexuality, a current flowing beneath her manifest homosexuality. That the girl might have been rivalrous not with her mother for her father, but with her father for her mother, that her mother was her first love—these are hypotheses he cannot entertain (see Fuss, Wineapple, and D'Ercole, in this volume). Dissociated, her love for her mother and rivalry with her father are unintelligible."Does Freud's reading of the mother as crotchety and competitive," asks Wineapple (p. 92, in this volume), "come from the girl's estimation—or his own?" According to Fuss and Wineapple in this volume, as well as Merck (1993) Freud cannot imagine being maternal; he probably doesn't like the girl's mother. Famously he has said to H. D. "I do *not* like to be the mother in transference—it always surprises me and shocks me a little. I feel so very masculine" (H.D. 1974/1956, p. 146–467). His countertransference is not only paternal, it is antimaternal. His discomfort with the oceanic feeling he finds in religious belief can be read also a *mal-de-mer* engendered by maternal and hence feminized feelings of relatedness (Benjamin, 1988.)

These essays must be seen in the context of a quarter century's worth of feminist retheorizing of mother as agent, sexual subject, principal childrearer, of woman as mother, of mothering as gendered or not. Many of the essays argue for a reversal of the classical psychoanalytic order of thought and interpretation. The Oedipal, with its battle of father and son, is not first in psychic formation. It is second, coming after and recasting through *Nachträglichkeit* the pre-Oedipal object world, with its complicated space between mother, or caretaker, and child. Only one essay in this volume, that by Moss & Zeavin with its focus on phallic disappointment as the root of male as well as female sexuality, is content to remain exclusively within the classical scheme of erogenous zones that fits so well with Oedipal theory. Others privilege instead the place of object-relations in psychosexuality, a task now being undertaken in increasingly widespread psychoanalytic quarters. That we take up where Freud left off, in the theorization of the pre-Mycenean floor of psychic development, does not, Fuss argues (this volume), require us to commit to the archeological metaphor now also being overhauled in relational theory (Ogden, 1994). Mother, maternity, femininity, and homosexuality are not only "the pre: the preoedipal, the presymbolic, the prelaw, the premature, even the presexual" (p. 55). They are instead features of human life altogether, always implicit in, fundamental to, and at one with conduct, intimacy, and sanity in maturity as well as infancy.

The mother and the lesbian, as figures of psychoanalytic fact and fiction, are not the same. Still, for de Lauretis (1994a; in this volume), their histories and futures in psychoanalytic and cultural and even political fantasy are interimplicated. If you restore mother to psychoanalysis, then you have to revise the Oedipal. Once the masculine is unseated from the throne of subjectivity, you have to make room not only for girls but also for female desire, for which homosexuality stands as symbol. Freud, de Lauretis proposes, has the sense that something is going on in homosexuality that he cannot grasp. His failure, she argues, rests in his deathlike grip on his founding "passionate fiction," the Oedipus complex. Ungovernably and unwillingly wed to the reproductive foundations of sexuality, he does not want to imagine anything other than heterosexual desire. If heterosexuality, however, is no longer the given of desire and the goal of development, then large sections of the psychoanalytic edifice begin to fall away. A massive remodeling effort is required. Oedipality can no longer dominate. Rather, as de Lauretis (1994) reasons, it must be moved to allow equal room for both pre- and post-Oedipal constructions.

How we think sexuality is constituted consequently undergoes a sea-change. Psychoanalysis classically posits a fateful fork in the road that must be taken on the Oedipal passage. It constructs "identification and desire as two mutually exclusive relations" (Schwartz, 1998, p. 20): To become adult—read heterosexual—you must identify with the parent whose sex is the same as yours and to desire the parent whose sex is opposite. If instead you both identify with and desire the same parent, you are on the road to illness—homosexuality. New psychoanalytic thinking says otherwise. You can, with no more ill effects than those suffered by the ordinary heterosexual (Chodorow, 1994), both identify with and desire someone of the same gender. Neither does choice of love-object determine one's gender identity, nor does one's gender tell one's desire. Postmodernist feminists like Fuss propose a fundamental revision in the psychoanalytic theory of sex and gender development. Like Butler (1990) and Jacobus (1995), Fuss in this volume argues against the seemingly fundamental psychoanalytic law holding that desire and identification are structurally independent of one another, so that "the possibility of one always presuppose[s] the repression of the other" (p. 63). Rather, given the fluidity and volatility of gendered and sexual identity, which Freud well knew and indeed introduced us to, the bond between identification and object-choice is always provisional and purchased at psychic cost.

All bets are suddenly off in this shake-up of sex and gender. What happens then when we think about identification and desire in Freud's nameless patient? "What might be helpful," Harris suggests in an essay in this volume that is one of the first to import feminist postmodernism into the psychoanalytic study of gender, "is to maintain a contradictory model of gender in which it is a serious, fully lived, conscious experience of self, often 'core' to one's being, and at the same time it can dissolve or transmute under our very gaze" (p. 177). Harris wonders about the girl's gender. Is she in fact female? Startlingly, Harris claims—and is echoed although not cited by Gagnon (a gap that makes clear how necessary and valuable is the interdisciplinary conversation taking place in this anthology)—that the girl is a boy:

> In formal identity terms, the patient makes a homosexual object choice. But in the more subtle terms of identity and unconscious meaning, I read this patient's love relation as a heterosexual object choice in which a fictive "boy" chooses a mother to idealize and save from an Oedipal father. (p. 166)

Not only is she a boy, she is not even homosexual: She has a boy's love, a son's desire for his mother.

Is this one more erasure of female–female desire, or is it an instance of gender's shape-shifting? We may wonder whether Harris here returns us to the masculinity Freud attributes to lesbians: If you love women, you must be a man. Lesbian feminist theory and practice have insisted on the wrongheadedness of this formulation. Woman-to-woman desire, the "woman-identified woman," does not require phallic mediation. Yet benefits accrue from gender crack-up: Thinking of gender as fluid and multiple allows more room for the individuality that surely marks sexual desire and fantasy (Chodorow, 1994; Person, 1980), more room for the particularity of individual experience and history that are, at least for many these days, the clinician's prime focus. Perhaps some lesbians love as this patient does. For others, object-choice is as woman to woman. *Mutatis mutandis,* the same goes for gay men and straight people and . . . whatever. Oedipal universality, move over.

. . . in a Woman

"Who was that girl?" asks Gagnon (in this volume). If she is the "girl-who-is-really-a-boy" whose rivalry for male terrain Freud combats, she is also the girl who refuses to abandon her "masculine protest" (Harris, pp. 166–67, in this volume). Many of our other essayists, especially clinicians, try to imagine her. Freud's case studies always inspire fantasy, for they present themselves as little dramas; one wants to write a play. Mostly they exercise this fascination because of the fullness of their detail and the narrative rendering Freud supplies. This case, in contrast, tells only enough to whet, but not satisfy, our appetites. Teased, our authors begin to invent. D'Ercole (in this volume) imagines the girl's struggle to please her parents while satisfying her own desire and sees her pain as the symptomatic outcome of this impossible fusion of contradictory desires. Others evoke film and drama (although not, curiously, fiction). In *hommage* to Max Ophuls, de Lauretis (in this volume) writes a "letter to an unknown woman." Meyers' (in this volume), self-appointed dramaturge to Freud, conjures a twenty-first-century revival of the "case" and imagines a cast of characters to fill out an oddly incomplete text, including Freud's father, Jacob, and the second of his homo-erotically invested colleagues and mentors, Wilhelm Fliess. We might note, as an aside, *Hugh Brody*'s (1985) film *1919,* which stars John Scofield and Maria Schell as two of Freud's most poignant patients, the Wolf Man and the homosexual girl, who fictionally meet up and fall in star-crossed love.

The road to hell is paved with good intentions. Not only the nameless patient figures in the authorial imagination. How these essays do go on about Freud's thoughts, feelings, life; the subtitle of Lesser's Introduction, "In the Shadow of Freud," is so right-on. Freud takes the case perhaps because he is hard up (see Fuss and Wineapple) or possibly because his challenged professional self-esteem drives him to support anyone who will support psychoanalysis in a time of its unpopularity (Fuss). He writes this admittedly unsatisfactory case up because of his ambition and competitiveness (Gagnon, Harris, and Woolwine), wanting to beat Abraham to the punch by publishing his manifestly half-baked ideas on homosexuality (see Wineapple) before Abraham publishes on masculine protest. Perhaps his hatred of his patient has to do with his analysis of his daughter Anna and his inability to handle his negative countertransference: He hates in his patient the "masculine" intelligence and strong-mindedness he encourages and cannot bear to hate in his daughter (see Meyers and Wineapple). Perhaps he pro-jectively identifies his own homoerotic sexuality in her: Is, as Meyers proposes, "the *cocotte* . . . to the patient what Fliess is to Freud" (p. 191)? Harris proposes a triangle among Freud, Victor Tausk, and Helene Deutsch and links it with "the

end of this young woman's treatment [which enacts] both castration and reparation . . . the father's punishment of a contesting son, a guilty repetition of Freud's
treatment of Tausk" (p. 168). Can we finally historicize Freud's relation to this
case, seeing at work in him the struggle with anti-Semitism (which also affects
the patient and her father) that is cognate with the patient's struggle with homophobia and misogyny (see Schoenberg, this volume)?

Notice the classic repudiation of woman, how male replaces female as protag-
onist in these several accounts of Freud's famously incomplete account. Freud's
"masterful" narrative, Woolwine argues, creates an interpretation of lesbianism
that gives pride of place to the male, the father, the brother, the girl's masculinity, while moving the female from the center to the margin. Even these essays
replicate the fault they themselves discover in the case: Freud emerges as the figure about whom we know most, by comparison with whom the patient is as
vague as she is sharp-featured, sharp-tongued, sharp-minded. He even becomes
a sympathetic character, suffering the anti-Semitism that Lesser sees as the shadow
story of this "case."

How striking, infuriating, and disturbing it has always been that Freud confesses, in several spots, to his helpless (see de Lauretis), bemused ignorance about
women. Dark continents, what do they want? Femininity is to him maternity
(see Fuss), and he can't relate. Some authors note his mistrust and pathologizing of female friendship (e.g., Harris). To what then can he resort to understand
this patient? If, as de Lauretis observes, only the biologists know for sure at the
end of this case history, later on he sends us to the poets (a challenge Bassin
[1982] quite beautifully took up). He throws up his hands, gives up, eventually
sends her off to a female analyst, and fantasizes about a male surgeon.

If Freud sees women in black and white, the contributors to this volume picture them in technicolor. Here in these essays passionately concerned about the
condition of women under conditions of gender hierarchy, women live, breathe,
are ample and vocal, are sexed, raced, and classed. Almost cinematic in this book
are depictions of women in wildly varying scenes, from Vienna to the Caribbean,
from rural New York to the Ivy League. As the twentieth century begins in
earnest in the post-1914 Old World, a girl suffers in Vienna: We see her prom-
enade with her *cocotte,* be turned away from her beloved's door where she has
importuningly gone, and throw herself down onto the railway tracks. Our
authors' close readings, informed by social and feminist theory, locate her
socially, economically, and culturally, winkling out critical details that address
Gagnon's title question, "Who was that girl?" "The girl," Fuss writes, "a member of the rising middle class, finds herself irresistibly attracted to 'fallen women.'
Her current object of desire [is] a 'demimondaine' who has lost her reputation
and fallen in to 'ignoble circumstances'" (p. 69). Fuss imagines the patient's aspi-

rations, a gender protest arising from the possibilities and demands suddenly opened up for her class and the women in it in the wake of World War I. Fuss notes the other women the patient has come across in her search for an identificatory object, an ego-ideal: "All three of these mother-substitutes—the prostitute, the actress, and the teacher—occupy a class below the girl, but they also represent collectively a class of women who earn their livings independently, outside of marriage and the heterosexual contract" (p. 69). Is she lured by the economic independence and social mobility they stand for? The girl, it seems (contrary to Grey's plaint in this volume), does have models, albeit acquired through pain and suffering.

At the other end of the century are several distinct New World scenarios drafted by four of our clinical authors, who call on the authority of personal experience, wishing to make up for what Freud omits by filling in with their personal lives. Recognitions leap gaps of race and nationality, although they circulate within the same socioeconomic, middle-class level. To Pérez Foster, patriarchy in her mid-century Caribbean childhood and in turn-of-the-century Vienna look very much the same: "It is the extreme autocentric reaction of these fathers that moves me to write this essay" (p. 130). She finds sisterhood across sexual preference in "the young woman's will; her insistence to love how and whom she wants; and her refusal to forswear her womanhood in the name of her father's wishes" (p. 130). Can we escape the "male imaginary?" Yes and no. Pérez Foster identifies for us the "gender habits" codified by the twin cults of *marianismo* and *machismo,* from whose confines she and her Latina patients do and do not escape in their immigration to North America: "The well-known secret among us [immigrants] is that we also use the 'Other' to disguise what still remains of an unresolved anxiety about saying no to the 'word of the father'" (p. 138).

In el Norte at the beginning of the Sixties, we find ourselves at a very heterosexual Wellesley College, where Grey listens dubiously to what her educators have to tell her about being a woman, still (though for not much longer) like the Viennese girl "without the protection and support of feminism" (Harris, p. 157, in this volume). There she is taught to fend off men's sexual advances by saying, "'I am a Wellesley girl, and, I hope, a lady!'" Grey's life, in a way, takes up where the patient's leaves off. Corporate wives to be—or so they, their teachers, and their parents thought and hoped—these daughters of privilege soon come to call themselves "neither 'girls' nor 'ladies' but women," as women's liberation movement bursts on the scene. Grey recounts her evolution from wifely-companion-in-training to failed career girl to divorcee to analysand: "It took several years of discouraged drifting and angry reliving of my mother's life to find my way to an independent sense of purpose" (p. 143).

Finally, in rural upstate New York close to the turn of the next century, Schoenberg valiantly struggles with this difficult text through her dreams, fantasies, and clinical experience. She would like to posit underground lines connecting Freud's experience of anti-Semitism, the homophobia enveloping the girl as well as Schoenberg herself, and the racism snaring her and her patients.

The Psychogenesis . . .

Questions of mental health, illness, and cure are implicit in this case and in these cross-disciplinary essays about it. Freud begins his title with "psychogenesis" because he intends to make a point about homosexuality: Its causes are not biological, they are psychological. This case, many of the authors in this volume point out, is to serve his cause, to advance the psychoanalytic movement with its foundational constructs of the unconscious and the Oedipus complex. In contemporary thought, however, the binary between psychology and biology no longer cuts it. The psyche, we see now, is so much more complicated: inhabiting intersubjective space, filled with intimations of social forces, made of culturally contoured representations, dynamically saturated with unvoiceable bodily experience. To say that Freud anticipates all this subtlety, as do many postmodernist Freudians in the academy as well as classically oriented psychoanalysts, is not to say that he limns its depths and ramifications. There is still more to say, as, despite his often conquistadorial mood, Freud well knew.

The essays in this volume collectively recognize that there are yet no answers to the conundrum of mental illness, health, and cure; it is an evolving question and many factors are active. The greatest mystery in this "case" is not homosexuality. Recall the opening quote of this essay: ". . . our patient, who was in no way neurotic . . ." Freud says on several occasions that she is not ill (e.g. 1920, pp. 150–151). Our essayists, surprisingly, disagree with him: The girl is suffering and they are determined to find out why. Shifting the locus of authority from center to margin, they listen very closely to what the girl does not say so as to hear what she wants and needs to tell. For them, the analyst is no longer the absolute master (to borrow from Borch-Jakobson's [1991] study of Lacan): If analysts have psyches too, so patients have answers that must always be listened to, even if, as Moss & Zeavin remind us, the psychoanalytic appreciation of the unconscious requires recognition that, in any communication, meaning is endlessly doubled.

The contributors herein draw particularly on object-relational explanations for the patient's suffering. Engaging the space between self and other, they hurt for her in a way that they find Freud does not. Harris, referring to contemporary literature on adolescent treatment, observes "Freud's rather chilling refusal to privilege the girl's despair, to see the integrity and seriousness of her hope-

lessness and her confusion" (p. 165). Our essayists insist we probe the intima-
cies of her family constellation as well as the intricacies of her inner object
world. Elsewhere, Merck (1993) wonders that Freud does not read her neglect
of her friends, studies, and looks as symptomatic: "The stated seriousness of the
girl's suicide attempt, and the severity of her feelings about her father, do not
fit comfortably with Freud's non-pathological diagnosis" (p. 23).

Perhaps, in a weird way, her gender really does make her ill; the radical feminist idea of femininity as the normal psycho-socio-sexual pathology of women's
everyday lives has found its way into psychoanalytic thought. Pérez Foster (in
this volume) cites Virginia Goldner on the link between gender and illness: As
a false self system, Goldner (1991) argues, the "maintenance of normative gender ideals" requires the "aggressive activation of pathogenic mechanisms [and]
the suppression, splitting off, and denial of human self attributes" (p. 139). The
rigidity Freud diagnoses in his patient, however perverse and mean-spirited he
is to do so, could then be interpreted as a normal response to gender as rigidly,
dually, and hierarchically constructed. Recall that, in his view, she is too lacking in normal bisexuality, too rigidly homosexual (see de Lauretis) or, on the
other hand, too normal, since she lacks hysterical symptoms (see Fuss). Pérez
Foster compares rigidities in contemporary patients: She treats two couples, one
lesbian and one heterosexual, and notes how they share restrictions in their ways
of being coupled. Despite one partner of each having made great changes in her
life via immigrating to the United States, each couple still lives out a patriarchal
relationship, one partner being dominant and the other compliant, each couple
clinging to "culturally sanctioned systems that offer meaning and organization
to their relationships" (p.137). Merck (1993) wonders whether Freud's patient's
masculine identification, which Freud presents as a singular, unproblematic concomitant of her object-choice, is at the source of her conflict. On the one hand,
it helps her, improving her relations with her mother, who seems to prefer her
daughter as homosexual confidante rather than heterosexual competitor. But
identifying with her father, an object she hates, causes the girl to suffer, like the
melancholic, from overweening self-denigration (pp. 23–25).

How do women contend with the normal psycho-socio-sexual pathology of
their everyday lives? Like Pérez Foster, D'Ercole is interested in how women
rebel. She turns to the social to understand (what classical analysis calls) the compromise formation from which the patient suffers. Holding agentic engagement
with the conditions of one's life as critical to psychic well-being, she reads the
patient's symptoms for their resistance to domination. She asks about Freud's
patient's conflict, her "wish to pursue her own desires without disappointing her
parents, resulting in her willingness to undergo treatment" (p.120). In comparison, D'Ercole writes of her own patient, who tries to stay connected to her fam-

ily while creating her own life, whose fears hide her conflicts and split her desire for autonomy from her longing for nurturing. How, D'Ercole and Pérez Foster want to know, are women affected by their resolve to be different from their mothers and to contest cultural codes for passion and action? D'Ercole sees Freud's patient's misery as the result of the sort of necessary contradiction that grounds all symptoms: "By choosing someone unavailable, the patient protects herself from having to face a stronger social rejection" (p. 121). Pushing the limits of her social milieu while remaining within it, she suffers "shame and guilt, not of autonomy but of compliance" (p. 121). The shame and guilt of compliance. What a novel idea!

In/Conclusion: Speak Truth to Power

All theory, some wag once said, is autobiography. Perhaps this proposition is nowhere more true than in psychoanalysis. Freud's analyses of his own dreams, his daughter Anna's of her own fantasies, and so on, are legendary. As analysts daily sit on the clinical hotseat and probe their own experience, they endlessly confirm or reformulate theories received or improvised. Laboratory-like, this investigation of mind is necessarily subjective. The problem with self-analysis, another wit quipped, is countertransference: In psychoanalysis, the utopian goal of scientific objectivity will have to be reached by some other means than controlled experiments. One such route might be the intersubjective back-and-forth of clinical psychoanalysis, where, it has been argued (Aron, 1996), analyst and patient together co-construct the meaning that helps. Another route may be the sort of colloquy this anthology permits.

Consider penis envy. In advancing their position on the primacy of the classical tradition—that theory is not and must not be autobiography—Moss & Zeavin (in this volume) treat us to a new riff on the idea, put forth by Benjamin (1988), that not only women have penis envy. Phallic disappointment, which Freud targets as the cause of female homosexuality, is not particular to women. Freud thinks it is just women's problem because he, reasoning in his own sincere voice (a mistake, in their view) from his personal experience of his own, male body, imagines how damaging it must feel to be a woman lacking the genitals that he has. Moss & Zeavin do not speculate, at least overtly, about what Freud might have thought had he consulted his own feelings about what women's bodies have and he lacks. Nevertheless, it is an implicit part of their reasoning that, had he done so, he would have seen what any man might: that phallic disappointment is a universal truth, not a special case. It is, in fact, "an element of genital sexuality, regardless of gender, and regardless of heterosexual and homosexual object-choice" (p. 199). To put it aphoristically, men have penis envy too, and the fact that they have it—that no one, to use a Lacanian figure, has the phallus—suggests that feelings of genital inadequacy constitute, so to speak, a shock heard round the world.

Still, the binary opposition between the authority of tradition and the authority of personal experience, which Moss & Zeavin set up, breaks down over and over again. Or rather, there is always dialogue between them. How otherwise should we understand that Moss & Zeavin reach, as we have earlier seen, the same conclusion as de Lauretis (1994), who tells us in no uncertain terms that her ideas about lesbian sexuality and perverse desire come equally from her engagement with theory, her studies of cinema, and her own personal experience? A politics of knowledge pulses in these pages, and shows up in this debate between the particularities of personal experience and the generalities of psychoanalytic tradition. Where Moss & Zeavin would have us re-establish the *status quo ante* and return to those pre-Sixties days when the authority of tradition ruled, de Lauretis resolves the contradiction between traditional and personal authority through a classic synthesis of opposites: not either/or, but both/and.

We get to the commonalities of human experience by moving back and forth between universal and particular. The project is one of simultaneous practices: to wonder about general truths; follow each individual's foray into the psychic depths; compare notes; correct for that problem of self-analysis, countertransference; propose truths; and then make emendations the next time the question comes up. If, encouraged by the authority of personal experience, men probe their feelings about their bodies, find that they too can be phallically disappointed, and add that to our store of knowledge of human life, surely that is a good thing. To be sure, once men and women compare notes and discover that neither feels particularly good about their genitals, we might then want to ask what their disappointments have in common. We might then come up with a primal sense of loss. But we might also find some very particular losses, of not only penises but wombs and clitorides, not only body parts but entire bodies, not the concreteness of body but the intangibility of relationship.

If you discredit the personal voice, the first-person narrative, you risk eliminating one of the most important resistances to disciplinary power. It is by now a commonplace that power structures inform social life; perhaps no one has the phallus, but some people—those with their fingers on the nuclear buttons or on the pulse of the stock market—sure look like they do. That power is knowledge—that systems of knowledge are, as Foucault demonstrated, central to practices of domination—is less well understood. That clinical psychoanalysis remains a principal, if not the emblematic, regulatory practice makes Gagnon's critique worth keeping in mind: "Perhaps the debate about the girl is actually a debate about Freud and his authority to tell her story to us" (p. 85, in this volume). Noting the power differential, he indicts Freud for exploiting his patients. Freud's archaeological metaphor is too passive, he says, because it omits the activity of the analysand, who, "like the native digger . . . unearths the psychic fragments for the analyst to evaluate and interpret" (p. 77).

While psychoanalysis does not always come up smelling like a rose, Gagnon's wholesale condemnation is perhaps a little out of date. There is more questioning and skepticism at play in the land of psychoanalysis than its popular and professional hold on authority would have it. Compare Gagnon's view to the clinical process detailed for us by three of the essayists herein (Harris, D'Ercole, and Schoenberg), whose respect for patients' desires and insights and whose self-reflexiveness constitute moments of resistance to unvarnished psychoanalytic authority. Unlike most of the essayists, Gagnon really dislikes psychoanalysis altogether and sees nothing liberating about it. His profound distaste is at the opposite extreme from Moss & Zeavin's implicit faith in the power of the classical to illuminate the truth or D'Ercole's trust in the power of the interpersonal to emancipate.

Elsewhere in these essays such abiding belief is tempered by ambiguity and doubts. How well the postmodernist appreciation of inconclusiveness suits contemporary psychoanalytic work. How do we know what is true? Freud counters the biological truth of homosexuality with a psychosexual truth. Now, in the days of uncertainty, we add the postmodernist truth: All knowledge, indeed truth itself, is an effect of discourse, of practices constituting a set of possibilities for knowledge (Flax, 1990, p. 206). Knowledge and truth are provisional, social constructions that, changing, also wait for correction. Perhaps most clinical accounts are not as incomplete as Freud's "The Psychogenesis of a Case of Homosexuality in a Woman." But all are always provisional: Who knows what will happen after a patient terminates analysis?

Uncertainty has different valences for our academic and clinical contributors. Wineapple hits the nail on the head: "[T]he analyst is . . . enmeshed in a world of uncertainty and apprehension, the world identified by the hip literary critic as a world of interpretative possibility" (p. 252, in this volume). That which is playful and fun for the critic is anxiety-producing, wrenching, and often draining for the clinician. The coherence of Freud's master narrative is one thing; the chaos of everyday clinical life is another.

We have been dealing here with a case that, like its title, keeps mutating before our eyes, fragmenting, enlarging, adding new difficulties. Likewise, this anthology, including my commentary, is necessarily an unsuccessful attempt to complete what amounts to a jigsaw puzzle from which a few key pieces are forever lost—or perhaps in which there are too many sets of equivalent pieces. Contemporary philosophy suggests that this sense of lack or excess, the feeling that you can't quite get it right, is a millennial commonplace. As Woolwine puts it, we live in "a period in which the dilemma of the exact relationship of the world to the word is philosophically insoluble" (p. 111, in this volume). In the generality of this account—"The Psychogenesis"—we may perhaps take comfort in some possibility of coherence. As Harry Stack Sullivan put it, "We are all much more human than otherwise." But in its particularities—"Case of Homosexuality in a Woman"—we find the overwhelming mess, the "primal stew" (P. Rose, 1983:2) of which any life is made. As the late Joseph Brodsky (1990) said, "Life is always a disaster, one way or another. Even the successful life is a disaster." In that sense, too, each of us may resemble Freud's patient: She can't win, but at least she tries, a bittersweetness savored by psychoanalysis, most famously by Freud (1937) but, half a century later, by Stephen Mitchell, too (1988). Life is an unfinished business.

Notes

1. Lacanians are justifiably critical of the emphasis in contemporary relational, clinical, and theoretical practices (object-relations theory, interpersonal psychoanalysis, self-psychology), on dyadic, mostly maternal relationships to the exclusion of triadic formations that bring in paternality. It is beyond the scope of this essay to do justice to this critique and its implications. Worthy of detailed attention is the interesting disparity in theoretical allegiance between those psychoanalytic feminist clinicians who locate their practices in relational thought and those psychoanalytic feminist literary theorists who draw on Lacan (Benjamin [1994] has made a beginning; see also Brennan [1989]). There are also convergences. Note how de Lauretis (1984; this volume), whose vocabulary is highly Lacanian, privileges the mother and the daughter's relation to her in a way not dreamt of in the Lacanian philosophy but certainly recuperated in the world of Klein and Winnicott. Note, on the other hand, how Pérez Foster (this volume) who works in relational mode, interprets the problem of patriarchy through the Lacanian metaphor of the phallus. Finally, while Lacanian and relational thought originate from different points of the classical tree, they have evolved not without mutual influence (see, e.g., Flax [1990] on Winnicott and Lacan). There are even echoes between intersubjective space and the Imaginary, as well perhaps as other coincidences/convergences, that are just now beginning to receive notice (e.g., Dimen [1998]). In any event, both evolutions belong to the larger reorganization taking placing in psychoanalytic thinking at the end of the century that may fit under this rubric: What goes on internally and what goes on externally are always already imbricated.

References

Aron, L. (1996). *A meeting of minds: Mutuality in psychoanalysis*. Hillsdale, NJ: Analytic Press.

Bassin, D. (1982). Woman's images of inner space. *International Review of Psychoanalysis 9*, 191–203.

Benjamin, J. (1984). The convergence of psychoanalysis and feminism: Gender identity and autonomy. In C. M. Brody (Ed.), *Women therapists working with women*. (pp. 37–45). New York: Springer.

Benjamin, J. (1988). *The bonds of love*. New York: Pantheon.

Benjamin, J. (1994). The shadow of the other (subject). *Constellations, 1,* 231–254.

Bersani, L. (1995). Foucault, Freud, fantasy, and power. *GLQ 2* (1–2) 11–34.

Borch-Jakobson, M. (1991). *Lacan: The absolute master.* Stanford: CA Stanford University Press.

Brennan, T. (1989). Introduction. In T. Brennan (Ed.), *Between feminism and psycho-analysis.* (pp.1–23). London: Routledge.

Brodsky, J. (1990). Interviewed. *The Threepenny Review, 43,* 24.

Butler, J. (1990). *Gender trouble.* New York: Routledge.

Chodorow, N. (1994). *Femininities, masculinities, and sexualities.* Lexington, KY: The University Press of Kentucky.

Corbett, K. (1993, February 3). Between fear and fantasy. *The New York Times.*

de Lauretis, T. (1994). *The practice of love.* Bloomington, IN: Indiana University Press.

Dimen, M. (1997). The engagement between psychoanalysis and feminism: A report from the front. *Contemporary Psychoanalysis, 33,* 527–548.

Dimen, M. (1998). Polyglot bodies. In L. Aron & F. S. Anderson (Eds.), *The relational construction of the body.* (pp. 65–96). Hillsdale, NJ: The Analytic Press.

Dinnerstein, D. (1976). *The mermaid and the minotaur.* New York: Harper & Row.

Drescher, J. (1997). From preoedipal to postmodern. *Gender and Psychoanalysis, 2,* 203–217.

Flax, J. (1990). *Thinking fragments.* Berkeley, CA: University of California Press.

Freud, S. (1913). Totem and taboo. In J. Strachey (Ed. and Trans.), *The standard edition of the complete psychological works of Sigmund Freud.* (Vol.13, pp. 1–164). London: Hogarth.

Freud, S. (1937). Analysis, terminable and interminable. In J. Strachey (Ed. and Trans.), *The standard edition of the complete psychological works of Sigmund Freud.* (Vol. 23, pp. 216–254). London: Hogarth.

Freud, S. (1953–1974). Leonardo da Vinci and a memory of his childhood. In J. Strachey (Ed. and Trans.), *The standard edition of the complete psychological works of Sigmund Freud.* (Vol. 11, pp. 63–137). London: Hogarth. (Originally published 1910)

Freud, S. (1951). Letter. *American Journal of Psychiatry, 107,* 786. (Originally written 1935)

Goldner, V. (1991). Toward a critical relational theory of gender. *Psychoanalytic Dialogues 1* (3), 249–272.

H. D. [Hilda Doolittle] (1974/1956). *Tribute to Freud.* New York: New Directions.

Jacobus, M. (1995). Russian tactics: Freud's "Case of Homosexuality in a Woman." *GLQ, 2(1–2),* 65–80.

Kohut, H. (1974). *The Analysis of the Self.* NY: International Universities Press.

Mayer, H. (1998). Reading Ralph Ellison. *The Threepenny Review, 72 (Winter),* 13–14.

Merck, M. (1993). *Perversions: Deviant readings.* London: Virago.

Mitchell, S. (1988). *Relational concepts in psychoanalysis: An integration.* Cambridge: Harvard University Press.

Nicolosi, J. (1991). *Reparative therapy of homosexuality: A new clinical approach.* Northvale, NJ: Jason Aronson.

Ogden, T. (1994). *Subjects of analysis.* New York: Aronson.

Person, E. (1980). Sexuality as the mainstay of identity. *Signs, 5,* 605–630.

Rich, A. (1980). Compulsory heterosexuality and lesbian existence. *Signs 5,* 631–660.

Rose, J. (1986). *Sexuality in the field of vision.*

Rose, P. (1983). *Parallel lives.* New York: Knopf.

Rubin, G. (1975). The traffic in women: Notes toward a political economy of sex. In R. Rapp (Ed.), *Toward an anthropology of women.* (pp. 157–211). New York: Monthly Review Press.

Schwartz, A. (1998). *Sexual subjects.* New York: Routledge.

Socarides, C. (1968). *The overt homosexual.* New York: Grune & Stratton.

Winnicott, D. W. (1975). *Through paediatrics to psychoanalysis.* NY: Basic Books.

LIST OF CONTRIBUTORS

〜

Teresa de Lauretis, Ph.D., is Professor of the History of Consciousness at the University of California, Santa Cruz. She is author of (most recently) *Technologies of Gender: Essays on Theory, Film, and Fiction* and *The Practice of Love: Lesbian Sexuality and Perverse Desire.*

Ann D'Ercole, Ph.D., is Clinical Associate Professor of Psychology at the Postdoctoral Program in Psychotherapy and Psychoanalysis and the Graduate School of Arts and Sciences, both at New York University. She is editor of both the *Journal of Gay and Lesbian Psychotherapy,* as well as editor of *Unconventional Couplings / Uncoupling Conventions: Reappraisals in Psychoanalytic Theory and Practice* (forthcoming).

Muriel Dimen, Ph.D., is Clinical Professor of Psychology and training analyst at the Postdoctoral Program in Psychotherapy and Psychoanalysis at New York University. The author of *Surviving Sexual Contradictions* and *The Anthropological Imigination,* she contributed to *Freud: Conflict and Culture* (ed. Michael Roth), the book accompanying the Library of Congress exhibit of the same title. She is also an associate editor of *Psychoanalytic Dialogues* and *Studies in Gender and Sexuality.*

RoseMarie Pérez Foster, Ph.D., is a psychologist/psychoanalyst who is an Associate Professor at the New York University School of Social Work and a faculty member of the New York University Postdoctoral Program in Psychoanalysis. She is author of *The Power of Language in the Clinical Process: Assessing and Treating the Bilingual Person;* and coeditor with M. Moskowitz and R. Javier of *Reaching Across Boundaries of Culture and Class: Widening the Scope of Psychotherapy.*

Diana Fuss, Ph.D., is Associate Professor of English, Princeton Univeristy. She is the author of *Essentially Speaking* and *Identification Papers.*

John H. Gagnon, Ph.D., is Distinguished Professor of Sociology Emeritus at the State University of New York at Stony Brook. Previously a Senior Research Sociologist and member of the Board of Trustees of the Institute for Sex Research, he is coeditor (most recently) with Martin Levine and Peter Nardi of *Encounters with AIDS: Gay Men and Lesbians Confront the AIDS Epidemic.*

Carolyn C. Grey, Ph.D., is a faculty member and supervisor at the New York University Postdoctoral Program in Psychoanalysis and Psychotherapy, an adjunct faculty member at the Clinical Doctoral Program, Fordham University, and Clinical Supervisor, Clinical Doctoral Program, Yeshiva University.

Adrienne Harris, Ph.D., is a faculty member and supervisor at the New York University Postdoctoral Program in Psychoanalysis and Psychotherapy. She is an editor of *Studies in Gender and Sexuality* and is coeditor with Lewis Aron, Ph.D., of *The Legacy of Sandor Ferenczi.*

Ronnie C. Lesser, Ph.D., is coeditor with Tom Domenici, Ph.D., of *Disorienting Sexuality: Psychoanalytic Reappraisals of Sexual Identities.* She is on the editorial board of *Studies in Gender and Sexuality* and the *Journal of Lesbian and Gay Psychotherapy* and is in private practice in New York City and Westchester County.

Linda I. Meyers, Psy.D., is a clinical psychologist and psychoanalyst in Princeton, New Jersey. She is a senior faculty member at the Institute for Psychoanalysis and Psychotherapy of New Jersey. She has written on culture and psychoanalytic theory, sexuality and countertransference.

Donald Moss, M.D., is a faculty member at the New York University Psychoanalytic Institute.

Erica Schoenberg, Ph.D., is Book Review Editor of the *Journal of Lesbian and Gay Psychotherapy.* She is a supervisor at the Institute for Human Identity and is in private practice in New York City and Westchester County.

Brenda Wineapple, Ph.D., is codirector of the New York University Biography Seminar and Washington Irving Professor of Modern Literary and Historical Studies at Union College. She is the author of *Genêt: A Biography of Janet Flanner, Sister Brother: Gertrude and Leo Stein,* and is currently working on a biography of Nathaniel Hawthorne.

David Woolwine, Ph.D., is Adjunct Professor at The New School University in New York City, where he teaches courses in the social sciences and humanities. He is the author of "Reading Science as Text" in *Vocabularies of Public Life.* He is also author of "Community in Gay Male Experience and Moral Discourse," forthcoming in *The Journal of Homosexuality.*

Lynne Zeavin, Psy.D., is a senior candidate at New York University Psychoanalytic Institute.

PERMISSIONS

~

INDEX

~